Kentucky's Rebel Press

KENTUCKY'S REBEL PRESS

Pro-Confederate Media
and the
Secession Crisis

BERRY CRAIG

UNIVERSITY PRESS OF KENTUCKY

Copyright © 2018 by The University Press of Kentucky

Scholarly publisher for the Commonwealth,
serving Bellarmine University, Berea College, Centre College of Kentucky, Eastern
Kentucky University, The Filson Historical Society, Georgetown College, Kentucky
Historical Society, Kentucky State University, Morehead State University, Murray State
University, Northern Kentucky University, Transylvania University, University of Kentucky,
University of Louisville, and Western Kentucky University.
All rights reserved.

Editorial and Sales Offices: The University Press of Kentucky
663 South Limestone Street, Lexington, Kentucky 40508-4008
www.kentuckypress.com

Unless otherwise noted, photographs are from the author's collection.

Library of Congress Cataloging-in-Publication Data

Names: Craig, Berry, author.
Title: Kentucky's rebel press : pro-Confederate media and the secession
    crisis / Berry Craig.
Description: Lexington, Kentucky : University Press of Kentucky, [2018] |
    Includes bibliographical references and index.
Identifiers: LCCN 2017043858| ISBN 9780813174594 (hardcover : alk. paper) |
    ISBN 9780813174600 (pdf) | ISBN 9780813174617 (epub)
Subjects: LCSH: American newspapers—Kentucky—History—19th century. |
    Press—Kentucky—History—19th century. | United States—History—Civil
    War, 1861–1865—Press coverage—Kentucky. | Secession—Kentucky. | Press
    and politics—Kentucky—History—19th century. |
    Presidents—Election—1860—Press coverage—Kentucky.
Classification: LCC PN4897.K723 C73 2018 | DDC 071.6909/034—dc23
LC record available at https://lccn.loc.gov/2017043858

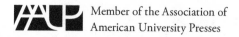

To Dr. Carl Jón Denbow, whose ancestors served in the 78th Ohio Veteran Volunteer Infantry, and who, forty years ago at Murray State University, broadened my interest in the Civil War to include Yankee and rebel newspapers in Kentucky, my home state.

Contents

Photographs follow page 92

Introduction

Historians have devoted considerable ink to Yankee and rebel newspapers during the Civil War. While they have examined Northern and Southern papers, they have written almost nothing in detail about the press in Kentucky and in the other border states. There, the press was unique in that it operated in a vast region where the people were divided to one extent or another. There were Southern sympathizers in the North and unionists in the South. Both groups were minorities in their regions. But in the borderland, especially in Kentucky, the war divided communities, friends, and families. Most border-state citizens wanted to stick with the old Union, although a vocal minority favored the new Confederacy. Kentucky was mainly pro-Union, but apparently its press was almost evenly split. The Confederate papers were every bit as feisty, caustic, and partisan as the state's pro-Union papers. Most of the rebel press supported Southern Democrat John C. Breckinridge, a Kentuckian, for president in 1860. Beginning with Abraham Lincoln's election in November 1860 and continuing for the next ten months, the rebel press battled the Union press word for word. The verbal combat ceased after September 1861, when the Bluegrass State abandoned its precarious neutrality and joined the war on the Union side. While the Lincoln administration grappled with the limits of free speech in wartime, federal authorities zeroed in on Kentucky's Confederate press. A handful of publishers and editors were jailed as traitors, but most were not imprisoned for long. Some publishers and editors fled to the rebels, including Walter N. Haldeman, owner of the *Louisville Courier,* the state's leading secessionist organ. Uncle Sam's punitive actions effectively silenced the disunionist press. But the unionism of Kentucky—and its unionist press—was qualified. Support for the Union did not mean opposition to slavery. Eleven other slave states seceded in 1860–1861 because their leaders feared that Lincoln and his "Black Republican Party" aimed to abolish slavery. Most white Kentuckians believed that staying in the Union was the safest means of protecting their interests, including their slaves. The unionist press,

1

led by George D. Prentice's *Louisville Journal*, reflected the simultaneous pro-Union and pro-slavery views of most citizens. The rebel publishers and editors countered that only secession and alliance with the Confederacy would save slavery. While the Confederate press failed to turn most Kentuckians against the Union of their forebears, several of the old rebel papers, notably Haldeman's *Courier*, enjoyed a great resurgence after the war. Such a turn of events was not surprising, given that many Kentuckians felt betrayed when the federal government abolished slavery. No sooner did the war end than the state idealized and embraced the "Lost Cause." Historian E. Merton Coulter famously wrote that Kentucky "waited until after the war to secede."[1]

Before Kentuckians marched off to bloody battle in the Civil War, Bluegrass State publishers and editors waged a bloodless, though heated, war of words. The stakes could hardly have been higher. Would Kentucky rally to the old Stars and Stripes or the new Stars and Bars? At the onset of the secession crisis of 1860–1861, it was hard to say which road Kentucky would travel. Slavery bound Kentucky to the South, although it was never a large slaveholding territory compared with the cotton states. The real Taras were in the Deep South; in 1860 slaves accounted for 19.5 percent of Kentucky's populace, and free blacks for 0.9 percent. Even so, almost all Kentucky whites were pro-slavery.[2]

At the same time, Kentucky was intensely nationalist and unionist. "United We Stand, Divided We Fall" was the state motto. Henry Clay, the state's most beloved prewar politician, put the Union above all other considerations. Though he was Speaker of the House, senator, secretary of state, and three-time presidential candidate, Clay was best known for helping to broker three crucial compromises to save the Union. He was the venerated "Great Pacificator" and probably Kentucky's most popular politician ever.

Clay died on June 29, 1852, almost nine years before the war started. When fighting flared, Kentucky desperately tried to remain neutral, but it was always neutrality within the Union. Ultimately, the state forthrightly declared itself for the Union and sent three to four times as many of its sons to war in Yankee blue as in rebel gray. Nonetheless, Kentucky's secessionist minority was conspicuous and voluble, notably in a significant pro-Confederate press.

At any rate, on the eve of the Civil War, the press in Kentucky and elsewhere in America "was a political, social, and economic force," Ford Risley wrote in *Civil War Journalism*. The country had 3,725 newspapers, twice as many as in Great Britain, and they accounted for about a third of the world's broadsheets. Per capita, newspaper circulation in America was considerably greater than that in any other country, according to Risley. Most newspapers in America were small weeklies, but almost every community boasted at least one or two papers; many cities had three or more. Risley's description of the national press was applicable to Kentucky. Most of its papers were weeklies, and almost all of them were published in county seats; in some cases, there were two rival papers. Louisville had a trio of battling broadsheets: the *Courier* (secessionist), the *Democrat* (unionist), and the *Journal* (unionist). All three had staffs of reporters, but newswriting was hardly less slanted than editorializing. The *Courier, Democrat,* and *Journal* were the state's only dailies; they circulated statewide through the mail. In Frankfort, the state capital, the triweekly *Commonwealth* (unionist) and *Yeoman* (secessionist) became daily papers when the General Assembly was in session. The *Paducah Herald* (secessionist) was also a triweekly. In Lexington, the *Kentucky Statesman* (secessionist) and *Observer & Reporter* (unionist) were semiweeklies.[3]

Accurate circulation figures for Kentucky papers—indeed, for all Civil War–era papers—are hard to come by, although historians avidly seek them. Scholars are skeptical of the figures available because they were provided by publishers, who naturally reported big numbers because the greater the circulation, the more they could charge for advertising. But based on one estimate, the total yearly circulation of all American newspapers between 1828 and 1840 more than doubled, from 68 million to 148 million copies. Some scholars peg the dramatic growth of the pre–Civil War press and of newspaper readership to increased political participation among the working and middle classes, rising literacy rates, and more leisure time. Also boosting circulation were improvements in printing technology, such as the Fourdrinier papermaking machine and steam printing presses. Such innovations allowed newspapers to be printed with greater speed and efficiency.[4]

But most literate Kentuckians, like most other Americans who could read, doted on newspapers, which were more accessible than ever in the Civil War era, thanks to a technology-driven communications revolution as significant as the one unfolding today. By the 1860s, papers were genuinely "mass media, with the power that term implies," Lorman A. Ratner and Dwight L. Teeter Jr. wrote in *Fanatics & Fire-Eaters.* "Newspapers came to be read widely, both in places of publication and, thanks to the railroads, farther away." The telegraph spread news fast and far, and the number of newspapers and newspaper readers grew dramatically. When Andrew Jackson was elected president in 1828, newspaper readership was largely limited to a relatively few men who were interested in government, politics, or business. By the time of Lincoln's election in 1860, the major papers had become cheap, popular, cash-and-carry commodities, Ratner and Teeter added. In 1840 America had 1,404 newspapers, only 138 of which were dailies. Of America's 3,725 papers in 1860, 387 were dailies. "The introduction of the so-called penny press, inexpensive publications aimed at a mass audience, forever changed newspapers, which for decades had largely been editorial tools of the country's political parties," Risley noted. For the first time, publishers hired reporters to cover the news aggressively. Nonetheless, antebellum journalism remained "geared to the leisurely pace of an age in which the stagecoach, the horse car, and the sailing ship were still being used in varying degrees," J. Cutler Andrews wrote in *The North Reports the Civil War*. Most Americans "were more accustomed to being regaled with somebody else's opinion of what had happened the week before than with the news of the previous twenty-four hours."[5]

Andrews followed his landmark study of the Northern press with *The South Reports the Civil War*. He found that in the decade preceding the war, relatively few Southerners read books and magazines published below the Mason-Dixon Line, and Dixie's papers were as good as those up north. Andrews used the Mason-Dixon Line—the old Maryland-Pennsylvania border—as the North-South divide, thus putting border-state Kentucky in Dixie. He cited George Prentice as among the "sectional spokesmen whose gifted pens were quite as influential as the rhetoric of clergymen and political orators in shaping Southern opinion and giving direction to Southern action." The sharp-penned Prentice may have been a "Southern" editor, but his paper did not represent the views of most white Southerners during the war. He made the *Journal* Kentucky's most influential anti-secession paper. Nonetheless, Prentice was unable to sway his wife and sons to his cause. Harriette Benham Prentice, whom George wed in 1835, was a secessionist. Their two sons, William Courtland and Clarence, were Confederate cavalry officers. Courtland was mortally wounded by friendly fire at the Battle of Augusta, Kentucky, on September 27, 1862. His parents witnessed his eventual death in a hospital; his father eulogized him in the *Journal* and memorialized him in a poem, "The Death-Day of William Courtland Prentice." The Yankees captured Clarence, but he survived the war.[6]

Of course, like everybody else involved in journalism during the Civil War, Prentice and his chief rival Haldeman seldom let the truth stand in the way of a good story, meaning a story that made their side look good and the other side look bad. Both papers—indeed, almost all Union and Confederate papers—shamelessly slanted the news. By twenty-first-century media standards, the 1860s *Journal* and *Courier* and the rest of Kentucky's press were guilty of multiple journalistic sins of omission and commission. Character assassination was a Civil War editor's stock-in-trade, to boot. Readers seemed to care more about the force and ingenuity of a paper's prose—the more pointed the better—than about its accuracy. Examples are plentiful. One of the *Journal*'s favorite targets was secessionist congressman Henry C. Burnett of Cadiz, who presided over the creation of Kentucky's bogus pro-Confederate government in November 1861. Burnett, according to Prentice's paper, was "admirably qualified for the office of Blackguard Extraordinary and Scullion Plenipotentiary to the Court of [Confederate president] Jeff Davis, for his brain is as feeble as his lungs are forcible and his mouth is as dirty as a den of skunks." But for sheer outlandish editorializing it would be hard to top Len G. Faxon of the rabidly rebel *Columbus Crescent*. He flayed Yankee soldiers as "bow-legged, wooden shoed, sour craut stinking, Bologna sausage eating, hen roost robbing Dutch sons of —."[7]

Civil War papers were not above flat-out lying in print. For instance, the *Courier* claimed that Kentucky-born Major Robert Anderson was "the man who bears the awful responsibility of having begun this most unrighteous war." Anderson was in command of Fort Sumter in Charleston harbor, where the Civil War began on April 12, 1861. The Confederates fired the first shot, sending an artillery shell screaming at the brick bastion at 4:30 a.m. Anderson's gunners fired back in self-defense.[8]

Polemical and even prevaricating editors and publishers were common in nineteenth-century America, especially in Dixie. "To an even greater extent than was true elsewhere in the country, the partisan political press dominated prewar Southern journalism," Andrews wrote in *The South Reports*. Before the war, the *Journal* was Kentucky's leading Whig organ. Prentice's paper was unswervingly loyal to Clay's unionist and nationalist party from the *Journal*'s advent in 1830 to the party's demise in 1854. Afterward, the *Journal* became the state's chief organ of the nativist, anti-foreign, and anti-Catholic American, or Know-Nothing, Party.[9]

While the circulation numbers for the *Journal* and *Courier* are unknown, they were almost certainly smaller than those of big-city Northern papers, if for no other reason than the states north of Kentucky were more populous and therefore had larger newspapers. Louisville, with a little more than 68,000 inhabitants, was Kentucky's largest city, but eleven other American cities were more populous. Despite being smaller than Northern papers, Southern papers were exceedingly important and had a virtual monopoly on disseminating the news, Donald Reynolds wrote. Whereas Andrews characterized the Southern media as political, religious, or literary, Reynolds found that it was also partisan. The Reverend Robert J. Breckinridge's stoutly unionist *Danville Quarterly Review* was all four. A Presbyterian theologian, Breckinridge was one of the state's leading unionists. He was a Kentucky delegate and president pro tem at the 1864 National Union Convention in Baltimore that renominated Abraham Lincoln for president. Breckinridge's rival, the Reverend Stuart Robinson, seasoned piety with a dash of politics in the *True Presbyterian.* In 1862 federal authorities shut down Robinson's paper and the Reverend Charles Y. Duncan's *Baptist Recorder* as treasonous. Duncan spent a short stretch behind bars; Robinson was out of the authorities' reach in Canada. The *Danville Quarterly Review* and the *True Presbyterian* are long gone, but the *Western Recorder,* the successor to Duncan's journal, survives as the country's second-oldest state Baptist paper.[10]

In terms of substance, size, and almost everything else, Civil War–era organs, religious or secular, looked almost nothing like modern newspapers. For their time, they were state of the art, albeit primitive by twenty-first-century standards. They lacked the technology to print photographs, although engraved images were common. Kentucky papers, regardless of circulation, were only four pages long and consisted of one large rectangular sheet folded once. Typically, each page had eight or nine columns of type. Readers today might find such papers gray and lifeless, if not downright boring. However, what the papers lacked in "reader appeal" they more than made up for in prose that was anything but prosaic. It was often sharp and stinging and peppered with references to classical literature, history, and Greek and Roman mythology. As in today's papers, editorials were unsigned. The owner of a rural paper almost always wrote his own editorials and functioned as business manager, press operator, and reporter. Prentice and Haldeman (especially the former) wrote their share of editorials, but they also employed staff editorialists. Many journalists were well versed and educated, either formally or through their own reading and study. Prentice graduated from Brown University in Providence, Rhode Island, at the head of his class in 1823. Haldeman did not go to college and started his newspaper career on Prentice's payroll, joining the *Journal* as a nineteen-year-old clerk in 1840.[11]

Today, college students enrolled in Journalism 101—or rookie reporters on the job—are taught to assume that readers do not know much about the subject matter and to write accordingly. Apparently, Civil War journalists believed that if the reader did not get the literary, historical, or mythological allusions, so be it. For example, the *Journal* decried Burnett as a "Kentucky Thersites." It seems likely that few readers would have known Thersites was an altogether unlovable Greek soldier in Homer's *Iliad.* But the writer deigned not to offer an explanation.[12]

Too, students in journalism class and neophyte reporters learn that a news story's lead, or introduction, is supposed to quickly draw readers into the who, what, when, where, why, and how of the news event. "Don't bury the lead!" journalism professors admonish students and city editors chastise greenhorn reporters. Leads on feature stories, editorials, news analyses, and opinion columns are supposed to be relatively short and punchy attention-grabbers. No such rules applied at Civil War papers. Prose was universally ponderous. Editorials often took up one whole column and continued onto another—and even another. Editors and writers seemed to take great delight in drawing out sentences, stitching them together with commas, colons, semicolons, and dashes—and sometimes a comma, colon, or semicolon and dash combination. Dependent and independent clauses were copious. Appositives abounded.

"Quote, quote, quote!" my editor admonished me when I was a cub reporter. "People often use lively language when they speak," advises the *News Manual* online. "Quotes allow you to put that lively language directly into your story." Likewise, Civil War–era journalists employed "lively language," though perhaps too loquaciously for today's newspaper readers. This book features a hefty helping of that "lively language" in quotations from the papers themselves—notably, the three Louisville dailies, and not just because they were the most widely read Civil War papers in Kentucky. The *Courier, Journal,* and *Democrat* are among the few papers that are readily available for study and research. Unfortunately, copies of most other Civil War papers are long gone, destroyed by fires or other mishaps or simply deemed not worth saving and thrown away. The *Courier* and *Journal* are on microfilm in several libraries statewide, including Murray State University's Pogue Special Collections Library, where I did most of my research. Many copies of the *Democrat* are available online through the Kentucky Digital Library. I also read microfilm copies of the *Frankfort Yeoman* at the University of Kentucky Library and microfilm of the *Kentucky Statesman, Lexington Observer & Reporter,* and *Frankfort Commonwealth* at the Lexington Public Library. In addition, I could access online copies of the *Covington Journal.* I hoped personal papers would provide additional insight for this study. The Filson Historical Society in Louisville has Haldeman and Prentice collections, and the Eastern Kentucky University Library houses the Major Family Papers. Samuel Ire Monger Major was editor of the *Yeoman.* Regrettably, none of these sources yielded significant information about the role of Haldeman, Prentice, and Major during the secession crisis of 1860–1861.[13]

At any rate, stories in the *Courier, Journal, Yeoman,* and other Civil War–era sheets were not "headline grabbers" in the modern sense. Headlines were seldom more than one column wide. They were boldfaced but set in relatively small type, which meant that it must have been easy for readers to miss stories. The big stories usually appeared on page two or three, not the front page, for practical reasons: they were usually printed last. The front page was mostly advertising, although there were ads on every page. In the 1860s it was not uncommon for ads to take up at least half of many papers. They were often illustrated with images of the products being sold, ranging from spectacles and buggies to patent medicines and false teeth. Page two was usually a combination of editorials, letters to the editor, other news (usually local or state), and more advertising. The third and back pages generally carried telegraphic news, marketing and other business stories and reports, sometimes serialized fiction, and more ads.[14]

Like most other newspaper editors, Kentucky's editors subscribed to out-of-town papers by mail. Much like rival football coaches swapping videos of each other's teams before a game, editors subscribed to the competition's publications. Uncle Sam helped by waiving postage on papers exchanged between editors. They routinely pulled stories from other papers to suit their own purposes, which were, of course, to praise newspapers and politicians that were friends and pillory those that were foes. Most Kentucky papers were heaviest on local and state news, but the Louisville, Frankfort, and Lexington papers regularly ran telegraphed stories on national and international topics. Papers frequently published letters to the editor as if they were news stories. Unlike modern editors, Civil War editors permitted their correspondents to use pseudonyms. Few writers signed their real names to their missives, and, like the editors to whom that correspondence was addressed, they were not bound by any self-imposed strictures of objectivity.[15]

Except for clipped stories, all other copy had to be handwritten before being set in type. Hence, quality penmanship must have been a plus for editors and reporters and greatly appreciated, if not prayed for, by typesetters. Henry Watterson, the famous postwar editor of the *Louisville Courier-Journal,* was a Pulitzer Prize winner, even though his handwriting was evidently almost illegible. He was blind in one eye, nearsighted in the other, and missing part of his thumb. In one case, "his expression 'forty miles of conflagration' became 'forty mules of California'" in print, historians Lowell H. Harrison and James C. Klotter wrote. Such miscommunication between the newsroom and the pressroom surely happened with lamentable frequency at many nineteenth-century newspapers.[16]

At any rate, this book concentrates on how the Confederate press argued for secession rather than how it reported the news. Civil War news gathering on the home front and the battlefield is amply covered in books by Andrews and others. This book also briefly places the censorship of the Confederate press in the context of a never-ending yet vital debate in free society: what are the proper limits on dissent in a democratic nation when that nation is fighting a war for its very survival? Many other books examine this critical issue in detail, and rightly so. At the same time, it is tempting to compare Kentucky's Confederate press to the modern media in terms of another seemingly ever-lasting debate: how biased is the media? The Civil War press—Union and Confederate—was a mother lode of media bias.

Any attempt to compare the media of the mid-nineteenth century with today's media comes with significant pitfalls. One could argue that all such comparisons are fruitless—of the apples and oranges variety. Civil War–era newspapers were virtually, and shamelessly, propaganda organs, according to Reynolds, who observed that "political partisanship was the *raison d'être* of most Southern newspapers." Northern papers were every bit as partisan. Such "sharp political divisions lasted through the Civil War and well into Reconstruction," David Sachsman notes in his introduction to *A Press Divided.* He added that Northern and Southern newspapers plainly reflected the clash of public opinion "and contributed to the division of the nation." Ratner and Teeter similarly observe that self-interest was the main motivation of publishers and editors. Thus, by manipulating how information was described and explained, the press "helped set the stage for civil war." The authors also maintained that "fighting words in newspapers, including those famous epithets *fanatics* and *fire-eaters,* applied name-calling not merely to handfuls of radicals but to whole societies. Such words provided sparks and tinder for the coming conflagration." In Kentucky, rebel editors commonly labeled unionists "submissionists." Union editors were wont to call secessionists "traitors."[17]

The partisan, or party, press was more than seventy years old by the time of the Civil War. As Harold Holzer wrote in *Lincoln and the Power of the Press,* "In the mid-1790s, the explosive growth of political enthusiasm and the slow but sure development of improved printing technologies coincided to make newspapers more widely available as well as more openly partisan, and served to connect politicians to both editors and their subscribers." As time passed, readers lined up "with party newspapers as routinely as they began aligning themselves with political organizations."[18]

Holzer pointed out that by the 1840s, newspapers were virtually a branch of political parties, "and in parallel fashion, politicians became full partners in newspaper publishing." To curry favor with publishers, politicians rewarded them with advertising, printing contracts, "and publicly financed subscriptions, not to mention well-paid nourishment from the patronage trough and choice seats at the tables of power." In kind, publishers provided their favored politicians "with unlimited news space and unbridled political support," Holzer wrote. "The inviolable line that today separates politics from the print press—at least as an ideal—had yet to be drawn."[19]

Ratner and Teeter acknowledge that "the mid-nineteenth-century lack of independence in political terms may be difficult to fathom now." Indeed, Prentice traveled to Kentucky from his native New England in 1830 to write a campaign biography of Henry Clay. He stayed and became editor of the *Journal,* which was founded to help Clay win the presidency. Some editors and publishers even ran for office. In 1859 William E. Simms, political editor of the *Paris Flag,* campaigned for Congress as a Democrat and won. John H. Harney, editor of the *Louisville Democrat,* was elected to the state legislature on the Union ticket in 1861. Thomas Bell Monroe Jr., the *Statesman's* editor, was Lexington's mayor and Kentucky's youngest secretary of state, the latter an appointed position. *Observer & Reporter* editor Daniel C. Wickliffe was secretary of state during the war. Other publishers and editors were leaders in local, state, and even national party organizations. Samuel Ire Monger Major Jr., editor of the *Yeoman,* was a member of the state Democratic Central Committee. One can trace the ebb and flow of nineteenth-century Kentucky politics by identifying the state's public printer. When the Whigs dominated, he was Albert Gallatin Hodges, editor of the Whiggish *Commonwealth.* Hodges was another Bluegrass State delegate to the 1864 National Union Convention, where he served as one of seventeen convention secretaries. After the Democrats gained supremacy on the eve of the Civil War, the state printers were brothers S. I. M. and Jonathan B. Major.[20]

With editors slanting the news, helping to run political parties, and even holding public office, it is no wonder that bias was so rampant in the Civil War–era media. But did such blatant bias sway public opinion? Or did the media only reinforce pro-Union or pro-Confederate predilections? Absent scientific polling, it is difficult, if not impossible, to prove what influence the media of the 1860s had on the body politic, North or South. On the one hand, Reynolds wrote that "newspapers may well have reflected public opinion on political issues even more than they created it, a possibility widely recognized by the press itself." On the other hand, he suggested that "many editors undoubtedly entered the crowded publishing field . . . because they expected to help shape the public mind on political issues." Ratner and Teeter concluded that newspapers "could and did shape public opinion." Yet they cautioned that "the extent of their influence has been and should be questioned." Indeed, one could argue that Kentucky's rebel press in 1860–1861 is an example of the media's inability to change public opinion because the state, which had been mainly Whig and unionist for years before the Civil War, spurned secession. It also seems possible, if not probable, that the partisan nature of most papers would not have helped editors win converts. Most people read papers that represented their viewpoints. Secessionists doted on the *Louisville*

Courier; they probably would not have been caught dead perusing the *Louisville Journal.* Conversely, unionists swore by the *Journal* and swore at the *Courier.* Such was true of newspaper readers elsewhere in America, according to Holzer, who wrote that citizens revealed their politics by the newspapers they got in the mail or bought and carried around town. "Voters embraced their newspapers to tout their convictions in much the same way they wore campaign ferrotypes and medals on their coats—or today affix bumper stickers to their vehicles." Holzer quoted historian Elizabeth R. Varon, who argued that "the function of antebellum newspapers, which were organs of political parties, was to make partisanship seem essential" to the lives and identities of men. Thus, publishers and editors knew they were preaching to the choir, and in Kentucky, the Union choir had the most singers. In any event, newspapers reflected the rampant partisanship of antebellum America.[21]

Such partisanship is common in today's body politic. Sachsman sees parallels between Civil War–era journalism and the current media. "The mass media of the twenty-first century may be just as partisan—and sharply divided—as the newspapers of the Civil War era," he wrote. "This is an ideological age that resembles in many ways the earlier divisions of the nation." Most newspapers maintain at least some semblance of separation between news and editorializing. The sharpest partisanship is in the electronic media, most notably on cable television. For example, MSNBC leans liberal, though increasingly less so. But even in its liberal heyday, MSNBC was not nearly as far to the left as Fox News, the Republican Party's virtual echo chamber, is to the right. Still, responsible journalists feel obliged to verify information in their pursuit of the truth, while their antebellum predecessors commonly reported rumors. In the 1860s "newspapers' words were often published with no sense of responsibility that would have provided readers with a full and fair view of what happened and why," wrote Ratner and Teeter.[22]

Yet newspaper publishers, like any other business owners, had to be attuned to their customers. Without customers, any enterprise will fail. Thus, to keep their presses running, Civil War publishers traded in "words and ideas that would attract the readers they sought," as Ratner and Teeter point out. The "media were driven in the 1850s by a hunger for profit and power—a distant, echoing predictor of the feral pursuit of profit by the merging communications conglomerates of the late-twentieth and early-twenty-first centuries."[23]

Though the nineteenth-century press was overtly biased and most modern media outlets profess to be objective, complete objectivity is impossible to achieve. News gathering and news reporting are not sciences conducted empirically in laboratories. The Civil War–era newspapers "often reinforced readers' traditional values and attitudes, encouraging them to retain faith in existing institutions and feel secure about the motives and skills of their societal leaders."[24]

Finally, I hope this book provides some insight into that never-ending debate over the media: does it reflect, or shape, public opinion? Kentucky's Confederate press may prove instructive. Confederate papers were about as numerous as Union papers, yet they were unable to coax most Kentuckians to take up the secessionist cause. The fact that they could not do so perhaps adds weight to the argument that the press mainly mirrors, not drives, public opinion.

1

The Rebel Press,
and Some Yankee Papers, Too

Kentucky's press reflected the deep division in the Bluegrass State in 1860–1861. Many communities had pro-Union and pro-Confederate papers. In Louisville, Kentucky's largest city, the *Democrat* and the *Journal* sided with the Union. The latter was the state's most important unionist organ. The *Louisville Courier* was Kentucky's leading Confederate paper. Frankfort, the state capital, was home to the unionist *Commonwealth* and the secessionist *Yeoman*. In Lexington, the principal city in the wealthy Bluegrass region, the unionist *Observer & Reporter* and the Confederate *Kentucky Statesman* fought a fierce war of words. Several other towns had rival Union and Confederate papers. Most of the pro-Confederate press supported Vice President John C. Breckinridge, the Southern Democrat, for president in 1860. The *Journal* and the bulk of the unionist papers backed John Bell, the Constitutional Unionist candidate. The *Democrat* was for Northern Democrat Stephen A. Douglas. Evidently no Breckinridge sheets went over to the Union side, but some Bell papers, notably the *Cynthiana News* and *Covington Journal*, tilted toward secession. The pro-Douglas *Hickman Courier* became one of the first Kentucky papers—if not *the* first—to endorse secession.

Ten years after the nineteenth century's midpoint, Kentucky, which had been admitted to the Union in 1792, still stood tall among the thirty-three states. Just six of them had more electoral votes than Kentucky; Kentucky and Tennessee were tied at a dozen each. The Bluegrass State's population included 919,484 whites, 225,483 slaves, and 10,684 free African Americans. Kentucky had helped populate several western states, notably Indiana, Illinois,

13

Ohio, Iowa, Kansas, and Missouri. All told, almost 332,000 former Kentuckians lived in other states. One hundred thousand of them resided in the Show-Me State, and Missouri governor Claiborne Jackson was a Fleming County native.[1]

Kentuckians, too, distinguished themselves in national affairs. Henry Clay of Lexington was Speaker of the House, secretary of state, senator, three-time presidential candidate, and broker of three compromises to save the Union. The "Great Pacificator" was beloved beyond Kentucky, too. One of Clay's most ardent admirers eulogized him in 1852 as his "beau Ideal of a statesman." That mourner was Kentucky-born Abraham Lincoln of Illinois, who would be elected the sixteenth president in 1860. Breckinridge, however, would continue to challenge him—as a Confederate major general and secretary of war. In any event, Kentuckians were often sought as presidential or vice presidential candidates because of the state's importance. In eight of the ten presidential elections preceding the Civil War, somebody from Kentucky ran as president or vice president. In the antebellum era, Kentucky had more key leaders in national politics than at any time before or since.[2]

Lincoln was a Whig member of the Illinois house of representatives when Richard M. Johnson, who hailed from Scott County, Kentucky, was sworn in as President Martin Van Buren's vice president in 1837. A War of 1812 veteran, he had supposedly killed the great Shawnee chief Tecumseh in the 1813 battle of the Thames in Canada, a feat with "scarcely a parallel in the heroic annals of our country." He was "perforated with balls, his bridle arm shattered, and bleeding profusely," yet he "continued to fight." A postwar senator and congressman, Johnson ran with Van Buren while Democrats crooned, "Rumpsey dumpsey, Rumpsey dumpsey, Colonel Johnson killed Tecumseh." Congressman Linn Boyd from Paducah was not as colorful as Johnson, but his colleagues voted "the Farmer-Statesman, the Statesman-Farmer—another hickory from the Democratic forest"—Speaker of the House in 1851, evidently as a reward for working on behalf of Clay's compromise of 1850. He served until 1855.[3]

A decade after Clay's last and greatest compromise, Kentucky was still largely agrarian, as was the nation. Most industry was up north, but Louisville, at the Falls of the Ohio, developed some manufacturing. Dubbed the Falls City, it prospered as a commercial center and as the state's largest and busiest river port. Louisville's 1860 population was 68,033. While it ranked twelfth in size nationally, Louisville was the fourth largest slave-state city, trailing only Baltimore, New Orleans, and St. Louis.[4]

Unlike in the Deep South, where cotton was king, Kentucky was a land of diversified farming. The state typified "the American term 'country.'" Most

of Kentucky "was isolated by land and forest barriers, and the local population was made up largely of yeoman farmers." The state's "basic land pattern
was of small farmers who owned from 50 to 200 acres of land." In 1840 the
Bluegrass State ranked first nationally in the production of wheat and hemp,
second in corn and tobacco, and fourth in rye. Kentucky farmers grew more
than half of the nation's hemp, a fiber used in making ropes, rough clothing,
and bagging for cotton bales. Livestock raising was also widespread in Kentucky—notably, horses, mules, cattle, and hogs. Only one other state bested
Kentucky in growing hogs and mules.[5]

In 1860 Kentucky ranked ninth in slave population among the fifteen
slave states. The South's peculiar institution had been declining in Kentucky
since 1830, when slaves accounted for 24 percent of the total population. In
1860 the percentage of slaves had shrunk to 19.5, while the percentage of free
blacks in the state had grown from 0.7 to 0.9. Several factors contributed to
the decrease in the enslaved population. The demand for labor dropped after
the frontier era passed. At the same time, Kentucky agriculture did not require
the large number of slaves used on cotton, rice, and sugar plantations in the
Deep South. This situation led to a large slave trade after 1830, when many
Kentucky slaves were "sold down the river." For the most part, Kentucky
whites were too poor to own slaves. On the eve of the Civil War, the average
slaveholder possessed about five slaves; only Missouri had a lower number.
But almost all slave-state whites, rich and poor, supported slavery as the foundation of white supremacy. Many poor whites in Kentucky and elsewhere
dreamed of becoming wealthy slave owners.[6]

No state faced the secession crisis of 1860–1861 with more trepidation
than Kentucky. Slavery and a common culture bound the state to the South.
Family ties and trade linked the state to both sections. In the end, unionism
prevailed. Most Kentuckians were too devoted to the old Union of their forebears to risk secession. Indeed, "for that aspect of Southernism that was identified with secession in 1860–1861 Kentucky had no heart," wrote historians
James G. Randall and David H. Donald. They explained that "Southerners
had long realized that Kentucky was 'different.'" The Bluegrass State's political heroes were senators Henry Clay and John J. Crittenden, men who "had
put the Union first and the state second; or, to put it more accurately, had
thought of the state in terms of the Union" explained Randall and Donald.
Yet by *Union*, almost all white Kentuckians meant a Union *with* slavery. Fearing that President Abraham Lincoln and his "Black Republican Party" would
abolish slavery, eleven slave states seceded in 1860 and 1861 and founded the
Confederate States of America on the twin pillars of black bondage and white
supremacy. Likewise, in border states like Kentucky and Missouri, white

supremacy was at the heart of universal white values "or, more specifically, a belief that Western civilization was a product of characteristics unique to the white race and that all interracial relationships must protect the white race from subjugation or degradation by the black race," historian Aaron Astor wrote. The touchstone of border-state thought was "the thirst for order in a region challenged by both abolitionism and secessionism. . . . It would trump all concerns about sectional honor in the ensuing crisis, revealing a population that embraced slavery and Union, or conservative unionism." Abolitionists were rare in Kentucky. Almost all unionists, both slaveholders and nonslaveholders, scorned secessionism and abolitionism with equal fervor.[7]

Indeed, nonslaveholding whites felt they had a stake in preserving slavery. They "recognized that the path to wealth, status, and power in the South was through the ownership of slaves," historian Gary R. Matthews wrote. "This understanding provided the non-slaveholder with an incentive to support an institution that he hoped someday would provide him with the means to join the ruling class." He added, "The only shift in the balance of power that these poor whites possessed when measured against the African Americans was race. If the slaves became free, the master class argued, they would be the natural competitors of the poor whites, both economically and sexually, a thought that threatened the very core of the Southern racial class structure." Therefore, according to Matthews, "whiteness became a property right that even the poor white had the 'right to use and enjoy,' along with the reasonable expectation to consider himself as part of 'a broadly construed ruling class.'"[8]

Thus, the Kentucky press, both Union and Confederate, reflected the deep racism of almost all whites in the state. The rebel newspapers claimed that Kentucky could remain a slave state only if it seceded and joined the Confederacy. Union papers countered that slavery would perish if Kentucky left the Union. In other words, the press largely argued over the means to an end—the preservation of slavery and white supremacy.

Kentucky's sons had fought, bled, and died in every American conflict. Yet when the Civil War came in April 1861, most Kentuckians were loath to spill the blood of their fellow Americans. In May the state proclaimed its neutrality within the Union, a stand most people welcomed with relief and thankfulness. Only after Confederate and then Union forces invaded the state in September 1861 did Kentucky enter the war on the Union side. Between 1861 and 1865, 90,000 to 100,000 Kentuckians fought for the Union, and some 25,000 to 40,000 joined the Confederate forces.[9]

In 1860 the bitter years of sectional strife over slavery and its growth climaxed in the presidential election. Indicative of a deeply divided nation, four candidates sought the office. Each took a different stand on the central issue:

the expansion of slavery into the federal territories. The Democratic Party split into Northern and Southern factions. Senator Stephen A. Douglas of Illinois was the Northern Democrat. Dubbed the "Little Giant," he called for "popular sovereignty." Let citizens of the territories vote slavery in or out, he proposed. Douglas's running mate was a conservative Southerner, Herschel Vespasian Johnson of Georgia. Southern Democrat John C. Breckinridge, the sitting vice president from Lexington, stood on a platform that supported the Supreme Court's notorious decision in *Dred Scott v. Sandford* (1857). The high court ruled that, free or slave, African Americans were not citizens and that Congress had no power to bar slavery from the territories. That decision only widened the rift between slave states and free states. To balance the ticket geographically, the Southern Democrats chose Joseph Lane of Oregon as their vice presidential hopeful. Abraham Lincoln, the Kentucky-born Republican candidate from Illinois, opposed any further spread of slavery into the territories. Because the Republicans were exclusively a free-state party, Lincoln's running mate had to be a Northerner—Hannibal Hamlin of Maine. John Bell of Tennessee rounded out the field. As the nominee of the Constitutional Union Party, he sidestepped the slavery-in-the-territories question and campaigned for "the Union, the Constitution and the enforcement of the Laws." He ran with a conservative Northerner, Edward Everett of Massachusetts.

The Kentucky press quickly chose sides, but only among Douglas, Bell, and Breckinridge. Nearly all whites in Lincoln's native state despised him and his anti-slavery party. Most papers that backed Bell or Douglas in 1860 turned out to be unionist during the secession crisis. The Breckinridge press, led by the *Louisville Courier, Kentucky Statesman,* and *Frankfort Yeoman,* became the pro-Confederate press. Likewise, the Breckinridge Democrats formed the core of the Southern Rights Party, an arm of the region-wide secessionist movement. Bell and Douglas partisans were the Kentucky Union Party's nucleus. The *Journal,* the *Observer & Reporter,* and the *Commonwealth* were typical of Bell papers that embraced the Union cause. The *Democrat* and most other Douglas organs were also pro-Union. Apparently, no paper that endorsed Breckinridge was unionist, but some Bell and Douglas sheets converted to secessionism.

The Confederate Press

Louisville Daily Courier

Walter Newman Haldeman published the *Courier* in Louisville from its founding in 1844 until federal authorities shut it down in September 1861. Fearing arrest as a traitor, he escaped to the rebel army at Bowling Green, where he resurrected his paper. In February 1862 Haldeman departed the Bluegrass State with the retreating Confederates, and the *Courier* rolled off borrowed presses now and then until the war concluded in rebel defeat in 1865. Despite his ignominious exit from Louisville in 1861, Haldeman returned in triumph to the Falls City in 1865 and restarted the *Courier.* Three years later, he bought the *Journal* and the *Democrat,* merging them with his paper into the *Courier-Journal.* The new editor was Henry Watterson, a Washington, DC, native, ex-Confederate soldier, and wartime editor of the *Chattanooga Rebel.* Dubbed "Marse Henry" after his hair and mustache turned a snowy white, Watterson made the *Courier-Journal* one of the leading papers not only in the South but also in the nation.[10]

Ironically, Haldeman learned the rudiments of newspapering from his future foe, George D. Prentice, the *Journal's* sharp-penned editor. Prentice, of course, had no idea he was nurturing an enemy-to-be when he hired the teen-ager as a clerk. Haldeman was born on April 27, 1821, in Maysville, a bustling Ohio River port in northern Kentucky. He attended Maysville Academy with two future foes: Yankee generals Ulysses S. Grant and William O. "Bull" Nelson. Maysville was Nelson's hometown, too; the Ohio-born Grant moved to town with his family. At age sixteen, Haldeman quit school and migrated with his father down the Ohio River to Louisville. While working at the *Journal,* Haldeman gained "a full knowledge of the printing business, and of journalism." After he left Prentice's employ, he borrowed $300 from his aunt and started a successful bookstore. Meanwhile, in 1843 a group of printers founded the *Daily Dime,* a newspaper that proved less than profitable. Even so, the *Dime* caught Haldeman's fancy, and in 1844 he sold his store and bought it. The original owners were probably glad to drop the *Dime* on Haldeman, as they had defaulted on loans to keep the enterprise going. Haldeman soon reversed the *Dime's* decline. After just four months, he bought new type and increased the paper's physical size. At the request of advertisers, he renamed it the *Morning Courier,* which debuted on June 3, 1844. Later, it became the *Daily Courier.* The paper was moderately Whig, but to attract Democrats and independents, Haldeman emphasized news. He was the first publisher west of the Appalachian Mountains to stress news gathering. Evidently, Haldeman left the job of penning editorials to staffers, at least at first. The publisher's 1902 obituary in the *New York Times* noted that he was "a good writer himself" but specialized in advancing the business end of his paper, "and for that line he had quite an unusual aptitude." The *Times* characterized Haldeman as "a man of unusual force of character, but remarkably modest, so that he resented any form of publicity about himself." Along the way, he had several different partners, including Reuben T. Durrett, who bowed out as the *Courier*'s editor in 1859. Durrett's successor was Robert McKee, a delegate to the fractious 1860 Democratic National Conventions in Charleston and Baltimore. McKee was editing the paper when federal authorities stopped its press. Durrett remained a *Courier* contributor and allegedly wrote the editorial that led to the paper's closure and his arrest and brief imprisonment for treason.[11]

Durrett was used to landing in hot water, having survived an 1857 gunfight with Prentice. Barbed words preceded the bullets. First, the *Journal* claimed that Albert Gallatin Talbott of Danville, a Democratic candidate for Congress, was "an Abolitionist and non-resident of the State"; then on July 20 it claimed that Democratic congressman John Milton Elliott of Prestonsburg was a drunk. The next day, the *Courier* blasted the *Journal*'s cheeky "Plug Ugly editor" and his paper, "the principal Plug Ugly organ in Kentucky." The *Courier* flayed the Connecticut-born Prentice as a hypocrite, accusing the "imported wooden nutmeg Yankee" of editing an anti-slavery paper in his home state. The *Courier* heaped on the race-baiting, claiming that Prentice had declared in the *Journal* "that *'all men have a right to liberty no matter what color.'*" He had "repeatedly uttered other Abolition sentiments equally as vile" and never missed "an opportunity to exhibit his sympathy for the Black Republicans and n—r-stealers of the North." The attack incensed Prentice, who immediately dispatched a letter to Durrett demanding to know whether he had written the retort and, if so, insisting that he retract it in the next issue of the paper. On July 21 Durrett returned fire, denying that Prentice had any "right to interrogate me as to the authorship of any article in the Courier unless you see my name at the head of its columns as editor." The rivals swapped more poison pen letters, but Prentice got in the last word: "I shall denounce you to your face the first time I see you upon the street. I shall be upon Third cross street myself in half an hour or less, and I hope I shall not have to wait for you long." Armed with pistols, the two men went gunning for each other, although the details of what really happened are as cloudy as gun smoke. Eyewitness accounts vary. Reportedly, Prentice squeezed off four shots to Durrett's three. They missed each other, but one of Prentice's bullets supposedly wounded a bystander. Naturally, the dueling editors disagreed on how their shoot-out went down. Thereafter, Prentice and Durrett were content to battle verbally. And when the Yankees shut down the *Courier* and hauled Durrett off to prison, Prentice was among those pleading for his release.[12]

Before the war, the *Courier*'s editorial slant gyrated with the mercurial Haldeman's wildly shifting politics. He endorsed the anti-Catholic and anti-immigrant American, or Know-Nothing, Party after the Whig Party splintered and collapsed over the controversial Kansas-Nebraska Act of 1854. He advocated abolitionism, but only briefly. By 1860, the erstwhile anti-slavery Haldeman, the master of the volte-face, was a rabid pro-slavery Southern Democrat. In 1861 he made the *Courier* Kentucky's loudest secessionist trumpet.[13]

Kentucky Statesman

When South Carolina seceded in December 1860, Thomas Bell Monroe Jr. sat behind the editor's desk at the semiweekly, devoutly Democratic *Kentucky Statesman*. An attorney and a journalist, Monroe was just twenty-seven years old. The *Statesman* had started as a Whig paper in 1849, but some Democrats bought it seven years later and hired Monroe as editor. In 1859 the voters elected him Lexington's mayor, and Governor Beriah Magoffin, a Democrat, named Monroe secretary of state, the youngest person to hold that office. Like the *Courier*, the *Statesman* championed Breckinridge for president in 1860. After penning fiery pro-slavery and pro-secession editorials for most of 1861, Monroe closed the *Statesman*, joined the Confederate army, and became a major in the Fourth Kentucky Infantry Regiment of the storied "Orphan Brigade." Monroe was fatally wounded on April 7, 1862, the second day of the Battle of Shiloh, Tennessee. His admirers in gray included Ed Porter Thompson, a brigade veteran who chronicled the Orphans' story. He wrote of Monroe: "The bold and uncompromising stand which he took for Breckinridge and State rights drew upon him not only the attention of Kentucky and contiguous States, but the malignant wrath of both the enemies of free government and the short-sighted of even the Douglas Democracy." Monroe was also a fearless editor, according to Thompson. "His pen became a barbed arrow, which penetrated all the flimsy defenses of the opposition, and galled them like the open play of a Damascan blade."[14]

Frankfort Yeoman

Established in Frankfort on February 13, 1840, the pro-Breckinridge and pro-secession *Frankfort Yeoman* normally came out three times a week, but it was a daily when the General Assembly was in session. During the secession crisis of 1860–1861, the *Yeoman* seemed to function as the semiofficial organ of Democratic governor Beriah Magoffin's administration. In 1852 twenty-two-year-old Samuel Ire Monger Major Jr. became its editor. Born near Frankfort in 1830, as a lad he had reputedly collected berries and nuts while other boys shot marbles and played ball. He supposedly sold his produce in town to earn money to buy books. Major received a classical education in Frankfort. When he took over the *Yeoman*, he crossed swords with the rival

Commonwealth and its editor, Thomas M. Green. Major so riled his competitor that Green challenged him to a duel in 1857. Major accepted, and both parties named seconds. Major's man arranged the time and place—June 11, "at or near the mouth of the Big Sandy river" in Virginia. "Weapons were to be the ordinary rifle known as the Kentucky or Western rifle carrying a ball not larger than sixty to the pound, the barrel of the gun not to exceed 38 inches in length; distance ninety yards." Green rejected the terms, and the affair of honor never came off.[15]

Local and Regional Confederate Papers

Several other papers championed the Confederate cause, often in towns that had unionist papers as well. In general, Union sentiment rose with the terrain in Kentucky. Secessionism was strongest in the flatlands of the Jackson Purchase, the state's westernmost region. Dubbed "the South Carolina of Kentucky," according to an 1885 history book, the Purchase was the state's only Confederate-majority region, and rebel journals ruled.[16]

Few, if any, of the Confederate journalists possessed pricklier pens than a Purchase pair: *Columbus Crescent* publisher Edward I. Bullock and his editor, Len G. Faxon. The latter once scorned Union troops based at nearby Cairo, Illinois, as "bow-legged, wooden-shoed, sour craut stinking, Bologna sausage eating, hen roost robbing Dutch sons of —." Faxon was an editor in Cairo before the war, having cofounded the *Cairo Times* with W. A. Hacker. "Hacker was the heavy editor, while Faxon with a dreadful long-pointed sharp stick, stirred up the animals." Their weekly paper was a supporter "of the old bourbon barefooted Democracy." On July 4, 1855, the flighty Faxon started the rival *Cairo Delta*. The new publication mostly eschewed politics, "but it wielded a free lance for every comer, and poked and prodded and put on a long-tail coat and would tread majestically around dragging this behind and begging some man to tread on it." Faxon's replacement at the *Times* was Ed Willett, a "poet, journalist and erratic young man." In November, when the *Times* and the *Delta* merged, Faxon discovered "what he lacked in Willett," and Willett discovered "certain essential qualities" in Faxon. The two "wooed and wedded and joined their two papers together." Faxon had fans far beyond Cairo. An admiring *Daily Nashville Patriot* proclaimed him "a gentleman" and his town's "one redeeming feature." He was also the local postmaster, evidence that he supported Democrat James Buchanan for president in 1856. Equally important, "the color of his politics is the best of proof that he is a judge of brandy." Faxon was a "brick" who, "in his efforts to build up the city . . . is neither daunted by dangers nor deterred by difficulties." When the Mississippi River overflowed its banks and flooded Cairo, the editor supposedly "sat a-straddle of his office with his feet dangling" in the water. His paper stock inundated, Faxon penned "editorials in praise of the town on a shingle." He was reputedly the mayor of Cairo when the Mississippi inundated the town again. Anxious to hear from his brother, Hank, Len scribbled "a telegram on a shingle, sitting astride of his housetop, and tossed it down to a chap in a boat with orders to pull for the telegraph office with it."[17]

Other papers frequently reprinted Faxon's humor. When Brosen's Comet streaked across the heavens above Cairo in 1857, Faxon claimed the citizens "have made arrangements to stop the comet" and use it to plug a hole in their levee, Tennessee's *Fayetteville Observer* reported. Up north in Bloomington, Illinois, the *Pantagraph* published Faxon's story about an unknown thief who broke into the *Times and Delta* office and stole five of his new shirts. The "miscreant," the editor concluded, "was most decidedly a hog, or he would have left us at least one for a change." Faxon wondered if the robber was editor Mose Harrell of the *Emporium* in nearby Mound City, Illinois, or maybe John C. Noble, editor of the *Paducah Herald*. "Whoever the rascal may be, we would like to take one look at him in order to gratify our curiosity to see a man who would assail a printing office for the sake of plunder."[18]

A little less than three months later, Faxon lost his shirt, figuratively speaking. He had borrowed money to buy some city lots, could not pay his creditors, and had to sell the real estate. He advertised the tracts in his paper, copiously adorning his half-column notice "with 'fists,' exclamation points, pictures, &c." The ad promised, "No joke! To the tallest bidder!! . . . Neighbor's wood piles convenient on three sides!! Out of sight of the Cairo Company's office and whiskey shops! No old newspapers taken for cash, particularly the Times and Delta. At a safe distance from the Mayor's residence!! Gold and silver taken at par. Banjo will be present, and wag his tail when the cash is paid. (Dog.)" Below the official for-sale notice, Faxon added a long description of the lots. The property overlooked "Joe Littlefield's onion patch" and was near Mose Harrell's old house. "The earth is of first-rate quality for making brick and cultivating snakes. Orange and Magnolia trees perpetually in bloom in the back yard (that is, they might be)." The soil was amply fertile for cultivating plum, peach, or apple trees, and it was "the healthiest location in the city for a small cemetery." Squirrels loved the lots, which, alternatively, could be the site of "a potato patch, a small saw mill, or . . . a monument." Faxon also suggested other uses: "a railroad station, a pasture for dilapidated cows," or a good spot "for a circus, elephant show, &c."[19]

The *Louisville Courier* mined another Faxon nugget—the tale of a "crazy man" wandering about Cairo at night and scaring people. "What is he crazy about—love or spiritualism?" the editor mused. Again, he poked fun at his editor friends. "Neither John Noble nor Mose Harrell, have escaped, and visited our city recently." Before the paper folded in 1859, the *Times and Delta* "flourished finely under its dual title, because it combined the materials of an almost certain success in its publishers."[20]

Edward Bullock, Faxon's boss in Columbus, was a Virginia-born lawyer and graduate of William and Mary College. He moved to Kentucky and was elected a commonwealth attorney and Whig state representative from Russell County. In 1841 he moved to the Jackson Purchase and settled in Hickman and then Mills Point, where he practiced law and ran the Whiggish *Hickman Argus*. He moved to Clinton in 1850 and then to Columbus in 1856. After the demise of the Whigs, Bullock switched to the Democrats. He and a partner founded the *Columbus Crescent* in about 1859. He became its publisher and editor after Faxon joined the rebel army, part of which occupied Columbus in September 1861. In honor of the rebels' advent, Bullock renamed his paper the *Daily Confederate News* and proved to be Faxon's equal, or perhaps his superior, in blood-and-thunder editorializing. "We want to kill a Yankee," he boomed, "must kill a Yankee—never can sleep sound again until we do kill a Yankee, get his overcoat and scalp."[21]

The Union Press

The *Journal, Democrat, Commonwealth,* and *Observer & Reporter* were the main unionist papers in Kentucky, but the Union press also included several small weeklies across the state. In many towns they sparred with Confederate papers. There were army papers at Paducah, Columbus, and elsewhere. In 1864 the *Louisville Daily Union Press* began as "the Official Paper of the United States for the State of Kentucky and the Southern portion of Indiana and Ohio." The publisher was Calvert, Civill and Company. The *Press* supported the war, Kentucky's Unconditional Unionist Party, and the Lincoln administration; it lasted until 1865.[22]

Louisville Daily Journal

Editor George Dennison Prentice's *Journal* represented the conservative unionism of most Kentuckians. Calling themselves Union Democrats, they favored a vigorous prosecution of the war against the Confederates, whom they detested as traitors, yet they denounced secessionism and abolitionism with equal fervor. In other words, the *Journal,* like the majority of white Kentuckians, was pro-war, pro-slavery, anti-Lincoln, and anti-Republican. Lincoln was never popular in his home state. Whites especially despised him because of the Emancipation Proclamation—even though it did not apply to Kentucky—and the enlistment of African Americans as Union soldiers. In

1863 the *Journal* endorsed Union Democrat Thomas E. Bramlette for governor, and in 1864 the paper backed Yankee general and Democrat George B. McClellan over President Lincoln.[23]

Prentice, a native New Englander, was only twenty-seven years old when he became editor of the *Journal* in 1830. Arguably, he was second only to longtime *Courier-Journal* editor Henry Watterson as Kentucky's most influential nineteenth-century journalist. Born in Connecticut on December 18, 1802, Prentice graduated from Brown University at the top of the class of 1823. He started his career as a journalist in Hartford, where he was the successful editor of the *New England Weekly Review.* He moved to Kentucky in 1830 to write a laudatory biography of Henry Clay, who still had presidential aspirations.[24]

While working on the Clay book, Prentice still found time to write for the *Review,* which published each of his missives as a "Letter of a Strolling Editor." In one especially lacerating communiqué, he lampooned a Kentucky election, gleefully informing Yankee readers that when the polls were open, "whisky and apple toddy flow through our cities and villages like the Euphrates through ancient Babylon." He conceded that the vote was "conducted . . . with tolerable propriety" in Lexington, Clay's hometown. Prentice was less charitable in describing Frankfort, which leaned toward President Andrew Jackson, Clay's political and personal foil. There in Kentucky's capital city, "Jacksonianism and drunkenness stalked triumphant—'an unclean pair of lubbery giants,'" Prentice punched. He recounted that there were several "'runners" at the polls, each one "with a whisky bottle poking its long neck from his pocket"; these individuals "were busily employed bribing voters." In addition, "each party kept half a dozen bullies under pay, genuine specimens of Kentucky alligatorism, to flog every poor fellow who should attempt to vote illegally." He figured "a half a hundred of mortar would scarcely fill up the chinks of the skulls that were broken on that occasion." One of the whiskey-toting toughs asked Prentice if he was a voter. When he said no, the brute replied, "'Ah, never mind,'" and offered Prentice a bottle. "'Jest take a swig at the cretur and toss in a vote for Old Hickory's boys—I'll fight for you, damme!" Prentice decided discretion was the better part of valor. "Here was a temptation to be sure; but after looking alternately at the bottle and the bullies who were standing ready with their sledge-hammer fists to knock down all interlopers, my fears prevailed and I lost my whisky." Soon afterward, Prentice "witnessed a fight that would have done honor to Mendoza and Big Ben." One double-fisted combatant belonged to the "Salt River Roarers." The other Prentice christened "Bullet Head," declaring that the man's noggin, framed with black hair, "looked like a forty-pound cannon shot" and that his bulging biceps resembled "a pair of cables knotted at the ends." The battlers "tugged and strained and foamed at the mouth, and twined like serpents around each other's bodies" until Bullet Head managed to pin his opponent. "Gouge him!" a dozen men yelled. As he prepared to pop out the Roarer's eye, "the prostrate man, roused by desperation and exerting a strength that seemed superhuman, caught his assailant by the throat with a grasp like that of fate," Prentice recounted. Thus throttled, Bullet Head's face "turned black, his tongue fell out of his mouth, and he rolled to the ground as senseless as a dead man." Prentice "turned away a confirmed believer in the doctrine of total depravity." His mockery doubtless delighted sophisticated New Englanders and confirmed their suspicions that Kentuckians and other westerners were brainless, brawling, besotted barbarians. In any event, Prentice's scorching style presaged his editorializing at the *Journal*. He would eviscerate his enemies—Democrats, disunionists, and "Black Republicans."[25]

Prentice's *Biography of Henry Clay* was more hagiography than history, but it impressed Kentucky Whigs, who beseeched him to start a party paper in Louisville as competition for Shadrach Penn's formidable and deeply Democratic *Louisville Public Advertiser*, the West's first daily paper. The *Journal* appeared on November 24, 1830, thus beginning an eleven-year editorial feud between Prentice and Penn that stopped only when the latter left to start a newspaper in St. Louis. Meanwhile, the wily Penn, who had begun publishing the *Advertiser* in 1826, launched a preemptive strike on September 10, 1830, after he heard that a rival paper was on the way. Prentice's snide account of the Frankfort election had reached the West; the *Cincinnati Advertiser* republished the letter under the headline, "PRICK ME A BULL CALF TILL HE ROAR." Penn was eager to share the maligning missive with his readers, in the expectation of discrediting his upstart competitor before he put out a single paper. Penn poured on the satire, claiming he wanted to publicize the letter so that Prentice "shall be known by the people whose patronage he is seeking." Penn proposed that Prentice's correspondence "may be viewed as a fair specimen of his 'fine literature,' his 'drollery,' 'strong powers of sarcasm,' and, above all his 'poetical capacity.' The respect and attachment he displays toward Kentucky (to say nothing of the Jackson party) must be exquisitely gratifying to the respectable portion of Mr. Clay's friends in this city." Penn reloaded and fired again: "To them we commend the letter of Mr. Prentice as an erudite, chaste and veritable production, worthy of the 'great editor' who is hereafter to figure as Mr. Clay's champion in the West. We may, moreover, congratulate them in consequence of the fair prospect before them; for with the aid of such an editor they cannot fail to effect miraculous revolutions or revulsions in the political world." The *Advertiser*'s boss was certain that "the occupants of all our fish markets will be confirmed in their devotion to the opposition beyond redemption." Penn's ploy ultimately backfired. It was likened to Francis Jeffrey's biting review of Lord Byron's first poems, which launched "his great career."[26]

Penn's withering rejoinder unsettled some of Prentice's patrons, but he soon proved that their faith in him was justified. After the Whig Party was founded in 1833, the *Journal* became Kentucky's "Whig Bible" and the most widely read paper in the state. The editor's "pen bristled like the 'fretful porcupine' and he shot the pointed quills in every direction." His prose "frequently made people laugh, sometimes stare, and often squirm, and he seemed ever equally indifferent as to which result flowed out from his pen."[27]

Prentice got even with Penn via a prank that almost brought the two editors to blows. The *Journal* chief came across a copy of a New Orleans paper that contained an article about a gruesome murder. The issue was about a year old, but still pristine. Prentice sprinkled it with water, neatly folded it, carefully ironed out the wrinkles, wrapped it, and had a messenger deliver it to Penn with the greeting: "Compliments clerk of the steamer Waucousta, five days, seventy-eight hours out from New Orleans. Quickest trip on record." Penn fell for the ruse. He literally stopped the press and had the murder story set in type, certain he had scooped the *Journal.* In an accompanying article, he thanked the clerk and complimented the captain for his record-breaking journey. Penn was doubly mortified when he found out that Prentice had tricked him. Not only was the slaying ancient news, but everybody familiar with steamboats knew that the *Waucousta* was a slow, leaky old tub that never could have made a record-setting run. Prentice kept rubbing it in. Henceforth, whenever the *Advertiser* published a big story, the *Journal* would needle, "Did that item come by the Waucousta?"[28]

Although Penn and Prentice crossed only pens, Durrett was not the only irate editor who dueled with the *Journal* chief. At one point, he engaged in three such affairs of honor on Louisville streets within a month. Another of Prentice's nemeses, Lexington editor George J. Trotter of the *Kentucky Gazette,* opted for an ambush. When he spotted Prentice, Trotter pulled his pistol and fired at point-blank range. He missed, but his intended victim did not. Like in an old cowboy movie, Prentice whipped out his pistol, shot the gun out of Trotter's hand, and strode away declaring, "I will not harm an unarmed man."[29]

After the demise of his beloved Whig Party, Prentice, like many Kentucky Whigs, settled on the Know-Nothings, who claimed Catholics and foreigners were destroying the country. The *Journal* framed "the general issue" as "between Americanism and foreignism." Prentice's nativist editorializing was blamed, at least in part, for the "Bloody Monday" Election Day riots in Louisville on August 6, 1855. Protestant mobs rampaged through Catholic neighborhoods inhabited by German and Irish immigrants; at least twenty-two people were killed, more were wounded, and property damage was heavy from arson and pillaging. Greatly discredited, the Know-Nothings faded away and were replaced by the "Opposition," a coalition of men unified mostly by their disdain for Democrats. Prentice established the *Journal* as Kentucky's leading Opposition paper.[30]

Louisville Democrat

John Hopkins Harney helmed the *Democrat* during the secession crisis. Though foes up to this time, Harney and Prentice made common cause in support of a war to put down the Southern rebellion and preserve the Union as it was, but not to abolish slavery. After the Emancipation Proclamation, Harney abandoned Prentice and the Union Democrats for the antiwar "Peace" Democrats. The *Democrat* endorsed Peace Democrat Charles A. Wickliffe for governor over Bramlette. Like Prentice, Harney boosted McClellan for president.[31]

Founded in 1843 as the *Advertiser's* successor, the *Louisville Democrat* took on both the *Courier* and the *Journal*. Born in Bourbon County, Harney was editor from the *Democrat's* start-up to its merger with the *Courier* and *Journal* in 1868. He had engaged in "practically a hand to hand fight with Prentice for nearly a quarter of a century, an intellectual combat on a high key, void of rude personalities unworthy of such a mind as Mr. Harney's." Like Haldeman, Harney had no experience in running a newspaper when he first started, and facing Prentice, "a less courageous man . . . would have quailed." But Prentice "always entertained the most unbounded respect for him, and personally they were warm friends." They became pro-Union allies during the secession crisis. In 1861 Harney, with the *Journal's* endorsement, ran for the state house of representatives and won on the Union ticket.[32]

Frankfort Commonwealth

While Harney's unionism waned, that of Albert Gallatin Hodges ultimately waxed. The *Commonwealth's* editor endorsed Bramlette for governor, then drifted to the minority Unconditional Unionists, who allied themselves with the Republicans. In 1864 Hodges endorsed Lincoln for a second term.[33]

Like the *Yeoman*, the *Commonwealth* was a triweekly that increased to a daily when the legislature met. Hodges, every bit as colorful as Prentice, helped start the *Commonwealth* as a Whig paper in 1833. Born in Virginia in 1802, he had moved with his family to Lexington in 1810. At age twelve, he went to work for the *Kentucky Reporter*. Six years later, he started the *Kentuckian* at Lancaster. When that paper failed, the teenaged Hodges was so cash-strapped that he had to walk home to Lexington. On the way, he swam the Kentucky River because he had no money to pay for the ferry. Hodges returned to the *Reporter* as a foreman, but in 1824 he cofounded the *Louisville Morning Post* with D. C. Pinkham. When Pinkham ran off with the paper's funds, Hodges partnered with William Tanner. For the next year, "these two young editors published a rollicking sheet, which was a house divided against itself." The duo took opposite sides in the famous Old Court–New Court fight of the 1820s. "Two pages conveyed Tanner's argument for the New Court Party, and two sheets proclaimed Hodges' faith in the Old Court group." Ultimately, Tanner and Hodges decided that just one of them should run the paper, so they flipped a coin; the loser would sell out, pack up, and leave. Tanner won, and Hodges moved to Frankfort and cofounded the short-lived *Commentator*. A year before the *Commonwealth* began, the General Assembly named Hodges the state printer, a post he held every year, save one, until 1858, when the Democrats finally gained the upper hand in state politics. After the Whigs were gone, Hodges embraced the Know-Nothings and the Opposition. Although his editorials were tough on the *Commonwealth*'s enemies, he was always genial and hospitable and earned their "respect and partiality," even "in times of bitterest strife." In 1860–1861 Hodges was the paper's publisher and J. M. Johnson its editor. Hodges and the *Commonwealth* were typical of much of Bluegrass journalism in the nineteenth century: "Hodges was the *Commonwealth*, and the *Commonwealth* was Hodges."[34]

Lexington Observer & Reporter

Daniel Carlisle Wickliffe's semiweekly *Observer & Reporter* defended the Union cause in Lexington. He became editor and owner of the paper in 1836, six years after it started. Born in Lexington in 1810, he "graduated with much honor" from his hometown's Transylvania University at age seventeen. He was editor of the *Observer & Reporter* for almost twenty-seven years, and during the Civil War he served as secretary of state under Governor James F. Robinson. Wickliffe was reportedly "in very many respects . . . the ablest [editor] . . . that ever wielded a pen in the whole commonwealth of Kentucky."[35]

In Louisville, Prentice's *Journal* and Haldeman's *Courier* squared off on Green Street, between Third and Fourth. Appropriately, the *Courier* was on the south side, the *Journal* on the north. The bearded Haldeman turned forty-nine in 1860; the beardless Prentice fifty-eight. Both were as fiery as ever. Prentice's paragraphs were "the stinging, hissing bolts of scorn," according to romantic poet and New York newspaper editor William Cullen Bryant. "His small round face was fringed with dark hair, a little silvered by age; his eyes gleamed with their early fire, and his conversation scintillated with that early wit which made him the most famous paragraphist in the world"—or so an admiring Civil War correspondent described Prentice. Evidently, nobody thought Prentice was handsome. His enemies often described him as "ugly," and his detractor Durrett called him "plug-ugly." An elderly farmer passed the same judgment on Prentice's looks when he laid eyes on the editor in 1860. That man and his companion of a similar age—apparently a man named Jim Dodd—dropped by the *Journal* office to meet the editor and settle a wager. The man warmly shook Prentice's hand while carefully studying his features. "So, you're old George D. Prentice, air you?" he asked. "Well I'm mighty glad to see you. Jim Dodd bet me you was good looking, and I bet you wasn't; and I think I've won it." Prentice was inclined toward stoutness. Clean-shaven, he was said to be of medium height and had sloping shoulders that made him seem stooped. But his dark brown eyes, set below a broad, sloping forehead, supposedly sparkled when he was happy. Though less famous than his foe, but an equally vitriolic "paragraphist," Haldeman fought Prentice tooth and nail, word for word. On the war's eve, the only thing Haldeman and Prentice had in common was their disdain for Lincoln and his party.[36]

Prentice "was devoted to the Union, yet a staunch advocate of slavery," but "to what extent Prentice molded that opinion, to what extent he was molded by it, is a debatable question." Yet Kentucky's behavior during the secession crisis proved that most whites in the Bluegrass State shared Prentice's simultaneously pro-Union and pro-slavery opinion. Like the *Journal's* editor, they failed to see any contradiction in that viewpoint.[37]

2

The Press and the Presidential Election of 1860

Voters chose from four candidates in the presidential election of 1860. The Kentucky press endorsed three of the hopefuls, the winner not among them. The Louisville papers reflected how the state split: the *Journal* endorsed Bell, the *Courier* rallied behind Breckinridge, and the *Democrat* lined up with Douglas. Bell carried the state, followed by Breckinridge, Douglas, and Lincoln. Apparently, no newspaper of any consequence—perhaps no paper at all—came out for Lincoln, who was elected. The war of words that broke out over the presidential race became even more heated in the secession crisis. The future of the Union was at stake in the former; Kentucky's future hung in the balance in the latter.

While the Whig Party was a casualty of the growing sectional split, the Democrats somehow managed to hold together until 1860. The party met in convention in Charleston in April. But after the pro-slavery Southerners bolted, the Democrats could not settle on a presidential nominee and agreed to try again in Baltimore in June. The rift became a chasm; more Southerners decamped, including Robert McKee of the *Courier*. They held their own convention and nominated Breckinridge. The rest of the party chose Douglas. Of course, both candidates claimed to be the true nominee.[1]

Meanwhile, in early May the Constitutional Union convention opened in Baltimore and nominated Bell. A week later, the Republicans gathered in Chicago and chose Lincoln.

Lincoln never had a ghost of a chance in his native state, and Douglas's prospects seemed poor. Most Kentucky papers boosted Breckinridge or

Bell. The *Courier, Statesman, Yeoman,* and other Southern Democratic sheets claimed that the Kentuckian Breckinridge was the genuine Democrat and the only candidate voters could trust to safeguard slavery and preserve the Union on Southern terms. The Southern Democratic press equated popular sovereignty with abolitionism and characterized Douglas as a power-hungry schemer whose candidacy had divided the party and threatened to hand the election to Lincoln. The Breckinridge papers dismissed Bell as an inconsequential has-been and a mere warmed-over Know-Nothing.

As the campaign progressed, the Breckinridge papers charged that the Douglas Democrats and the Bell men were virtual Republicans who would throw in with Lincoln's party if he won. After the Bell party's candidate finished first in a special election for court of appeals clerk in August, the Breckinridge press grew desperate. They stopped denouncing the Douglas men and begged them to come over to their side. The Breckinridge papers argued that Douglas could not win and urged his partisans not to waste their votes. As the presidential election drew nigh, the Southern Democratic press sought the votes of immigrants, linking Bell to the rabidly anti-Catholic and anti-foreign Know-Nothing Party and reminding them of "Bloody Monday."

The *Journal, Observer & Reporter,* and *Commonwealth,* along with the rest of the Bell press, agreed that Breckinridge was the main competition and focused their fire on him. They appealed to Kentucky's historic unionism, claiming that Bell was the authentic Union candidate and branding Breckinridge a willing accomplice of the fanatical "fire-eaters," whose ultimate aim was an independent slave-state confederacy. Naturally, the Breckinridge press hotly denied that he was a disunionist. The *Democrat* and the handful of other Douglas papers also claimed that Breckinridge was a secessionist at heart, that Bell was a nonentity, and that only the "Little Giant" could beat Lincoln and hold the Union together.

Meanwhile, the pro-Bell *Covington Journal,* published by Samuel Davis, delighted in the enemy's disarray. The paper claimed the Baltimore & Ohio Railroad was offering cheap round-trip tickets to Baltimore-bound Democrats. The *Journal* suggested, "Those of our Democratic friends who desire to witness the last grand conflict between the *Squatter Sovereigns* and the *Fire-Eaters,* led respectively by *Little Dug* and *Old Buck* [President James Buchanan]," should take advantage of the bargain.[2]

In contrast, the pro-Breckinridge *Yeoman* lamented the Democratic rupture but failed to "see that much can be gained in the expression of vain regrets." The paper blamed the division on Douglas and his followers, who were "determined to rule or ruin," and it predicted the Kentucky Democrats would rally to Breckinridge. At the same time, the *Yeoman* tried to spin the schism: "The chances for beating Lincoln, although clouded by this unexpected and unfortunate split in the Democratic ranks, are still far from hopeless." Samuel Major's paper calculated that Breckinridge could count on all fifteen slave states, plus the free states of California and Oregon, while "neither Bell nor Douglas can claim a single state with the least indication of certainty." Yet to defeat Lincoln, the paper admitted, Breckinridge must—and would, according to the *Yeoman*—pocket some Northern states by rallying "enough of the conservative men of all parties . . . to his standard." The *Yeoman* forecasted that the various state Democratic gatherings would ratify Breckinridge's nomination, thus forcing Douglas to bow out. The Kentucky convention backed Breckinridge, but the paper was wrong on almost every other count. Nearly all Northern Democrats got behind Douglas, who stayed in the race. Breckinridge ended up with only eleven of the states the *Yeoman* had predicted he would win, and Kentucky was not among them. Most Northern men, conservative or otherwise, voted for Lincoln, who won the election by triumphing in every free state except for New Jersey, whose electoral votes he shared with Douglas.[3]

The nearly brand new *Woodford Pennant* also gave its nod to Breckinridge, headlining him "the Big Gun—the Favorite Son of Kentucky." Published in Versailles, the Woodford County seat, the paper praised the Southern Democrat for standing "upon a platform which guarantees constitutional protection to the rights of all the citizens of the United States, and a just and equitable administration of the laws in every section." W. O. Coppage and Jonathan H. Shrum, who had announced their paper's start-up on June 1, were sure their candidate would win. They promised the *Pennant* would be "ardently devoted to the maintenance and dissemination of DEMOCRATIC PRINCIPLES," while endeavoring "to conduct all discussions in such manner as will secure the confidence of our own party, and the respect of those whose opinions may be at variance with our own." Coppage and Shrum concluded by warning that "all attempts to impair" the sovereignty of the states or to trample on states' rights would "be resisted with all the power we possess."[4]

The *Owensboro Democrat* was also expected to come out for Breckinridge and his running mate Joseph Lane, although the western Kentucky paper was hesitant about endorsing the Southern Democratic duo, the *Yeoman* said. It reported that if Breckinridge and Douglas both stayed in the race, the *Democrat* had promised, "of course, [we] will be found doing [Breckinridge] . . . all the good we can." Isaac C. Washburn, said to be illiterate, founded the *Democrat* in the Daviess County seat shortly before the war.[5]

In the Bluegrass region, the *Bardstown Gazette* had "given strong intimations, in its last issue, that it intends to give its support to the only national ticket, though it has not as yet hoisted the names of Breckinridge and Lane to its mast-head," the *Yeoman* claimed. The seat of Nelson County, Bardstown was in the Fifth Congressional District, where two other papers seemed to be straddling the fence, the paper reported disapprovingly. "We would like to hear all speak out promptly and take a definite position. We think it is their duty to do so; and any delay at this time might weaken the force of their future advocacy of the claims of either ticket," apparently meaning Breckinridge or Douglas.[6]

In Franklin, the seat of Simpson County in south-central Kentucky, the *Southern Democratic Banner* was all in for the Southern Democratic ticket. The *Yeoman* quoted the *Banner*'s entreaty: "Democrats of the South, rally to the support of your *conservative* men and measures; let 'principles, not men' be your motto. Ward off every element the least tinctured with antagonism to sound, conservative Democracy. Stand firm and unshaken by your cherished mementoes, and our word for it, the victory will be won under the lead of Breckinridge and Lane."[7]

Likewise, the *Statesman* applauded the Breckinridge-Lane team as the candidates "unanimously nominated by all that portion of the Convention not estranged from Democratic principles, and not crazed by fanatical or interested devotion to the fortunes of a favorite." Editor Thomas Bell Monroe, who never missed a chance to declaim Douglas, claimed that the "Rump Convention" had nominated Douglas, while Breckinridge was the choice of the "National Democracy." Breckinridge and Lane stood "upon a platform of principles which must command the cordial endorsement of every true Conservative Democrat, North or South." The Lexington paper was confident that Breckinridge would carry Kentucky and the South because he was "a fit exponent of the great principles of the Constitutional right and State equality."[8]

On the country's eighty-fourth birthday, Walter N. Haldeman's *Courier* advanced the states' rights theme while pondering Independence Day, 1861. "Will the clouds have passed away and the sky be clearer and the sun shine all the brighter for having been temporarily obscured? Or will the storm have gathered in strength and power until even the fool cannot shut his eyes to its rapid and dreaded approach?" The paper mulled "these things, with mingled feelings of hope and fear," while begging citizens to "resolve to stand by the Constitution, to stand by the Union, to stand by the rights of the States, and haply all will be well." In other words, if the North conceded to every Southern demand with regard to slavery and its expansion, the firmament would be everlastingly blue.[9]

Also on the Fourth of July, the *Louisville Democrat* skipped the weather analogies but rained on the *Courier*'s candidates and their followers as "bold and reckless men, inspired by prejudice, [who] have concentrated and organized a party whose ultimate object is avowedly the dissolution of the Union." John Harney's paper expressed the view of almost every Kentucky Unionist during the secession crisis and throughout the war: "We believe Disunionism and Abolitionism to be equally wrong."[10]

On July 4 the *Courier* had congratulated another ally, the *Princeton Bulletin,* for backing Breckinridge and Lane. The *Courier* prophesied that the western Kentucky paper "will do gallant service" for the Southern Democratic ticket. The *Bulletin,* published in the Caldwell County seat, was confident that many Bell backers, including well-known congressman and diplomat Humphrey Marshall of Frankfort, would go over to Breckinridge. "When such support is yielded to that ticket, combined with the present strength in this State, what can be the vote of Kentucky for Bell or any other candidate?" the *Bulletin* crowed. "Nothing more than a 'corporal's guard.'"[11]

In Louisville, "Corporal" George Prentice was having a high time sniping at Breckinridge, Douglas, and Lincoln. The *Journal* hooted that Breckinridge was moving to California and staying until after the election. "Perhaps he thinks that he can better hear the news of his defeat if it comes to him softened by some thousands of miles of distance," the paper suggested. The *Journal* also demeaned Douglas, recalling that in his acceptance letter the "Little Giant" had promised that "he is fully impressed with the responsibilities of the Presidency. We guess he has as ample opportunities of being impressed with them as he ever will have." The *Journal* jabbed that the Breckinridge partisans were calling "the Douglas convention at Baltimore the Rump Convention and are kicking it mercilessly. How long will the Douglas party submit to have its rump so outrageously kicked?" Douglas, sneered the *Journal*, "is no longer a prophet to the Democratic party, and the party will no longer profit to him." The state's chief Bell organ also lampooned Lincoln: "The rail-splitter . . . must look to his laurels, for the census takers in Williamson County, Tennessee, have found an old lady 75 years old, who built 300 yards of good rock fence within the last year with her own hands, and what is more, she gathered and carried in her arms all the materials of which the fence is built." The *Journal* even made fun of the first names of Lincoln's and Douglas's running mates: "Hannibal comes down from remote antiquity and Herschell [*sic*] from away off in the most distant portion of our planetary system; one is nearly lost in old legends and the other cannot be seen without a telescope."[12] Of course, Prentice's paper lambasted the enemy press, too: "The Democratic organs are great fools to undertake to make people think Mr. Bell an Abolitionist. Hate's labor is oftener lost than love's." Meanwhile, the Breckinridge press had trimmed Douglas's name, declared the *Journal*. He was born Stephen Arnold Douglas, but the Southern Democratic editors had now dubbed him "Arnold Douglas"—an obvious comparison to Benedict Arnold.[13]

On July 6 the *Courier* quoted from a trio of Breckinridge papers: the *Cadiz Organ* in western Kentucky, the *Georgetown Gazette* in the Bluegrass region, and the *Lebanon Democrat* in the central part of the state. John S. Spiceland's *Organ* charged that Douglas and his allies had sabotaged the Baltimore convention. He waxed biblical when he wrote, "They have sown the wind and must now be content to reap the whirlwind." Alluding to John Milton's epic *Paradise Lost,* the editor groused that the convention's breakup "and the partial disorganization of the Democratic party are justly chargeable to the mad ambition of an arch demagogue, who would rather reign in hell than serve in heaven." The Northern Democratic nominee, "with all the pride of his lofty talents and brilliant public career, with all his eloquence and popularity, is now swallowed up and lost in his new character, the representative and embodiment of Squatter Sovereignty and as an apostate from Democratic principles." Published in the Trigg County seat, the paper was all for letting Douglas "slide" because "his friends cannot rally a corporal's guard in the South to his support." The *Cadiz Organ* pledged to stand by "the nominees of the National Democratic party—Breckinridge and Lane." The Southern Democrats commonly styled themselves "National Democrats."[14]

The *Georgetown Gazette* forecast a Breckinridge triumph, at least in Scott County. The paper boasted that "Douglas men are like angels' visits—few and far between," and it claimed, "There are more Opposition men in this county that will support Breckinridge than there are Democrats that will support Douglas." According to the *Gazette,* probably a dozen Douglasites dwelled in Georgetown, the county seat, but "they will be 'all right' before the election." Nonetheless, the *Covington Journal* printed a story from the *Gazette*'s rival, the pro-Bell *Georgetown Journal,* disputing claims that "the Yanceyites"—a reference to former Alabama congressman William Lowndes Yancey, the "Prince of Fire-Eaters"—were winning. The *Georgetown Journal* sneered that "a grand demonstration" to ratify Breckinridge's nomination had included only a trio of voters parading through town. Earlier, the *Gazette* had dismissed Bell as "a lifeless old fossil Know Nothing," prompting the *Covington Journal* to reply, "We have no quarrel with our contemporary in regard to the opprobrious epithets he may choose to make use of, but it is due to all concerned to say, that John Bell is not, and never has been, a member of the Know Nothing organization." Even so, the *Georgetown Gazette* and the other Breckinridge papers kept pressing the charge that Bell was an unrepentant nativist. The *Courier* reported that the "Douglasites" had claimed the *Leba-*

non Democrat as one of their own. But the editor of the Marion County paper concluded, "the only hope left to us to defeat Lincoln is to give a united vote for the most available man, and in our present judgment, Breckinridge is that man."[15]

The *Louisville Courier,* to be sure, concurred with all prognostications of Bell's and Douglas's demise in Kentucky. "For the candidacy of Douglas, there is not one sane man in the State [who] would entertain any doubt, or set up any conflicting claim on the subject." The paper jeered at Kentuckians who "profess to think that Bell will carry the State, in consequence of the Democracy being weakened by the Douglas defection." It added, "We anticipate no danger from this source." Predicting election outcomes is risky business for any newspaper at any time. Estimating vote totals is even more perilous, but the *Courier* took the plunge, declaring that "to-day Douglas' vote would not exceed, at the outside 7,500 or 8,000." Haldeman's paper claimed this total was too skimpy to hurt the Breckinridge-Lane ticket and that the Southern Democrats would gain supporters "with each rising of the sun."[16]

While the Kentucky papers panned and praised the various candidates, they simultaneously scorned one another. The *Covington Journal* challenged the *Louisville Courier*'s boast that the Democratic Party was united. The *Journal* had faith that "the reader will not pronounce the foregoing an 'awdacious fabrication' without due investigation," even though "the Courier believes every word of it." Haldeman's sheet, according to the *Journal,* bragged that "wherever the flag of the country floats, there Democracy is found." The exultation was too much for the *Journal.* "Yes; and is generally found wanting," the Covington paper rejoined.[17]

Naturally, the state's most powerful Breckinridge trumpet wanted everybody to think that most state papers were behind the Southern Democrat. Under the headline "Spirit of the Press," the *Louisville Courier* quoted from the *Kenton County Democrat* and the *Owensboro Democrat.* The former, published in Covington, the county seat, by J. A. Slaughter and J. A. Gravenor, confessed it would have endorsed Douglas had he won the nomination of a united party. But the *Democrat* felt duty-bound, like the state party, "to work with all the strength we have for the noble statesmen from Kentucky [Breckinridge] and Oregon [Lane]." Besides, the *Democrat* predicted, Douglas had no chance to carry the Bluegrass State.[18]

Breckinridge was always the *Owensboro Democrat*'s first choice, but the paper admitted swinging toward James Guthrie of Louisville when he was proposed as a compromise candidate. Guthrie was president of the Louisville & Nashville Railroad and had been President Franklin Pierce's treasury secretary. But when Guthrie got nowhere, the *Democrat* hopped back on the Breckinridge bandwagon, calling him the nominee of "the true conservative and National Democracy of the Nation" and the faction that had nominated him "the true National Convention."[19]

Up the Ohio River at Louisville, the *Courier* aimed a double-barreled blast at Douglas and Lincoln. Haldeman's paper claimed the Northern Democrats and the Republicans were in cahoots. A *Courier* reporter wrote that the "Douglas wing of the Black Republicans" and "the Lincoln wing of the same party" met at the Jefferson County courthouse on successive nights to ratify their presidential hopefuls. Speakers at the Lincoln rally included Cassius Marcellus Clay, the fearsome, bowie knife–toting Madison County emancipationist, whose address focused on "the subject of slavery, and the position of the Presidential candidates thereon." The *Courier* scribe guessed that about a thousand people came to hear Clay, most of them out of curiosity. The correspondent characterized Clay as "a man who is believed to be honest, though known to be wrong; and whose sincerity is doubted less frequently than his sanity is questioned." Clay denounced Breckinridge as "a fire-eater and disunionist of the worst sort" but "had little to say of Bell, and that little not unfavorable." Clay said of Lincoln that "he had 'split rails,' and moved from Kentucky to Illinois, both of which he appeared to think indicative of a fitness for the Presidency." The reporter was certain that some of Clay's address "would have been applauded warmly" by the city's Douglas and Bell faithful.[20]

The *Courier* claimed that even some Bell backers were putting money on Breckinridge to capture Kentucky. "One of the most active, influential, and sagacious" Bell men in central Kentucky wagered $2,500 on a Breckinridge victory, the paper boasted. "He will not vote for Breckinridge himself, but he is betting to win, and will win. Straws show which way the wind blows." The editor of the six-year-old pro-Breckinridge *Paris State Flag*—evidently W. W. Pike—announced that "he is authorized to bet any amount from $1,000 to $10,000 that Breckinridge will carry Kentucky at the November election." The Bluegrass paper's ex–political editor, Democratic congressman William E. Simms of Paris, hoped Breckinridge would join him in Washington.[21]

Pike's ally Haldeman was also busy trying to tie Douglas and his camp to the Republicans. In a story headlined "Fusion of Douglasites and Abolitionists," the *Courier* reported that in the Oregon legislature, Douglas Democrats and Republicans combined to form an anti-Breckinridge majority. As a result, Oregon's next two senators would be "a Freesoil Democrat and an Abolitionist." This type of "fusion" was happening all over the North, the *Courier* charged. It claimed that in the South, where there were no Republicans, the

Douglas "orators are proposing a fusion with the members of the late Know Nothing party," meaning the Constitutional Unionists. The paper reported that a speech by a "Capt. Gibson" at the Douglas ratification meeting in Louisville "contains a fair expression of their views and wishes upon the subject." The *Courier* also appealed to the city's immigrants to reject Bell and Douglas, crying: "Are they ready to resign themselves, bound hand and foot, to this coalition between their implacable foes, the Know Nothings and the deserters of the true Democracy!"[22]

The pro-Breckinridge *Harrodsburg Press* proposed that the Douglas and Bell camps might as well unite in Kentucky, given that both groups had been charging that the administration of Democratic president James Buchanan *"was the most corrupt and infamous of all in history."* Presumably, the accusations of wrongdoing also covered Vice President Breckinridge. In any event, a union of the Northern Democrats and the Constitutional Unionists would be consistent, claimed the Bluegrass paper. The *Harrodsburg Press* was descended from the *Harrodsburg Ploughboy*, started in 1846. Owner A. E. Gibbons changed the name to the *Transcript* after 1854. When Gibbons died in 1860, John Carter bought the paper and hired Charles Smedley to edit it. Ultimately, Van Carter, the owner's son, took over as editor and ran the paper as the *Harrodsburg Press*.[23]

On July 16 the *Courier* spread what it considered glad tidings from western Kentucky: the *Henderson Reporter* was off the fence and supporting Breckinridge. "We believe they [Breckinridge and Lane] are the only true representatives of the great Constitutional principles that are at the very foundation of our Government—upon the faithful carrying out of which depends the equality of the States, the preservation of the Constitution, and the perpetuity of this glorious Union," the *Reporter* stated. C. W. Hutchen and E. W. Worsham had started the paper in the Henderson County seat in 1853.[24]

Additionally, the *Courier* was heartened to learn of the *Southern Yeoman*'s start-up in Mayfield, the seat of Graves County in the Jackson Purchase, the state's westernmost territory. Published by C. C. Coulter and J. T. Ingram, the *Yeoman*, which debuted on July 7, 1860, was the county's first newspaper. The "eight-column folio, intensely Democratic in politics," advised that its corner of Kentucky was solidly for Breckinridge. "Only a few political croakers are heard to raise the Douglas note, and that sounds more like the dying wail of intriguing but thwarted demagoguery than the clear notes of whole souled Democracy." The *Yeoman* deprecated Douglas as a fraud and an opportunist, arguing that "the convention which nominated him was not the *true* National Democratic convention." Breckinridge was "the peerless candidate of the National Democracy" and "emphatically the true nominee of the

Conservative Democracy." The *Yeoman* compared Breckinridge to President Andrew Jackson, for whom the Purchase was named.[25]

Although the *Journal* backed Bell and his running mate Edward Everett, Haldeman's *Courier* accused its foe of saying nothing about "the Old Woman's candidates." Indeed, he charged that Prentice aimed to outdo the *Democrat* in supporting Douglas. "In a few weeks it will be acknowledged as the mouthpiece of the little Squatter," the *Courier* scoffed and sneered. "How will the Democrats who have been deceived into the Douglas movement like their new leader?" The *Journal* stuck with Bell, but after Lincoln's election, the Bell and Douglas men united to form the core of the Kentucky Union Party.[26]

As the summer wore on, the Breckinridge, Bell, and Douglas papers insisted that the fortunes of their candidates were rising with the thermometer. The *Paris Citizen* reported that Breckinridge and Douglas supporters were rare in Bourbon County. The paper claimed that local Breckinridge partisans had tried and failed to manufacture support for the Southern Democrat with "raw materials" that included "gunpowder, music, whisky, huzzas," and a false claim that Douglas had quit the race. The rumor that the Northern Democrat had dropped out "was like a small shower in a dry time, soon evaporated." The Bell organ challenged the Douglas supporters to "try their hand." Should they fail "in making a pretty good show upon a small capital, they are very far behind their brethren elsewhere in the business of producing counterfeit enthusiasm."[27]

Likewise, Breckinridge men were scarce in Mason and Clark Counties, to hear the local Bell papers tell it. A meeting of "Yancey's Breckinridgers" in Maysville, the Mason County seat, "was a beggarly account" and "a *fizzle*," according to the hometown *Eagle*. "The Charleston *bolt*, it is now apparent here at least, was not the true electric fluid, but a sort of stage thunder and lightning, made up of the rattle of sheet iron and the fizzle of wet powder." Breckinridge's fortunes, reported the northern Kentucky paper, had sunk "to Davy Jones' Locker." An apparent Breckinridge ratification meeting in Winchester, the seat of Clark County in the Bluegrass, was even more of a bust, reported the Bell-boosting *Winchester Union*. "After all the puffing, brag and bluster of the Seceders here, they did not dare have a public meeting, but crept, a forlorn, and desperate struggling few, into the back room of Mr. Tucker's law office, and there in the shades of privacy, did their work." When a Breckinridge man arrived from Lexington to speak for the candidate, the "disunionists" dissuaded him after hearing that an elderly Douglas man was ready to take the stump and rebuke the out-of-towner. Thus vanquished, the Breckinridge men retreated to "the back room of Tucker's office and nothing was heard but one vociferation of 'thank God!' and two cries of 'mighty!' 'mighty!'"[28]

Two more Bluegrass papers, the *Nicholasville Democrat* and *Mount Sterling Whig,* also barbed Breckinridge and his followers. The *Democrat* reported that James B. Beck of Lexington, another Baltimore seceder, was coming to town to fire up the Breckinridge loyalists. The Jessamine County seat paper observed that Beck would have a hard time explaining why he had joined the "Yanceyites." The *Whig* claimed that "some of the Breckinridge men in this section publicly avow themselves Disunionists and assert this as a reason why they support Breckinridge." The Montgomery County seat paper queried, "Is this the party to defeat Lincoln and save the union?"[29]

The pro-Bell *Russellville Herald* exulted that the Democrats were in disarray in nearby Christian County. This posed a double dilemma for the editor of the *Hopkinsville Press,* published in the county seat. The Breckinridge-Douglas divide put the paper's purportedly pro-Douglas chief in a tight spot. According to a local Democrat, the *Press* chief was waffling. "Each wing of the party threatens a withdrawal of patronage if he does not go with it." The *Herald* hooted, "Alas! for the once 'harmonious' and united, but now divided Democracy! Even the 'cohesive power of public plunder' fails now to hold them together."[30]

Nonetheless, the *Courier* insisted that the Democrats were solid for Breckinridge as well as for Clinton McClarty, the Southern Democratic candidate in a special August 6 election to replace the clerk of the court of appeals who had died in office. The Bell party put up Leslie Combs, a former speaker of the Kentucky house of representatives. The Douglas faithful rallied to Robert R. Bolling. The *Statesman* did more than join the *Courier* in endorsing McClarty. Editor Monroe was ready to wager $500 on a McClarty win. "The amount will be increased to four or five times the above," the *Courier* exulted. "Face the music!"[31]

At the same time, the *Courier* challenged the Bell partisans, including Prentice, to face up to history—namely, the old "corrupt bargain" charge that supporters of Andrew Jackson had leveled against Henry Clay during the 1824 presidential election, a four-man race between Clay, Jackson, John Quincy Adams, and William Crawford. Jackson got the most electoral votes but not the requisite majority, so the election wound up in the House of Representatives, where Clay was Speaker. Clay supported Adams, the runner-up, and the House elected him president. Adams named Clay secretary of state—a stepping-stone to the White House. As a result, the Jacksonians shrieked "bargain and corruption." Foes of the Democrats were constantly invoking Clay's memory "to create or increase prejudice against those who differed from him while living," the paper declared.[32]

The *Journal* and other Bell and Combs papers claimed that Clay would have endorsed their candidates. But Bell, according to the *Courier*, had joined the Jacksonians in accusing Adams of appointing Clay as a quid pro quo. As proof, the *Courier* published a letter Bell had supposedly penned to the people of Nashville, Old Hickory's hometown, in 1827, in which he agreed that Adams had gained the presidency through a deal with Clay "formed upon the basis of mutual benefits to be received and conferred." The paper chortled, "The old Whigs of Kentucky, who really and honestly revere the memory of Mr. Clay, and who consider themselves the custodians of his good name and honest fame, are scarcely prepared to learn that John Bell" disdained the Great Pacificator.[33]

On July 31 the *Statesman* also delved into history to refute charges made by Breckinridge's "slanderers." The paper vehemently denied a story circulating "in some of the more extreme Southern States" that Breckinridge had signed a petition seeking a pardon for John Brown, the fiery Kansas abolitionist who had raided the federal arsenal at Harpers Ferry, Virginia, in 1859 in the hopes of arming a slave rebellion or sparking a civil war over slavery. Brown had been captured, convicted of treason in a pro-slavery Virginia court, and hanged. Anxious to burnish his pro-slavery credentials, Breckinridge's hometown paper denounced the story as "a malignant lie, without the slightest shadow of foundation." The *Statesman* dismissed another accusation that Breckinridge had wanted Kentucky's 1850 constitution to outlaw slavery. In addition, the paper discounted a claim that in the 1848 presidential election, Breckinridge had voted for Whig Zachary Taylor over Democrat Lewis Cass. The *Statesman* explained that although Breckinridge favored Cass, he did not vote for him because, on Election Day, he was off on a hunting trip with eight Taylor men. Breckinridge and the Whig octet had cut a deal—none of them would vote, the *Statesman* said. "Mr. Breckinridge remarked at the time, that if a number of Democrats in the State did as well as he, Cass would carry the State by an overwhelming majority." Taylor won Kentucky and the presidency. Finally, the paper disputed the assertion that Breckinridge was a disunionist. "When challenged to the proof, his slanderers cannot find in all the speeches he has made, one word, one sentiment, which, by the most forced construction, can be found to militate against the Union."[34]

As the day of the special election neared, Bell, Douglas, and Breckinridge partisans hoped—and simultaneously feared—that the contest for court clerk would be a harbinger of the momentous presidential balloting on November 6. The *Courier* knew the stakes were high, warning, "The result will have a mighty effect on the November election." Citing a story in the pro-Douglas *Cincinnati Enquirer*, the paper also raised the specter of a Douglas-Bell fusion. The *Courier* claimed that the duo would soon form a joint ticket in the South and that Douglas and Lincoln would make common cause in the North. "How many Kentuckians, we ask again, will 'aid and abet' this treasonable movement?" Haldeman's paper challenged.[35]

Naturally, the pro-slavery *Courier* considered the anti-slavery Republicans the worst traitors of all. On July 26 the paper mockingly reported on "the 'grand rally' of the Black Republicans of Louisville . . . there being twenty-eight persons present, all told." It charged that the Republicans were scheming to distribute German-language copies of Illinois congressman Owen W. Lovejoy's "infamous Abolition speech." Nationwide, most German immigrants were against slavery.[36]

A few days later, the *Courier* was happy to hear a prediction from the pro-Breckinridge *Paducah Herald*, founded in 1857 by John C. Noble, "the Nestor of the Kentucky press." The Purchase's leading paper predicted that the First Congressional District "will give Breckinridge and Lane from three to four thousand majority—we think four thousand—over Bell." The "outsider" Douglas was out of the running, the paper promised.[37]

In the meantime, Combs handily won the clerkship. He received 68,165 votes to 44,942 for McClarty and 10,971 for Bolling. As it turned out, the vote was indeed a predictor of the presidential election.[38]

The Breckinridge press soldiered on, professing to be confident of a different outcome in November. The *Courier* claimed it was not discouraged, and it tried to cheer the crestfallen. "Truth will prevail. Coalitions brought about by the 'arts of intrigue and management' which are 'fit only for the minions of princes,' cannot last long." Haldeman's paper also sounded the tocsin for renewed political war, entreating Democrats to "fall into ranks. Close up the gaps. Remove the killed and wounded. . . . Delay not for a more auspicious moment; but gird on your armor, draw your swords, throw the scabbards away, and meet the enemy at all points, prepared to triumph or perish nobly battling in behalf of the cause you have espoused."[39]

Monroe's *Statesman* alibied that McClarty lost because in several counties many Breckinridge men had not gone to the polls. The paper asserted that there had been widespread confusion: "The position of McClarty and of Bolling was not understood, and Bolling was voted for under the impression that he was the regular nominee." Perhaps so, but the combined McClarty-Bolling vote was well shy of Combs's total. Nonetheless, the *Statesman* held out hope. "Every day brings us encouraging intelligence for the November contest."[40]

Naturally, the *Journal* was ecstatic—and perhaps relieved—over McClarty's defeat and what it portended for the fall election. The paper also declared that several Douglas Democrats had voted for Combs, presaging the fusion of

Bell and Douglas men as the Union Party during the secession crisis. "What is to be the effect of this signal and utter prostration of John C. Breckinridge in his own State and in the person of his candidate and his party's candidate?" the paper asked, giddy to answer its own rhetorical query. "All intelligent men have perfectly understood for many weeks past that the disunion candidate for the Presidency could not by the remotest possibility obtain a solitary electoral vote in any non-slaveholding State; and now, when his party is miserably and hopelessly routed in his own State, the State where his hopes and the hopes of his friends have been highest, it is evident that nothing can be accomplished for him even in the slaveholding portion of the confederacy." Then came the coup de grace: "Politically he is as dead as if he had lived before the flood and not been admitted to the ark."[41]

In addition, the *Journal* poked fun at the *Courier*'s saber rattling: "Well, let them throw their scabbards away, and we can afford to throw our swords away and keep our scabbards to sheath their swords in when we disarm them. Our opponents are so weakened, that we, armed only with empty scabbards, can thwack them over their heads and shoulders till they bawl lustily for quarter." Partisanship aside, the *Journal* was right. Breckinridge had almost no chance to win the election or even to carry Kentucky.[42]

The *Courier* conceded that many Douglas men had voted for the *Journal*'s candidate, but it did its best to woo wayward Democrats to Breckinridge. The paper dug up more history, this time linking Bell to the Know-Nothings and "Bloody Monday." The *Courier* backed up the charge that Bell had been pro–Know-Nothing by quoting a speech in which he had reportedly concluded, "The best mode in which I can serve my country at the present time, is to stand by the American [Know-Nothing] party." Bell was not a party member but felt *that at heart I am as true to the great and leading principles of the party as I could be were I formally initiated into one of its councils.* The *Courier* claimed that Breckinridge had opposed Know-Nothingism.[43]

At the same time, the *Courier* kept charging that Bell and Douglas supporters were "acting together as a band of brothers, voting for the same candidates, rejoicing over the same successes, and opposing the same party." The *Journal* and the *Democrat* were allies "in the same cause, use the same arguments, attack the same men, and agree as lovingly as twin brothers."[44]

Yet the *Courier* was pleased that the *Southern Democratic Banner* was not for "brother" Harney's candidate. Irate that "some 'Shanghai' Douglas admirer" had claimed the *Banner* was for the Northern Democrat, the Franklin paper fumed, "We denounce such a charge; it is false. It has been our good fortune to battle against the Little Giant ever since July, 1857, and it is our intention to war against him until the sun shall set behind the Western hills on the day of election in November." Supporting Douglas for president "would be an unblushing sin and shame—would haunt us to our grave!" The *Banner* would "rather be a *dog* and bay at the moon, a *toad* and feed upon the vapors of a dungeon, than such a fellow." Not until "the moon is turned to blood and the sun refuses to give light," not before "heaven is converted into a place for the refuge of scoundrels and hell is regenerated and disenthralled," and not until "all nature is shrouded in gloom and horror sits upon the throne of perpetual night" would the *Banner* "in all probability, entertain a very *faint* idea of supporting Mr. Douglas, after our body shall have been devoured by worms and *crawling* reptiles!" The paper had "more decency about our carcass" than to ride the Little Giant's bandwagon.[45]

The *Banner*'s man Breckinridge had been nominated in order to elect Lincoln, thus precipitating Southern secession and disunion, according to a controversial speech Douglas made in Norfolk, Virginia, in August. The *Courier,* of course, took umbrage at this declaration. "It is a calumny upon each and all of those who participated in the proceedings of the Convention that placed Mr. Breckinridge before the people."[46]

The *Courier* switched back to the offensive on September 20, editorializing that Douglas and Bell were helping to push Lincoln to victory and that the Douglas Democrats were Republicans-in-waiting. "The Black Republicans are delighted with the present position of Douglas, and with the Bell-Everetts are earnestly encouraging him to persevere in his efforts to defeat the Democratic party." The paper predicted, "Where Squatterism is preached today, Black Republicanism will be tolerated a year hence, and before the next Presidential election it will be seen that the bulk of those who now support Douglas will occupy front seats in the Republican Church."[47]

"Reverend" Lincoln observed the long-standing tradition of presidential candidates and stayed home during the campaign. So did Breckinridge and Bell. Douglas became the first presidential candidate to personally campaign nationwide. After speaking in Norfolk, he wended his way to Louisville on September 29 and spoke in shady Preston's Woods. Not surprisingly, the *Courier* gave him less than rave reviews in another blatantly biased "news" report. Upon arriving in the Falls City, "Mr. Douglas and cortege passed down Main street, and were received everywhere with those manifestations due those more honest and patriotic." He spent an hour in a hotel before being "again put underway by the engineers of his corps." Most people had come to see Douglas out of curiosity, it claimed. "The procession from the city thitherward that accompanied Mr. Douglas amounted to seven carriages and four furniture wagons," the scribe sneered. Taking the stump, Douglas touted popular sovereignty and claimed that Breckinridge was leading "a disunion party." But the reporter noted that Douglas had failed to tell the crowd that Johnson, his running mate, "has avowed what are called the broadest disunion sentiments," be they "right or wrong."[48]

As Election Day neared, the *Courier*—and much of the Southern press— was filled with dire warnings that Lincoln's election would sound the death knell for slavery and the Union. If Lincoln got in, the South would go out, publishers and politicians in Dixie warned. The Republicans were sure the South was bluffing; they had heard secession threats before. Nonetheless, some conservative Republicans wanted Lincoln to issue a statement to placate the South, but he refused. In October the candidate explained in a letter that he had already promised not to interfere with slavery in the slave states. "A repetition of it is but mockery, bearing an appearance of weakness," he wrote. Besides, the well-publicized Republican platform pledged to leave slavery intact where it was established; it only opposed the extension of slavery into the territories. None of that mattered to the *Courier* and the rest of the Breckinridge press in Kentucky or elsewhere. They portrayed Lincoln and his party as uniformly abolitionist.[49]

"The party of which Mr. Lincoln is the representative is based upon one idea alone—that of hostility to African slavery," Haldeman's paper declared in an especially frenzied editorial less than a month before the election. The *Courier* scoffed at compromises, deriding them as "concessions." The paper disdained Douglas and his "Squatter Sovereignty" platform, positing that it "concedes to the Black Republicans every thing they demand in regard to slavery in the Territories, save only and except Congressional action for its prohibition." The *Courier* repeated its warning that barring slavery from the territories was "the first, but not the last, step, in the Black Republican programme." The paper argued that the anti-slavery movement "can not be met and driven back by concessions. If we would not ultimately succumb to its demands, we must encounter it face to face, with fire and steel, and exterminate it from the land."[50]

Piling on more blood-and-thunder prose that sounded like it came from the pen of a fire-eating editorialist in a cotton state, the *Courier* pleaded that vanquishing opponents of slavery "is our only safety; and either wittingly or unwittingly, every man who folds his arms in the pending conflict between the friends of the Constitution and the cohorts of Abolitionism, and every one who concedes a single point to the demands of the latter, and every one who shrinks from the maintenance of the right for the sake of a delusive peace, is strengthening the hands of the enemy, and increasing the perils of the country."[51]

The *Courier* concluded that when "slavery is hemmed in on all sides, and an anti-slavery sentiment established, and the chains fastened securely on the victim, then will come in rapid succession the last acts of the grand drama." It direly predicted, "The fugitive slave law, already nullified, will be repealed; slavery will be abolished in the District of Columbia; the inter-State slave trade will be prohibited." Finally, "either by 'unfriendly legislation' or by direct action," the South's peculiar institution would perish, resulting in economic ruin, the *Courier* claimed. "Our sugar and rice fields and cotton plantations, will be converted into one vast desert, giving no indications of what it has been or might have been—a desolation and a heritage of woe!"[52]

Bell and Douglas, too, were Kentucky's enemies, argued the *Statesman*. Bell was "the slanderer of Clay and the sympathizer with the Republicans of the North." Douglas was "not in the race in Kentucky, except as a cause of discord and strife in the Democratic party." The choice on November 6, sneered Lexington's Southern Democratic organ, was "Breckinridge or Bell; principles or empty generalities; the Union and the Constitution or vague platitudes."[53]

Just two weeks before the election, the *Yeoman* saw the candidates of the *Democrat* and the *Journal* falling farther behind Breckinridge. "We have reason to assert that we are on the eve of a victory to be made doubly sweet from the reverse in August," the paper chirped. The *Yeoman* boasted that nothing could stop Breckinridge in Kentucky short of "a complete fusion of the Bell and Douglas forces, and this would be difficult to bring about, no matter how willing the leaders may be to see it accomplished." Yet, "something else might also deprive us of the realization of our hopes," the paper cautioned. "Shall we say it? Culpable inactivity and neglect on the part of our friends, whose duty it is to see the vote brought out."[54]

The *Statesman* appealed to naturalized citizens to vote for Breckinridge: "When the storm of Know-Nothingism swept over the State in 1855, and your rights were attacked, yourselves denounced, and many of you cruelly assaulted without cause, the Democratic organization defended your rights, and in many instances the greatest dangers were met to screen you and your families from plug-ugly violence." At the same time, the paper appealed to white supremacy, claiming that popular sovereignty empowered a territorial legislature "to take a man's negroes from him, set them free, and not pay the owner one dollar for them." The *Statesman* argued that Bell and Douglas were bound to lose and that Breckinridge was "the only man that stands between Lincoln and the Presidential chair."[55]

With time running out, Harney's *Democrat* trumpeted for Douglas. It argued that Kentucky's vote was crucial; the Bluegrass State alone could determine the Union's fate. "Kentuckians, upon your vote on Tuesday will, in all probability, depend whether the 'cotton States' are 'precipitated into revolution' or not," the paper warned. If Breckinridge wins Kentucky, "the Fire-Eaters will take it as evidence that she is with them, and once assured that they can have Kentucky for a frontier, and Kentucky riflemen to defend it for them, they will not hesitate to consummate their threatened treason." Harney's paper was confident that "Breckinridge has no more chance of carrying Kentucky Tuesday than he has of getting the vote of Massachusetts." The *Democrat* demanded more than Breckinridge's defeat. "He must be rebuked. He and his treasonable band of conspirators must be told, in no unmistakable tones, that hemp is the only offering Kentucky has to make to treason."[56]

On November 1 the *Yeoman* characterized Breckinridge as the nation's savior. "Democrats! Remember your country, in her hour of need, if you would preserve the Union and the Constitution." Major's paper was still predicting a Breckinridge victory, but it reminded every man inclined to vote his way of "the vast importance of devoting the few remaining days to the work of redeeming Kentucky from the disaster brought upon us by the union of the Bell-Douglas party in August." Meanwhile, from all across Kentucky, the *Yeoman* was "receiving the glorious tidings that the standard of Democracy, upheld by Breckinridge and Lane, is advancing step by step to a decisive victory." All the Southern states "must be united to defeat Lincoln!" the paper warned. But "it would be a burning shame upon the cheek of Kentuckians, if the native State of Breckinridge should be the only one of all the South to refuse to rally to his standard—to the only standard, too, which is raised in defense of Southern rights and Southern honor."[57]

The *Journal* saw a Union imperiled by both Breckinridge and Lincoln. Of course, neither candidate saw himself as a threat to the Union. But perception is reality, and that perception would be mirrored on Election Day. Kentucky would back Bell, the candidate who assiduously steered clear of the slavery-in-the-territories issue and merely called for preservation of the Union. It was a hedge, but one that was welcomed in Kentucky, whose state motto is still "United We Stand, Divided We Fall." Meanwhile, the *Journal* saw "two sectional candidates before the people." It warned, "If the Northern sectional candidate be elected, the supporters of the Southern sectional candidate will go for the dissolution of the Union. If the Southern sectional candidate be elected, his supporters will still go for the dissolution of the Union unless they obtain a score of concessions, not one of which they have the least earthly chance or hope of obtaining." The paper also lamented, "The Black Republicans are shouting for a united North, and the fire-eaters for a united South." Both parties wanted disunion, the *Journal* claimed. "The

Breckinridge men have done even more than the Black Republicans to make a united North, and the Black Republicans are scarcely less anxious than the Breckinridge men to make a united South." The *Journal* concluded, "The two parties or factions are playing into each other's hands like confederated pickpockets."[58]

At the same time, Prentice's *Journal* made an eleventh-hour plea for Bell, arguing that only he could beat Lincoln. "Every Breckinridge man knows this, and, were he not either unscrupulous or half or wholly insane, he would acknowledge it." It concluded that "the issue to-morrow is peace or civil war, prosperity or ruin, Union or Disunion. What are all the questions of banks, tariffs, internal improvements, public lands, sub-treasuries, vetoes, and slavery in the Territories, compared with such an issue?"[59]

On November 5 the *Courier* made a racially charged last-minute pitch to all Democrats: "Remember that Abolition traitors would trample your most sacred constitutional rights underfoot." Foes of slavery "hold that the Constitution of your fathers—that instrument that made the Union, that preserves it, and to-day holds it together—is a 'covenant with death and a league with hell.'" William Lloyd Garrison of Boston, editor of the *Liberator,* the famous abolitionist newspaper, publicly burned a copy of the Constitution, which he called "a covenant with death, and an agreement with hell" because it did not abolish slavery. The *Courier* charged that abolitionists "clamor loudly for an anti-slavery Bible, an anti-slavery Constitution, and an anti-slavery God." Pro-slavery whites could rely only on Breckinridge "for safety in this hour of danger." The Southern Democrats were "the only party that meets and drives back Abolition treason at the ballot-box."[60]

To the chagrin of the Bell, Breckinridge, and Douglas press—and almost every white person in Kentucky—Lincoln won the election. He swept the North, carrying every state except New Jersey, whose electoral votes he divided with Douglas. Breckinridge was the runner-up, pocketing the cotton states plus the border states of Maryland and Delaware. Bell finished third, taking Virginia, Tennessee, and Kentucky. Douglas managed to win only Missouri outright. Bell triumphed in Kentucky with 66,051 votes to 53,143 for Breckinridge. Douglas finished a distant third with 25,638, and Lincoln garnered a mere 1,364. The hometown of the *Journal, Courier,* and *Democrat,* as well as the rest of Jefferson County, went for Bell over Douglas, 4,896 to 3,441. Breckinridge received 1,122 votes, and Lincoln 106. Bell also triumphed in Fayette County and its seat, Lexington, home of the *Statesman,* the *Observer & Reporter,* and Breckinridge. But the vote was fairly close: 1,411 for Bell and 1,051 for Breckinridge. Douglas trailed with 99, and Lincoln got only 5 votes. Breckinridge bested Bell in Franklin County, home of the *Yeoman* and the

Commonwealth, by a vote of 907 to 790. Thirty-seven voters chose Douglas; nobody cast a ballot for Lincoln.[61]

In the last analysis, Kentucky's significant Breckinridge press was unable to sway the state to the Southern Democratic ticket. The *Courier, Yeoman, Statesman,* and at least eleven county papers endorsed Breckinridge, but he won only five of those counties: Caldwell, Graves, Mercer, Scott, and Trigg. The balance went for Bell, except for Marion, where Douglas ran best in the state.

At the same time, the Breckinridge press woefully misjudged Kentuckians' choice for president in 1860. Yet these pro-Breckinridge editors did not have to worry about losing either credibility or readers. After all, the editors were partisans, as were almost all their readers. Likewise, accurate predictions by the *Journal, Democrat, Commonwealth, Observer & Reporter,* and other Bell papers probably did not win their editors many new readers. They too were preaching to the choir. Yet surely the Breckinridge editors were mortified about being so wrong. Even today, newspaper editors pride themselves on being in the know. They must have expected that Breckinridge was doomed in his home state after Combs handily won the clerkship over McClarty. At the same time, the editor of the *Paris State Flag* was so confident of a Breckinridge win that he offered to bet serious money on the Southern Democrat. Perhaps he proposed the wager as a publicity stunt, believing that nobody would take him up on it. But that would have been risky business, as Kentuckians were given to gambling on almost anything from horse races and shooting matches to cockfights and cards. As for the other Breckinridge editors, one wonders whether they really believed their prognostications or were simply trying to rally the troops, especially after Combs won. In any event, faith and intuition were about all any of these editors had to go on in 1860. Scientific polling was about a century away. Nonetheless, the Breckinridge editors were correct in claiming that Douglas would fare poorly in Kentucky. Their claims of a Douglas-Bell merger were correct, if premature. Still, the Breckinridge organs and the few Douglas and Bell papers that embraced disunion were even more misaligned with popular opinion during the secession crisis. Not even the election of a "Black Republican" president and a civil war between North and South could push Kentucky out of the Union.

3

South Carolina, Secession, and Lincoln's Inauguration

In declaring Lincoln's election deplorable yet insufficient grounds for secession, the Breckinridge press mirrored the views of almost all white Kentuckians. Yet the Southern Democratic papers argued that states had the right to leave the Union. In any event, while spurning secession at first, the papers stepped up their criticism of Lincoln and his anti-slavery views and warned the president against using military force against states that might choose to depart. But after South Carolina and the Deep South seceded, the pro-Southern press began to call for a sovereignty convention to take Kentucky out of the Union and put it into the Confederacy.

The cotton states had threatened secession if the "Black Republican" Lincoln won the election. With his victory confirmed, they prepared to exit the Union. But the *Statesman* was not ready for Kentucky to go with them. "No intelligent man in the South will fail to deprecate the election of Lincoln and therein the success of the Republican party as the most serious and lamentable calamity which could have befallen our Republic," the paper mourned on November 9. The *Statesman* feared for slavery and declared that Lincoln was "the author of the infamous 'Irrepressible Conflict' doctrine," even though it was Republican senator William H. Seward of New York who had uttered the phrase "irrepressible conflict" in an 1858 speech. Seward had argued that because slave states and free states were naturally incompatible, strife was unavoidable. At any rate, the paper claimed that the president-elect had declared war on slavery. Lincoln, it noted, had warned that the Union "can not exist as a confederacy of part free and part slave States," a reference to Lincoln's 1858 "House Divided" speech in which he said he doubted the country could last for long "half slave and half free."[1]

The *Statesman* also decried Republican-majority legislatures in nine free states that had passed personal liberty laws. These measures prohibited state authorities from helping slaveholders recover runaway slaves, as required under the federal fugitive slave law. In enacting the personal liberty laws, the Republicans had "nullified the Constitution" and arrayed themselves "in open rebellion against the Federal government." Thus, the *Statesman* was not surprised that "the Southern States grow restless." Even so, the paper grudgingly conceded that Lincoln was "constitutionally qualified" and had been lawfully elected. "Though we deprecate his principles and well understand the purposes of his party, we hope and trust his inauguration will be acquiesced in by all the States." The paper saw "as yet no just cause for revolution or dissolution" and appealed "to our Southern friends . . . to await the full development of Lincoln's policy before striking the fatal blow to the Union."[2]

The *Statesman* maintained that because Kentucky was a border state, it would be "the first and greatest sufferer by abolition ascendancy." In addition, Kentucky was "a barrier of protection to the cotton States against antislavery aggressions." Consequently, "our friends in the South can certainly bear the administration of Lincoln as long as we can." The *Statesman* was confident that "a Democratic Senate, a Democratic [Supreme] Court, and an anti-Republican House" would keep Lincoln from carrying out "the purposes of his party, even if madly determined upon their execution." Thus, the paper challenged, "why be precipitate?" The *Statesman* pledged its love for "the South and her institutions; we have labored to avert this calamity by the election of Mr. Breckinridge." The paper despised "the Republican party" and "its nullification and treason." But the *Statesman* loved "the Union, and would still cling to it with strong hope of yet wresting it from the traitors, and cling to the Constitution with sanguine expectations of preserving it intact."[3]

The next day the *Courier* predicted that Kentucky would not secede just because Lincoln had been elected. "We do not suppose there is one man in it who thinks she will take such a step." However, the paper warned that Kentucky would not become the hangman for Lincoln or the federal government should they decide to punish citizens for obeying the Constitution, meaning defying federal authority. The paper agreed that the "Black Republican party" had "alarmed the South" by endorsing "the war upon slavery." Thus, it was "right and proper that the threatened States should place themselves in an attitude to prevent a violation by a Black Republican administration of their rights or the rights of their citizens under the Constitution." But

Kentucky was not going anywhere—not yet. However, the *Courier* warned, Kentucky "*will never permit an army of Northern mercenaries to be marched across her territory to force one of her Southern sisters to remain in a Union from which in a proper manner she has determined to withdraw.*" Meanwhile, the state "will advise moderation, counsel prudence, urge forbearance, use all her influence, to induce the Southern States to remain in the Union until there is no hope for peace, or justice, or safety in it; she will and can and ought to do no more."[4]

On November 10 the pro-Bell *Covington Journal* began its retreat from unionism by bemoaning "for the first time in a contest for the Presidency the triumph of a purely sectional party." Lincoln and Hamlin "are Northern men; they represent Northern principles, and they are elected by Northern votes exclusively." Lincoln, the paper charged, had countenanced "the infamous sentiment that there is an irrepressible sectional conflict. There is of necessity no such conflict; but a fearful conflict may be created by a President who believes there is or ought to be such a conflict." His party was united "by a common feeling of hostility to the institutions of the South." The *Journal* feared such hostility was spreading and intensifying. "This feeling is the more dangerous because it is based upon prejudice and thrives by misrepresentation. Thousands of demagogues scattered over the North, have an interest in keeping this feeling alive. It is the hobby [horse] upon which they hope to ride into office."[5]

At the same time, the *Yeoman* agreed with the *Statesman* that Lincoln's election "would not, of itself be cause for secession or a dissolution of the Union." The paper urged the South to "give Lincoln's administration a fair trial" while "holding it to a rigid accountability for its acts, and holding itself ready to resist any unconstitutional aggression upon Southern rights." Kentucky, according to the *Yeoman,* "has perhaps suffered more from Northern fanaticism than any or all of the other States combined." The state's "losses in slave property have been heavy," claimed the paper. The *Yeoman* faulted personal liberty laws and decried Ohio Republican governor William Dennison's refusal to extradite to Kentucky Willis Lago, a free African American who had been indicted for theft after "enticing a slave to escape from its owner."[6]

Despite its worries over the future of slavery, the *Yeoman* was confident that Congress and the Supreme Court would "hold Mr. Lincoln in check, until we can make another appeal to the sense of justice of the North to guaranty our constitutional rights." The paper predicted that Lincoln and his party would ultimately "fall to pieces and be driven from power." Nonetheless, "the sectional vote by which [Lincoln] . . . was chosen and the principles upon which he was elected are wrong, and aggressive upon the South." The

Yeoman made it clear that in acquiescing to Lincoln's election, "we give allegiance, not to him nor to his principles which we shall continue to oppose, but to the Constitution."[7]

From the start of the secession crisis and throughout the war, almost all Kentucky unionists made the same distinction cited by the ultimately secessionist *Yeoman*. Union supporters stressed that their fealty was to the federal government, not to the president and his party. At any rate, in late 1860 and early 1861 the *Journal* and other unionist newspapers called on citizens to show their conservative, pro-slavery, and anti-Lincoln unionism in mass meetings. Throughout November and into December, many such gatherings were held, usually without party distinction, in many towns. This movement included Louisville, the bastion of Bluegrass State unionism.[8]

The unionism of Kentucky's pro-Southern papers was always qualified. They favored a Union where slavery was safeguarded and free to expand. Thus, editor Monroe was not willing to mingle the *Statesman*'s "voice in senseless shrieks of 'Union' without foreseeing the effect of such cries, or understanding how the movement is to redound to the advancement of the object." Kentucky was "true to the Union at heart, and however much opposed to the principles of the party lately foisted in power," it would not resort "to revolution." At the same time, the *Statesman* emphasized that the state "has no compromise to make with the Republicans; she has no blind submission to pledge to Lincoln's administration, nor has she harsh words for" states considering secession, however "premature and ill-advised" that might be. Therefore, the paper argued that unionist meetings and "any loud-mouthed and unqualified professions of love for the Union in Kentucky" were neither appropriate nor beneficial. Rather, they "would encourage our common foes in their treason and exasperate our friends to the completion of their fatal work."[9]

Not surprisingly, the *Courier* was similarly skeptical of these unionist gatherings. "Has any leading politician in Kentucky asserted that the election of Lincoln, threatening, menacing, alarming as it is, of itself warrants an immediate disruption of the Confederacy?" it demanded. The *Courier* argued that "Union meetings in Kentucky will only and can only be used to place our people in a false position." Kentuckians were not unconditionally unionist, the paper maintained. "They all stand by it and maintain it as long as is consistent with their own rights—until their honor and safety requires them to go out of it—until the Constitution is violated and trampled under foot by a dominant and hostile sectionalism, and all other remedies have been denied them." Of course, Haldeman's paper expected that Lincoln and the "Black Republicans" would soon deny the slave states "their own rights"—meaning white citizens' right to enslave African Americans. Obviously, the *Courier* believed in the right of secession, characterizing the United State as a "Confederacy" of sovereign states and not a federal republic.[10]

The pro-Breckinridge *Cadiz Organ* also chimed in against unionist meetings, citing a gathering organized by "Bellites" in neighboring Christian County. "There is no danger of Kentucky's seceding," the paper asserted, and it wondered, "Do those self-styled, complacent, hypocritical Union-savers imagine that anyone is deceived in regard to the ultimate design and real end contemplated by them?" According to the paper, the meetings were purely political and calculated to build up the Bell party for the August 1861 elections for a new state legislature. Anyway, the *Organ* doubted that "a string of magniloquent, glittering, and '*highfalutin*' resolutions, passed by a county meeting" in Kentucky, would have any effect on South Carolina and Georgia, which were on the verge of secession. The Bell backers "might as well attempt to resolve the laws of gravitation into a nullity."[11]

The *Henderson Reporter,* another Breckinridge journal in western Kentucky, cited the Old Testament and Roman history to pillory the president-elect: "We have cause to fear that he will prove to the Union what blind Samson proved to the Temple of Dagon, when that mightiest of men was allowed to embrace its lofty pillars—except that Lincoln, unlike Samson, will have no hope of expiring in the midst of the awful ruin he has wrought." The paper also predicted, "What the 'Ides of March' were to Julius Caesar, so the time may prove [the presidential election] to have been to the country we inhabit. . . . We cannot pretend to say whether the Union of these States will stay intact." The *Reporter* decried Douglas for splitting the Democratic Party and thus handing victory to Lincoln, "whose record is as foul as that of Giddings or Garrison—who for more than twenty years has advocated the odious tenets of the radical anti-slaveryites of Great Britain." It predicted, "If the dagger of faction is sheathed in the great heart of this nation, the finger of scorn will undeviatingly point to Stephen A. Douglas of Chicago, the arch demagogue that catered to the success of a party who burned him in effigy from the margin of the St. Lawrence to the shore of Lake Michigan, as the man who stabbed the victim."[12]

Lincoln's election also caused the unionism of the *Cynthiana News* to waver. The paper had supported Bell but feared "that Lincoln will attempt to carry out his obnoxious principles, and enforce them upon the South." If he tried "to pursue that policy towards the South, which would endanger the rights in property and otherwise abridge Southern privileges, it will then be time for the slave States to part company with the North, and not until then."[13]

Personal liberty laws were high on the *Bowling Green Standard*'s list of what the *Cynthiana News* decried as northern "obnoxious principles." The south-central Kentucky paper asserted that because Lincoln had been elected "upon one idea—the idea of anti-slavery," the South was right to be alarmed. It reminded readers that he "has said—*deliberately writing down his views before delivery*—that the public mind of the North would never be satisfied until slavery was put in the course of ultimate extinction—that the Union could not endure with slave and free States, but they must be all slave or all free." The *Standard* warned that no Northern army would be permitted to "march across our State to murder and assassinate our brothers of the South." If such a force showed up, everywhere it camped "will be converted into a grave-yard and Kentucky will re-baptise her soil in the proud and melancholy title of the '*Dark and Bloody Ground.*'"[14]

Meanwhile, the pro-Breckinridge *Paducah Herald* reported that Lincoln's election had turned many local citizens toward "unconditional disunion, while a still larger number are in favor of demanding guarantees of safety from the North, and disunion if such guarantees are not given." The paper vowed that "the sentiment is almost unanimous upon the point, that, if the Southern states go out of the Union, Kentucky must follow." Yet most locals believed "there should be no hasty action on the part either of Kentucky or the South—that conference on the part of the State and the people should take place first." Then "an attempt should be made by the united South, to get such guarantees from the North as would hereafter insure the safety of the South—and that in default of such guarantees, the whole South should secede from the Union in a body, and form a Southern Confederacy."[15]

The *Georgetown Journal* was not yet in favor of an independent slave-state confederacy, but the paper's unionism was wavering. "We are for the Union, forever and inseparable, *so long as our rights are respected and maintained.*" Yet the erstwhile Bell organ warned, "When we are to be subjected to the whims and caprices of a Northern power, without the power of redress, simply because it has the numerical strength, the Union is not worth preserving."[16]

While the *Statesman* and the *Courier* liked the idea of a slave-state convention, the two papers disagreed on whether Governor Magoffin should call a special session of the General Assembly. The *Courier* was for it; the *Statesman* and *Yeoman* were not. "Gov. Magoffin *should at once convene an extra session of the Legislature, and let the people through their representatives determine the position they will take, and in the event of a Southern Convention being determined on, select their delegates, and give them such instructions as they may deem prudent and proper,*" the *Courier* argued. After endorsing an extra session, the paper reported that it had "conversed with a number of the most eminent gentlemen in the State, representing all parties as heretofore constituted," and all of them supported "a convocation of the representatives of the people." The *Courier* claimed that "Northern aggression, culminating in an open declaration of war against slavery" and Lincoln's election, had convinced several Southern states that "resistance is necessary to their own safety." At the very least, the paper argued, no harm could come from an extra session. Besides, if the legislature met and if "the worst fears of the friends of the Constitution and the Union" came true, Kentuckians could not "blame those in authority for withholding from them an opportunity to try at least in a formal authoritative manner."[17]

The *Statesman* disagreed. It asked, "What can the Legislature do at such a juncture? We much fear that whatever its course, the moral force of its action will be lost by the violent partizan [*sic*] profits which will go up." However, the Lexington paper was in favor of having the legislature send delegates to represent Kentucky in a slave-state convention, but it conceded, "There seems to be no unity of opinion in the State on this subject." The *Statesman* was certain that "political sentiment was never more unsettled in Kentucky than at this time." Declarations "that 'Kentucky is for the Union, but will demand her Constitutional right,' . . . is about as definite an enunciation of her position as the Bell-Everetts platform in the late canvass." The paper argued, "What is meant by demanding our rights is not understood by even those who clamor for the Union and the Constitution. Is Kentucky disposed to confer with the slave States and demand new guarantees of the North, or is she disposed to submit to Lincoln and trust to luck?"[18]

Meanwhile, Magoffin drafted a plan to preserve the Union on Southern terms, and on December 9 he mailed copies of his proposal to the other fourteen slave-state governors, soliciting their support. The package called for amending the Constitution to guarantee slavery in the slave states, force the free to states return escaped slaves, divide the federal territories into slave and free sections along the thirty-seventh parallel (free above, slave below), and ensure free navigation of the Mississippi River for all states in perpetuity.[19]

On December 18 Senator John J. Crittenden of Kentucky, in true Clay fashion, offered a plan similar to the governor's. His proposal also protected slavery where it existed and extended the old Missouri Compromise line (thirty-six degrees, thirty minutes latitude) through the territories to the state of California. The Crittenden Compromise generated little support beyond Kentucky and the other border states, and it ultimately failed. South Carolina left the Union on December 20 and invited the other slave states "to join us, in forming a Confederacy of Slaveholding states." The lower South was ready to go; Kentucky was not, much to the dismay of the *Bowling Green Standard*. "Hurrah for South Carolina? Hurrah for a Southern Confederacy!" the paper cheered.[20]

After the Palmetto State departed, commissioners from Alabama and Mississippi conferred with Magoffin and urged him to work for Kentucky's secession. The emissaries argued that only secession could save slavery and white supremacy. That line would be repeated time and again by secessionist politicians, pastors, and publishers—indeed, by disunionists of every occupation. The Alabama representative was Stephen Foster Hale, a Kentucky native born in Crittenden County in 1816. Hale wrote to Magoffin on December 27, accusing the North of "waging an unrelenting and fanatical war" against slavery "for the last quarter of a century." He praised slavery for cementing "not only the wealth and prosperity of the Southern people, but their very existence as a political community." Lincoln, said Hale, "stands forth as the representative of the fanaticism of the North" and of the Republican Party, whose claims to popularity rested "upon the one dogma—the equality of the races, white and black." Hale demanded, "What Southern man, be he slave-holder or non-slave-holder, can without indignation and horror contemplate the triumph of negro equality, and see his own sons and daughters in the not too distant future associating with free negroes upon terms of political and social equality, and the white man stripped by the heaven-daring hand of fanaticism of that title to superiority over the black race which God himself has bestowed?"[21]

On January 3 the *Yeoman* published the correspondence between Magoffin and Hale, noting the Alabaman's Kentucky birth. "His appointment was in some measure a compliment to this State, while his official and social intercourse with the authorities of the State and the citizens of the capital has been of the most pleasant character." Hale "has left a good impression here and we trust that he will carry with him a better opinion of the soundness of the people of Kentucky upon the issues dividing the country than is generally entertained in the extreme South."[22]

Meanwhile, nothing came of Magoffin's proposal. So on December 27 he called the legislature to convene on January 17. By then, the *Yeoman* predicted, eight states would have already seceded, and "the Legislatures of four or five others will have been in session long enough to develop their policy." Thus, Kentucky would be able to "act with all the light of events up to that period." The paper maintained that the state "ought to be a unit, and we believe we will." The latter notion was wishful thinking, or perhaps Major was simply clueless about Kentucky opinion, which was anything but unified.[23]

A trip to Washington had convinced Monroe of the *Statesman* that the Kentucky legislature should meet. "The impression made by a brief sojourn at the Capitol precludes all hope for a maintenance of the Union as now constituted," he wrote home on December 15. "No man dreams of any other result of all consultation now going on than separation, but speculation commences when the extent of the dismemberment is discussed." He believed the states that followed South Carolina out of the Union would meet in convention in February and "set in operation by the simple adoption of the present Constitution . . . [a] new Government [by] the name of the 'United States of America.'" If Virginia threw in with any such Southern nation, Monroe mused, "how soon before Kentucky will sever her present relations, thus become intolerable, and unite her destiny with those to whom she is bound by all the ties of kindred sympathy, business and a common interest"? Thus, he concluded, "The Legislature of Kentucky should be called." That body's "main duty" would be to call a convention, Monroe added.[24]

The *Yeoman,* heretofore skeptical of a special session, had changed its tune. On December 29 the paper was positive that Magoffin's call for the General Assembly to convene "will meet the hearty indorsement of the people of all parties." The state "cannot with either safety or honor, remain longer a silent and indifferent spectator of the dismemberment of this glorious Union. It is high time that she should take position and speak in an authoritative manner." The *Yeoman* was certain the legislature would prove itself "equal to the emergency" and had "confidence in the patriotism and ability" of lawmakers and in "our patriotic Executive."[25]

South Carolina seceded via a so-called sovereignty convention composed of delegates elected statewide. On New Year's Day the *Statesman* again called for such a convention in Kentucky. "As events thicken upon us, and revolution approaches with fearfully increasing rapidity, many of our wiser and more conservative citizens are realizing the importance of having Kentucky assume an attitude wherein her people, by virtue of their original and inherent sovereignty, can control the destinies of the state." The paper noted that although the legislature was scheduled to meet on January 17, lawmakers had no power to determine Kentucky's position vis-à-vis the United States and the seceded states. "But we adhere to the opinion that the subject of our relations . . . should be left to the control of a Convention fresh from the people."[26]

The pro-Breckinridge *Maysville Express* also wanted a convention. "It is utterly inconceivable to us how the rights, the safety, the peace and the honor of Kentucky can be protected and preserved, without convening the Legislature in order to call a Convention of the people in their sovereign character to assume the armor and the attitude befitting the awful crisis impending." Neither federal nor state legislation "contemplated such an extraordinary state of case." The paper argued that, "in the absence of lawful power and authority applicable to the case," neither the governor nor the courts could "conduct the State through such a crisis."[27]

Kentucky secessionists hoped a convention would put Kentucky out of the Union. Unionists feared such a gathering might indeed vote for disunion. So the latter adopted a simple strategy and stuck to it throughout the secession crisis: prevent a convention, come what may. The secessionists knew that the sooner a convention met, the better their chances of wedging Kentucky out of the Union. They understood that the disunionist ardor triggered by Lincoln's election would invariably fade. Likewise, unionists believed that the longer Kentucky stayed in the Union, the less likely the state was to secede. Both sides were correct.[28]

At the same time, the Union men were rightly skeptical of the General Assembly and the governor. Breckinridge Democrats were leading the secession movement in the South, and Magoffin was a Breckinridge Democrat. In the Kentucky house, the Democrats had a fifty-nine to forty-one majority over the opposition—ex-Whigs and former Know-Nothings. In the state senate, the Democratic edge was twenty-four to fourteen. Most Democratic lawmakers were Breckinridge men.[29]

Before the legislature met, friends of the Union organized themselves to stave off a convention and disunion. On January 8 leading Bell and Douglas supporters met in separate conventions in Louisville. The meetings jointly resolved that Lincoln's election was an affront to the South but not cause for disunion. They endorsed the Crittenden Compromise and held out the possibility of forming a central confederacy if the Union splintered. In addition, the groups formed a ten-member Union State Central Committee to coordinate unionism across the state. Throughout the secession crisis, the Bell and Douglas men were the Union Party's base.[30]

The *Courier* published the resolutions of these meetings and concluded that they were "in some respects . . . better than we hoped." Yet "other resolutions are less satisfactory; and some of them are so utterly indefensible that we are surprised that they were reported by the Committee or adopted by the Convention." The paper singled out for scorn the idea of a central confederacy of slave and free states, predicting it "will not meet with favor in Kentucky, and does not express the sentiments of one-fifth of the Convention. The ambiguous language in which it is expressed alone secured its passage." The *Courier* believed the real action had taken place behind closed doors: "It is probable that in secret caucus something was done towards a union of certain antagonistic political elements in one party." It did not elaborate.[31]

The *Covington Journal* also had misgivings about the central confederacy because it might include free states. "The people of Kentucky may well hesitate before assenting to a proposition which will again connect them with that great disturbing element which has already ruptured the best government ever formed by man." Yet the *Journal* was gratified that some of the resolutions "come much nearer the popular sentiment of Kentucky than the resolutions of many of the county meetings." Nonetheless, the paper regretted "that the Conventions did not more distinctly and emphatically denounce coercion."[32]

The *Statesman* claimed that the deliberations of the Bell and Douglas meetings "were not harmonious. Violent coercion, and anti-coercion speeches were made, developing a material difference of opinion on that subject." The resolutions "are not calculated to do good, and at some points are far from a true utterance of Kentucky feeling."[33]

The "true . . . Kentucky feeling" was anti-secession, to one degree or another, in every part of the state save one: the Jackson Purchase, Kentucky's westernmost territory and its only Confederate-majority region. There in the counties beyond the Tennessee River, almost every Bell and Douglas man joined the majority Breckinridge Democrats in embracing the rebel cause. Among the most outspoken converts was Ed K. Warren, editor of the *Hickman Courier*. Before it shut down in 2017, it was one of the oldest papers in Kentucky still publishing under its original name. George Warren, apparently the editor's brother, had founded the paper in the Fulton County seat in 1859. Although the *Hickman Courier* embraced Douglas, it was one of the first Kentucky newspapers—if not *the* first—to endorse secession. "We have waited patiently and with anxious hearts to hear what our representatives in Congress would or could do to restore peace and confidence to our distracted country," the paper announced. "Our hope has been in vain. Our representatives have been denied everything they demanded. The Republicans have been firm and unwilling to make any concessions or compromise. The South, therefore, who has considered herself aggrieved, who has been denied her rights in the Union, is bound, in order to have her rights, in order to maintain her honor, and the honor of her citizens, *to secede*. Therefore, we say, all honor to the Southern Confederacy." Later, the Hickman paper blasted the Bell and Douglas conventions as "the expiring effort of defunct political organizations, whose great object can only be the spoils of office." It ridiculed the gatherings as "a grand congregation—from all accounts—of Fourth of July, Hail Columbia, Yankee Doodle orators, who delivered themselves of speeches red with blood *spilt* by their patriotic forefathers. All such Conventions are fustian, bombast and nonsense." The paper demanded, "Why in the first place did they not look the issue in the face, whether Kentucky would remain as the tail of a Northern Black Republican Union, or would join a Confederacy of her Southern sisters, upon the principles of State equality." It warned, "This is the living, vital issue, and all who attempt to impede or retard the triumphant march of the people—determined to assert and maintain their own honor will be crushed and trampled to death beneath their feet." The *Hickman Courier* challenged, "It would be a blot upon the escutcheon of the proud old Commonwealth of Kentucky to doubt her loyalty to the South and her institutions, which no time could wipe out."[34]

The pro-Breckinridge *Columbus Crescent, Owensboro Democrat, Woodford Pennant*, and *Henderson Reporter* also sided with the South. "The Rubicon is crossed, and Kentucky may as well prepare immediately to go with the Southern States into a separate Confederacy—the sooner she does so the better it will be for her," the *Crescent* urged. The *Owensboro Democrat* hoped "the Submissionists [unionists] will see the error of their ways; renounce their allegiance to Black Republicanism; maintain the Constitution as good citizens in all its requirements; and, lastly, stand by the South in defending those rights as handed down to her by our revolutionary fathers."[35]

The *Pennant* trumpeted, "The time has come for action—prompt and decisive action. . . . The Rubicon has been crossed—the die is cast." Southern secession was already hurting the Northern economy, but the worst was yet to come, the paper observed. "When their manufactories begin to crumble—sails fall tattered and weather beaten upon deck—the solitary spider spreads his web upon the loom—the spindle stands motionless in its socket—the hammer corrodes upon the anvil—and the lonely twitter of the swallow is heard in place of clashing machinery—we shall then hear a wail going up from the bleak hills of New England that cannot be mistaken!" The paper declared, "*A dissolution of the American Union is as inevitable as the rising of the sun on the morrow, and the powers of a confederated Government will go back to the sovereignties from which they came.*" The Versailles paper concluded, "The alternative is now left Kentucky and her sister border States to choose between the North and the South, or to establish a confederacy of their own."[36]

The *Henderson Reporter* numbered itself among "those who opine that the present is a most opportune time for an editor to take a bold stand—a decided position." The paper explained, "Enough is known to warrant us in believing that the Northern members of Congress are fully determined to maintain the ultra position they occupied during the late campaign. . . . We have no hope of any concession on the part of the Northern states." Thus, the paper was "for SECESSION, and shall abide the issue, satisfied that no one having an interest in Southern institutions desires to perpetuate a form of government under which the equality of the South is denied."[37]

Not surprisingly, the *Reporter* pandered to white supremacy. It claimed that the value of slaves—"the most valuable item of Southern property"—was declining and that the institution was "becoming more and more insecure."

The *Reporter* also took a swipe at anti-slavery Yankees, who "always meddled in our private affairs, to the neglect of [their] own concerns." Northerners had "stolen negroes from homes of comfort and contentment, and doomed them to a life of want, misery, and shame, while the poor white men and women of her cities, destitute of friends or employment, were compelled to resort to beggary, theft, and prostitution or perish in the streets, or die in drunkenness and sin." The *Reporter* turned up the racist wick: "The Abolitionist is to the negro what the Hooduman is to the snake of the banyan—his inveterate enemy—with this exception, that the monkey makes quick work of snake-destruction, while the Abolitionist destroys *his* victim by the slow, but none the less deadly process of want, disease, and the life-lasting pangs of viperous regret." The paper called "the monkey . . . more humane than the negro-thief and little less intelligent." The *Reporter* blamed "Northern traitors and their fanatical followers" for destroying the Union, charging that they "made war upon and attempted to free the blacks, and enslave the free whites of the South," thus leaving the South no choice but to secede.[38]

The *Reporter* endorsed disunion on January 10, apparently spurred by a unionist meeting five days earlier. On January 17 the paper printed notices calling for a pro-secession meeting at the courthouse on January 19, convinced that the Union get-together "did not express the sense of the people of this county." The paper challenged, "Let us see if the people of Henderson County are ready to say to their Southern brethren, and their Northern enemies, that they are for the Union whether the South is equal under the constitution or not." The paper printed and distributed notices that urged, "People of Henderson County, read this bill, and see if you will not come out on Saturday and rebuke the conduct of the men who have endeavored to place you in such a position." On the appointed day, the citizenry jammed the courthouse. A large majority favored sticking with the resolutions passed at the unionist meeting, but pandemonium ensued. "Every fellow who could speak, and many more who could not, were yelling at the top of their voices Mr. Chairman! Mr. Chairman! while in this tumultuous uproar, and broad field of disorder, an old grey haired patriot entered the crowded auditorium, waving over his head a large flag." Strong men cried "like little children" at the sight of the Stars and Stripes. The throng rose "seemingly en masse, and fairly rent the building with screams for the Union." Not until ex–lieutenant governor Archibald Dixon, a staunch unionist, took "the rostrum, and waved his arm could a composed looker-on, determine whether this wondrous crowd, was a convention of intelligent men, or an asylum of howling lunatics." After relative calm returned, "the flag was taken to the speaker's stand, and the announcement made that it had been presented by thirteen patriotic ladies of the city. This was the occasion for another outburst." The crowd adopted resolutions, but not the kind desired "by those who had been instrumental in calling the convention." When the meeting adjourned, the flag was paraded around town, "followed by hundreds of men and boys," until late at night. There was "music . . . in the air, and every man who could speak and had a good word to say for the flag, was serenaded, and called to the front." A crowd gathered in front of Dixon's house, "and after listening to several pieces by the band," he came out "and for thirty minutes held them spell bound by his matchless eloquence." The crowd ultimately dispersed, but "in three weeks afterwards, many of them were yelling the loudest for the Southern Confederacy." One of them might have been John W. Crockett, who had chaired the gathering. He helped organize Kentucky's bogus secessionist government in Russellville in the fall of 1861 and "represented" Kentucky in the Confederate Congress.[39]

Undaunted by the results of the mass meeting, the *Reporter* stuck to its pro-Confederate line, even arguing that secession would boost the economy, which the paper claimed was sagging locally. Others disagreed and said business was fine; some locals later recalled that money was never more abundant nor wages higher than during the war. Nonetheless, the *Reporter* could not "remember when times were harder than at present, money is almost entirely withdrawn from circulation, and we are told is worth an almost fabulous per-centure per month." Real estate could hardly be sold at any price, according to the paper. It added, "The question is not how much a man is worth, but how much can he raise. *Negroes* sold on New Years Day at ruinously low figures, and the best of servants hired at prices vastly below the usual standard." The *Reporter* claimed, "Confidence cannot be restored in commercial circles until the National difficulties are settled, and the sooner the *odious union* between North and South is severed the better. *Capitalists will not relax their purse strings before the establishment of the Southern Confederacy, which we believe will be born about the fourth of March next.*" Lincoln's inauguration would take place on March 4.[40]

By January 17, when the Kentucky legislature convened, Mississippi, Florida, and Alabama had also seceded. But was Magoffin, the pro-slavery Breckinridge Democrat, prepared to lead the Bluegrass State out of the Union? In his opening address to the legislature, the governor repeated his call for a border-state convention; he suggested they meet in Baltimore in early February. Magoffin also endorsed a sovereignty convention for Kentucky. State senators and representatives had abandoned the old party labels; they were now either "Union" or "Southern Rights" men. Magoffin was on the Southern Rights side, which found itself in the minority. Friends of the Union managed to cobble together majorities in the Kentucky house and senate and prevent a state convention. Instead, the legislature voted to send representatives to a peace conference in Washington on February 4. That gathering was poorly attended and a failure. Meanwhile, on the day the conference convened, the *Yeoman,* to no avail, called for a Kentucky sovereignty convention "as a purely practical position, to be determined alone by the exigencies of the times." Seven days later, the General Assembly adjourned until March 20. The Union Party had won round one. Kentucky was still under the Stars and Stripes.[41]

Before the lawmakers went home, Georgia, Louisiana, and Texas seceded and joined South Carolina, Mississippi, Florida, and Alabama in the Confederate States of America. Birmingham, Alabama, became the capital of their self-proclaimed Southern nation, which they formed in February. Kentucky-born Jefferson Davis of Mississippi was their president, and Alexander H. Stephens of Georgia was vice president. The Confederate constitution specifically protected slavery and guaranteed its unlimited expansion.[42]

Naturally, Kentucky unionists were relieved that the legislature had spurned a convention. "Hurrah for our last Legislature!" Harney's *Louisville Democrat* exulted on February 14. "They have acted nobly in the present crisis." Lawmakers "have refused to precipitate at the instigation of politicians whose only salvation was in secession. The State will stand firm." The paper quoted the inscription on the stone the state had donated to the Washington Monument: "Kentucky will be the last to leave the Union." The state would do more, the paper predicted. "She will, with Tennessee and Virginia, be the first to save the Union." Kentucky, of course, rejected secession; Tennessee and Virginia did not.[43]

The *Hickman Courier* was so angry with the General Assembly that it threatened regional secession if Kentucky stayed in the Union. On February 6 the *Louisville Courier* published an editorial from Kentucky's westernmost newspaper under the headline "What Is Thought of the Legislature—Threatened Secession of Southern Kentucky." The editorial claimed, "The Kentucky Legislature has not, and is not, doing a thing towards the adjustment of our national difficulties." The Purchase paper maintained it would have been "better, far better for the State, that this Legislature had never been convened, than that it should thus mock the pride and wishes of the citizens of Kentucky. We know not what are the feelings of the citizens of the upper portion of Kentucky, but we can not believe that their representatives are reflecting their feelings in the present Legislature." The *Hickman Courier* was certain "that Southern Kentucky feels humiliated at the present proceedings, and if the State does not afford some redress, and that too quickly, Southern Kentucky will per force link her destiny with that of chivalrous Tennessee." The editorial continued, "Wild as the assertion may appear, thousands of hearts have long anxiously favored such a transfer. Only a State pride separates us now, when that is wantonly abused by those who adorn it, where is the link that binds us?"[44]

The new *Winchester Review*, started by Messrs. Clayton and Taylor in the Clark County seat, also denounced the legislature for what the publishers saw as disgraceful dithering. "Its action (if action it can be called) is humiliating to the pride of the citizens of the State," the paper chided. "Called together to look after the safety of the Commonwealth at a time of imminent peril, it ignores its weightier responsibilities, and turns its attention to the consideration of insignificant corporation and relief bills. What excuse can be offered for such indifference at a time like this, when the very ground on which we stand seems to be giving way beneath our feet?" The *Review* demanded action: "If the Government is broken up beyond reconstruction, and the people of the State wish to adhere to the remains of the old Confederacy, their will should be done. Or if they should prefer a Central or Southern alliance, or even a lone independent Government of their own, no one, we presume, would question the omnipotence and right of their preference." Yet the legislature interposed "its little brief authority against the very essence of Republican liberty, the right of every people, at all times, and especially in times of revolution, to determine and fix their own destiny." The *Review* warned: "If the Commonwealth *should* receive serious detriment on account of their inaction, the responsibility will be a terrible one."[45]

Similarly, the *Southern Kentucky Register* of Madisonville complained that nothing had been done for Kentucky's defense. In its words, the state "must either become the accomplice of Black Republican tyranny, or, in her own defense, in the emphatic language of Lincoln, when it will, we fear, be too late, 'prepare for war.'" The paper saw nothing to gain "by inaction and delay. . . . If we are to stand by the North in her advances to despotism, then the sooner we signify our determination to do so, the better. If we are to share the toils, the glory, the dangers of our Southern brethren in their self-devoted attempt to uphold our domestic institutions and our integrity, then why procrastinate the moment of action until all shall be irrevocably lost?"[46]

Meanwhile, on February 11 the president-elect climbed aboard a train in Springfield, the capital of Illinois and his hometown, and began his circuitous journey to Washington. He received a warm welcome at stops in the free states. However, the Lincoln party was warned of a possible assassination attempt on the president-elect when he changed trains in Baltimore. Lincoln prudently, though reluctantly, took the advice of his aides and passed through the city, arriving in Washington on a night train. The murder plot was probably real, although Lincoln later regretted the decision to enter the capital "like a thief in the night." Anti-Lincoln newspapers North and South ridiculed the president; some, including the *Yeoman,* claimed that when he reached slave-state Maryland, he "assume[d] a disguise and clandestinely [made] his entrance to the capital city." The Frankfort paper could not "believe that any real danger was to be fairly apprehended." Lincoln's behavior would have insulted Kentuckians, the *Yeoman* claimed. "Had it been necessary or convenient for Mr. Lincoln to have passed through Kentucky, and had he chosen the same means of making the transit of our State as he did that of Maryland, we are certain that he would have lost all the sympathy and most of the friendship which may exist in this State for him and his administration."[47]

While the *Yeoman* lampooned Lincoln's arrival in Washington, the *Paducah Herald* fulsomely praised Davis and Stephens. "These are familiar names, and represent the two parties into which the people of the Southern States were recently divided—Immediate Secessionists and Co-operationists." Davis had supported Breckinridge for president, and Stephens had been a Douglas man. The *Herald* claimed that Davis and Stephens were "two of the wisest, calmest, firmest, and bravest men in the South," and "Heaven must have inspired the [Confederate founding] Convention with wisdom in making the selection." It added, "May God continue to be with them, and to inspire them with like wisdom and the same moderation that has so far characterized their action."[48]

The *Statesman* argued that only a blind man could fail to see that "the Union is dissolved, effectually and permanently." Thus, the peace conference was bound to be unsuccessful. The federal government could free the nation "from further apprehensions of war," it stated, by recognizing the Confederacy. Surely, Monroe knew that Lincoln and Congress would refuse do so. At any rate, the *Statesman* claimed that the only question was "where shall the division of the States be made?" Kentuckians "do not yet sufficiently realize the fact of disunion to meet this question. But we do not care to avoid it." To the *Statesman,* the situation was clear: there were two governments—one "non-slaveholding" and the other "slaveholding."[49]

In a similar vein, the heretofore pro-Bell *Russellville Herald* pronounced the peace conference a failure and proclaimed "the Southern Confederacy . . . a fixed fact." The paper, published in the Logan County seat, referred to a recent speech by Lincoln in Indianapolis in which he had given "the country to understand that he will use the Army and the Navy to retake the Forts in the seceded states and to collect the revenue in their ports." The *Herald* thundered, *"This, of course, is nothing but coercion, and must result in a final dissolution of the Union, and a long and bloody war."* The paper warned, "If Old Abe attempts to carry out this policy, he is a fool, and a madman, too. . . . The election of Lincoln has proved to be a great national blunder."[50]

Predictably, Kentucky's secessionist press—indeed, secessionists everywhere—saw Lincoln's inaugural address as a dire threat to the South and tantamount to a declaration of war. But people read into the March 4 speech what they wanted or expected to hear. The president presented both a sword and an olive branch. He promised to use his power as president "to hold, occupy, and possess the property and places belonging to the Government." Yet he again promised not "to interfere with the institution of slavery in the States where it exists" and pledged to uphold the constitutional injunction for the return of escaped slaves. Lincoln had no objection to a proposed constitutional amendment that would permanently prevent the federal government from interfering with slavery where it existed. He said such an amendment would simply make explicit what the Constitution already "implied." But Southerners bristled at what Lincoln considered the central issue in the sectional controversy. "One section of our country believes slavery is right, and ought to be extended, while the other believes it is wrong, and ought not to be extended," he said, refusing to compromise on the key dispute. Lincoln also rejected the legality of secession and affirmed federal sovereignty and majority rule. But, he concluded, "In your hands, my dissatisfied fellow-countrymen, and not in mine, is the momentous issue of civil war. The Government will not assail you. You can have no conflict without being yourselves the aggressors."[51]

The *Louisville Courier* branded Lincoln the aggressor. "We have heard but one opinion of the Inaugural expressed; and that opinion is, that it is a Declaration of War," the paper claimed. "Though it bears some traces of the Jesuitism of their Premier, it is too clear, too direct, too explicit to be misunderstood, or to leave room for hope of peace." Not a single word Lincoln uttered offered "consolation" to "the patriotic and peace-loving friends of his country," the paper protested. By using phrases such as "their Premier" and "his country," the *Courier's* retort sounded like the newspaper, if not Kentucky, had seceded. In any event, Haldeman's paper was sure that citizens of the border states would read the address "with care and attention." Of course, the *Courier* was happy to offer its own interpretation: "It will teach them the hopelessness, the folly, the madness of trusting to the honor, to the love of justice, or to the patriotism of the people of the Free States." The paper predicted that Lincoln's speech "will do more to fire [border-state] . . . hearts, than all the Southern writers have penned or Southern orators spoken. It will dissipate the hopes of the sanguine, clear the doubts of the undecided, and nerve all for what is to follow."[52]

The *Courier* followed its cutting commentary on Lincoln's speech with a blistering account of the inaugural ceremonies, which it described as "a shameful spectacle to be presented in this capital of a free and enlightened country." The paper claimed that "mercenary sharp-shooters" were stationed on rooftops, not to protect the president from harm but "to overawe the multitude assembled as witnesses of the ceremony of inauguration and to mock the memories of the past." The *Courier* characterized the proceedings as "despotism . . . installed into power in the midst of bristling bayonets and scowling policemen." Never before had the swearing in of "the Chief Magistrate of a Republican people required such demonstrations of physical force to tranquilize the fears of the trembling leaders." But "never was there a worse despotism than Black Republican despotism," the *Courier* groused. "The Union of our fathers has departed, and the degraded dynasty of sectionalism has begun."[53]

Not surprisingly, the *Yeoman* lambasted Lincoln's inaugural speech, luridly denouncing it as "a declaration of war upon the South" that "foreshadows a line of policy which if carried out will drench the country in blood." The address "has aroused the indignation of conservative men even in the North. The Democratic papers of the free states criticise it in severe terms." Not all did, and Douglas himself took a decidedly different view of Lincoln's speech: "I am with him," he said of the president's remarks.[54]

Of course, the *Statesman* was not with the president. "The exposition of his policy is received in the Southern States as a *Declaration of War*. That it will end in civil war, is so manifest as to need no argument." The paper refused to accept Lincoln's assurance that "there need be no bloodshed or violence, and will be none, unless it be forced upon the national authority." The *Statesman* failed to "understand the importance he would attach to the mode in which, or the party by whom hostilities are commenced." In its opinion, it would not matter who fired the first shot, because "the horrors of civil war are not averted by shifting the origin from one party to another." If civil war came, the paper predicted, America and the civilized world would blame Lincoln. The *Statesman* also ridiculed its rival, the *Observer & Reporter*, for counseling "submission" and urging Kentuckians to "wait for future developments." Monroe's paper argued that if the state "submits now; and if she does not rise to the vindication of her rights and honor; if she does not shake off her lethargy, slavery is doomed" and the state will be everlastingly dishonored.[55]

The *Observer & Reporter* characterized the inaugural address not as a war declaration but as "temperate, peaceful, and as national as we expected." It argued that Lincoln had no power to disturb slavery in the slave states nor to keep slavery from spreading into the territories. "Is there any thing in the

Inaugural ominous of evil or injustice to Kentucky?" the *Observer & Reporter* asked, obviously believing there was not. Hence, why should Kentucky, "hitherto the Union's champion, now desire to destroy it?" Kentucky's heart "still throbs for the glorious Union and its patriotic memories, its national music, and its charming stars and stripes," the paper declared.[56]

Down in western Kentucky, the *Cadiz Organ*'s dander was up over Lincoln's speech. Editor John Spiceland hurled down the gauntlet: "The great and most important question for Kentucky to decide at this time, is whether our traitorous enemies of the Northern States shall, after they have by their unconstitutional and treasonable aggressions against the well defined rights of ourselves and Southern States driven our friends out of the Union, force them back at the command of Lincoln, and require them to bow their heads and receive again the yoke of free negro Black Republican despotism and inequality." The paper demanded to know whether Kentuckians would "stand as idlers and behold an army of Abolition minions, with hearts festering with treason as black as hell itself, attempt to force our friends, our neighbors, our brothers of the South, into ignominious SUBMISSION TO NORTHERN RULE AND TYRANNY?" The *Organ*'s faith "in their bravery, their chivalry, nay, their patriotism" led it "to hope better things." Spiceland also wondered whether any son of Kentucky would hesitate "to enrich Southern soil with the last drop of his heart's blood, rather than see the heroes of the South who are struggling for 'life, liberty, and the pursuit of happiness'" vanquished and captured "by an army of law-nullifying, law-despising political desperadoes, fighting under the black banner of Lincoln, Seward, Greeley & Co." (Horace Greeley was the anti-slavery Republican editor of the *New-York Tribune*.) The *Organ* hoped there was no such man in the state, but if there was, "he is unworthy of the soil he treads!" In any event, the paper demanded that when the General Assembly reconvened on March 20, lawmakers immediately call a sovereignty convention to prepare for war.[57]

The *Princeton Bulletin* was also vexed at Republicans in general and at Representative James McKean in particular. The Saratoga Springs, New York, lawmaker had submitted a resolution that border states should be sounded out on the idea of abolishing slavery through compensated emancipation. "A careful scrutiny of that resolution will show that it is the design of the Black Republicans, first to endeavor to obtain the consent of the slaveholders for the emancipation of their slaves; then, if this is not voluntarily given, to *force* it by their numerical strength." The *Bulletin* claimed that more than a million and a half slaves lived in still loyal Kentucky, Tennessee, Virginia, Delaware, Maryland, and North Carolina. (For some reason, the paper left out Arkansas.) Under McKean's proposal, the slaves would be freed "in our midst," granted "all the privileges and immunities of American citizenship, and placed upon an equal footing with the white population." The paper ginned up the race-baiting: "How does this '*feeler*' suit you? Whilst considering the subject, reflect how you would like [the freed slaves] . . . to become as they would by this step, the every day companions and associates of your wives and children; your peers at the ballot-box, and your legislators in public assemblies; and give a moment's thought, too, as to what has been the effect of a similar movement upon the once beautiful and prosperous island of San Domingo." The *Bulletin* was referring to Haiti, which, upon winning its independence from France in 1804, became the only country established through a slave rebellion—a turn of events that horrified white Southerners, who lived in mortal fear of slave revolts.[58]

The *Bulletin's* overt racism was typical of Kentucky's Confederate press— indeed, the Confederate press everywhere—during the secession crisis. The editors knew that almost all whites—including almost all unionists—were also pro-slavery. The rebel press pandered hard to white prejudice, repeatedly claiming that if Kentucky remained in the Union, the abolition of slavery was inevitable, and equality between whites and African Americans would surely follow. While the *Bulletin* went after McKean, the *Hickman Courier* scorned another anti-slavery Republican from the Empire State: Senator Seward. The Purchase paper claimed that when it looked like some border states were about to secede, "Seward delivered a long speech in the Senate, moderate in tone and redolent in its love for the Union, but without, as the Republicans say, sacrificing a single cherished principle of the Black Republican party." Southern unionists seized on Seward's words "like hungry dogs," convinced the address was "the oracular declaration of 'the better time coming.'" The *Courier* scoffed, "What protection will Lincoln's government give to a citizen of Kentucky in the enjoyment of slave property in the Territories, when the creed of his faith, the Chicago [presidential] platform, has denounced the institution of slavery as a 'relic of barbarism.'" The Republicans "will afford that protection which the lion gives to the lamb and the jackal to his prey." Kentuckians, the paper argued, "will not be cheated or duped any longer. They have exhausted the argument, and will assert their honor and independence regardless of consequences."[59]

While other secessionist organs devoted multiple column inches to their pro-slavery and anti-Lincoln editorials, the *Elizabethtown Democrat* had "neither time nor space for extended comment" about the president's inaugural speech. Even so, the paper could not "but express our disappointment at the tone of the address. It looks to us like a manifestation of the President's utter inability to rise to the elevated position of statesman, and to look at matters as they exist." The paper dismissed the address as "a miserable dodging of the great questions on which the people desired to know his views." The president "seems too stupid to know that revolution has already disrupted the connection of these States with the Union, and seems fatally bent on the insane idea of enforcing the laws of the Union in these States," it argued. The *Democrat* warned that if Lincoln tried to "conquer and hold in subjugation" the seven Confederate states, Kentucky and the seven other slave states still in the Union would secede.[60]

The *Paris Flag* sneered at more than the substance of Lincoln's speech. "The diction and style of it are so inferior that his friends make all manner of excuses, and hope that the telegraph may have aggravated its imperfections. The matter of the address is worse than the poor verbiage in which it is clothed." The *Flag* figured "the cunning and erudite Seward would have dressed up the performance in more creditable comeliness, and would have procured some amellorations of the darker shades of the Chicago platform." It faulted "Mr. Lincoln's anti-slavery party" for breaking up the Union and denounced his address as "war without disguise." Meanwhile, the paper would wait and see what steps Virginia and the other border states took, while doing "what we can for peace, both for its own sake, as also for the hope of reconstructing the Union, which is impossible without peace." Yet if secession "is to be a fixed fact, and war must come, we shall advise our people to array themselves *with the South, and fight for the South.*"[61]

The *Louisville Journal* was no friend of Lincoln, but the state's most important pro-Union paper was somewhat charitable toward the new president. It published a telegraphic dispatch of the inaugural address, which it described as "most imperfect, but the substance is tolerably clear." The *Journal* understood the president to mean that he was not considering "the recapture of the forts and other impossible achievements." Rather, he was following the policy of President James Buchanan, but with the proviso "that 'current events and experience' may induce him to modify or change even that." The address was "not everything we could desire," but it was "at least much more and better than we were tempted to fear." The *Journal* commended the address "to the just and fearless consideration of the public."[62]

The *Louisville Democrat* pronounced the inaugural address "about what we expected." The president "denies the right of Secession, and, of course, he holds the laws of the United States valid in the seceding States. The Constitution says, 'he shall see that the laws are faithfully executed.'" Lincoln swore to uphold the laws "*as far as practicable,*" and "what he will do, depends on the meaning he will attach to the practicable." The start of America's deadliest war was now a little over a month away.[63]

4

Fort Sumter to Neutrality

From the onset of the secession crisis, the pro-Confederate press misjudged Kentucky sentiment. By championing a convention they believed would lead to secession, the editors and publishers claimed they were speaking for most citizens. But a majority of Kentuckians never embraced disunion. After the war began, the rebel papers blamed the conflict on Lincoln and clamored even more loudly for secession. The editors and publishers figured that in a shooting war between North and South, Kentucky would naturally side with the South. They were wrong again. The legislature opted for neutrality, a position that nearly every Kentuckian embraced. The rebel papers condemned neutrality as cowardly and foolish. They also stepped up their central argument in favor of secession—that slavery and white supremacy were doomed if the state stayed in the Union. All the while, the Confederate press continued to look toward the state elections in August 1861, when they expected the voters to elect a pro-secession legislature.

The *Columbus Crescent* was still fuming at faraway Frankfort. The paper groused that the majority-unionist legislature had gone out of its way to thwart the people's will. Thus, editor Len Faxon asked, were Kentuckians "to be bullied by a few men, who represent them in our legislative halls—men who were elected before there was a thought that the present state of affairs would exist?" Were Kentuckians' near "unanimous requests" for the legislature to summon a convention "to be shouted at and treated with contempt, and [the people's] . . . rights to be trampled under foot by these traitors to the Commonwealth?" Faxon let fly: Were the people idiots, cattle, or children? Who would "still shriek 'Union!' when Abolitionists and traitors" were stalking the state in broad daylight? "Will you not, can you not, see the dangerous ground upon which you are standing?" The *Crescent* also flayed a *Louisville Journal* correspondent who, according to Faxon, claimed that Kentucky should remain in the Union even if all the other slave states seceded. The scribe was "no doubt a true blue Abolitionist." The *Journal* not only failed to rebuke him but even seemed to agree with him, the editor charged, harrumphing, "Such a thing was to be expected from a sheet which has for years been exhibiting the cloven hoof of abolitionism."[1]

The *Crescent* did represent the popular will in the Jackson Purchase, the state's only disloyal region. But Faxon was dead wrong about majority opinion statewide. He was not alone. Throughout the secession crisis, Southern Rightist editors and politicians believed that Kentucky was really secessionist at heart and that the voters would prove it in the August elections for a new state legislature. To boost their chances at the polls, the secessionists started Southern Rights clubs statewide. Members were directed to talk up secession and circulate petitions demanding a convention. The Southern Rights Party also called a state convention in Frankfort on March 20, the day lawmakers were scheduled to return. Obviously, the idea was to sway the legislature.[2]

The Union Party, too, was girding for the coming fight in the state capital. It found a powerful spiritual ally in the Reverend Dr. Robert J. Breckinridge of Danville, a Presbyterian theologian and one of Kentucky's most learned men of the cloth. On January 4 he gave a long speech in Lexington in which he counseled moderation and warned against secession. His remarks were later printed in a pamphlet, distributed across Kentucky, and widely read.[3]

A professor at Danville Theological Seminary, Breckinridge essentially preached the same anti-secession line in his new *Danville Quarterly Review*, which debuted in March 1861. The bespectacled, long-bearded Breckinridge dominated the publication, and he became a major border-state spokesman for the Union cause. He owned as many as thirty-seven slaves yet advocated gradual emancipation and colonization. Breckinridge scorned abolitionism and secessionism as anarchistic and fatal to the Union, a stand he made abundantly clear in his inaugural article "Our Country—Its Peril—Its Deliverance." He wrote, "Both at the North and at the South, there are great parties thoroughly organized and acting in precisely opposite directions as to opinion, but one direction as effective as the other toward the common object of their labors—namely, the tearing of the nation to pieces." Breckinridge believed that every state had the right to make itself slave or free. He claimed that neither free states "nor the government which is common to all the States" had the power to interfere with slavery in a slave state. At the same time, he seemed to endorse the Crittenden Compromise, arguing that "if the nation survives," the federal territories "must necessarily be, and ought to be, partly slave and partly free." Breckinridge maintained that neither Lincoln and the Republicans nor the secessionists represented the majority opinion in their sections. He was convinced that most Northerners and Southerners wanted the Union back together. Therefore, the federal government must peacefully "pilot the ark" to that end. He entreated a united citizenry to "stir itself as a giant, waking from his slumber," and "let the voice of God be heard amongst us, as the voice of many waters, and as the voice of a great thunder." Breckinridge encouraged his readers not to hold their peace or rest until "the peril is overpassed" and "our country be as a crown of glory in the hand of the Lord, and as a royal diadem in the hand of our God!" His prose was ponderous and sounded more like a scholarly sermon than a newspaper editorial. Nonetheless, there is no doubt that Breckinridge spoke for the great majority of his fellow Kentuckians in early 1861. They, too, abhorred abolitionism and disunion with equal intensity, and they disparaged both positions as being deadly to the Union they revered.[4]

Meanwhile, the secessionist press beat the drum for the Southern Rights convention. The *Louisville Courier* published an invitation to the conclave signed by thirty-five men, including editor Robert McKee and ex-editor Reuben Durrett. They welcomed "all who love the South and are determined to maintain her rights; who advocate resistance to the coercion of the seceded States by the Federal Government; who prefer an alliance with the Slaveholding States to Northern aggression; and who desire a reconstructed Confederacy of the Slaveholding and loyal Free States rather than the rule of an abolitionized and centralized despotism." It is interesting that the invitation included supporters of a reunion with free states. Many secessionists were cool to that notion.[5]

The *Courier* expected the *Journal* and "all of the little organs of Cassius Clay's 'left wing of the Liberal party'" to denounce the Southern Rights gathering. "Without objection from the Journal, we should have doubted" the meeting's propriety, Walter Haldeman's paper sneered. "Without its abuse and denunciation, which are so freely poured out on anything that is not intended to consolidate the power and to further the purposes of anti-slavery-ism, we would have feared that the suggestion lacked some important element of loyalty to the institutions and honor of the South." The *Journal's* opposition left "no doubt that the Convention will accomplish all the ends for which it has been asked." The *Courier* was confident that the conference would confirm "the worst fears of the semi-Lincoln papers and Submission leaders" and lead to "the final overthrow of the 'left wing' of the Abolition army which is encamped on our soil," and it would ensure that "the voice of Kentucky will be potent where now her uncertain utterances are received with neither consideration nor respect."[6]

The *Statesman* advised that the convention was a crucial first step toward a Southern Rights victory in the state elections and Kentucky's subsequent secession. Only by joining the Confederacy could Kentucky hold on to slavery and white supremacy, according to the paper. Because the dissolution of the Union was "already a fact, patent to the world," it was time for the state "to determine to which faction . . . she will unite her destinies." The *Statesman* put the question squarely: Will Kentucky "by an alliance with States whose interests, sympathies and institutions are identified with her own, maintain and conserve African slavery, or place that institution under the ban of moral, religious and political proscription by entering a family where it is condemned by an overwhelming majority of those in power?" It argued that in the elections, the central issue had to be stripped "of unnecessary verbiage and conditions until it presents itself in the simple form of African Servitude or Free Labor, *Emancipation or Slavery.*" Such was "really and practically the issue now upon us."[7]

The convention failed to sway the legislature. Even so, the secessionist press, led by the *Courier,* pronounced it a great triumph. The Louisville paper published dispatches from the conclave that said the delegates had resolved in favor of restoring the Union along the lines of the Crittenden Compromise. It was an empty gesture; the secessionists knew the proposal was dead and beyond resurrection. The venerated Crittenden lived in Frankfort, and perhaps to further polish their unionist credentials, the convention delegates recessed for three hours so that they could attend a reception for him, the scribe reported. The delegates also endorsed a border-state convention but insisted that Kentucky "make common cause with the South, should the Administration attempt to collect revenue or retake the forts or other public property'" in the Confederate states. In addition, the convention pressed Davis and Lincoln not to start a war. But if war came, Kentucky "must go with the South."[8]

The *Courier*'s "Special Reporter" counted the delegates in the hundreds and wrote that they were "of all the old parties, representing every section of the State." They had come to Frankfort to get organized and thwart "the systematized efforts of the desperate men in our midst who are struggling to separate Kentucky from her Southern sisters in a crisis in which is staked their rights and honor and liberties." The correspondent summarized a series of speeches, including a crudely racist peroration by state representative George Washington Ewing, a former Whig and Know-Nothing from Logan County. The lawmaker "drew a parallel between the two heads of the Republics.

Davis—brave, manly, high-toned—with his little command drawn up in the form of a V to meet the rush of the foe on the bloody field of Buena Vista [a battle in the Mexican-American War]." He described Lincoln as a "n—r-stealer afraid to pass through a Slave territory to the Presidential chair—leaving his family to be blown up by the infernal machine, and enveloped in a Scotch cap and military cloak, sneaked into a baggage car in making his way to Washington." Such charges—patently false—commonly circulated in the South and in the anti-Lincoln circles of the North.[9]

In its story about the conclave, the *Frankfort Yeoman* cited a speech by party leader Humphrey Marshall, a former congressman and US minister to China. Marshall, according to the paper, "thought our chances of obtaining our constitutional rights in the Union were few enough." The Black Republicans were hewing to the Chicago platform, and Lincoln was hiding his intentions toward Kentucky until after the August elections, he charged. Meanwhile, "it was his policy to debauch the country with the offices within his gift; to raise in the border States a Union party with Black Republicanism as a base," Marshall claimed. Such a party was intended to "secure the fruits of" Lincoln's election. The *Yeoman* paraphrased the popular poem "The Spider and the Fly:" "*In the calm the spider secures his web; take care you are not the fly.*"[10]

The rival *Frankfort Commonwealth* lampooned the convention, equating the Southern Rights men to snakes that quickly slithered away and claiming that "the Ophidians" were all gone from Frankfort by the next morning. "But how they went and where they have gone, is a mystery." The *Commonwealth* figured they were "teaching somewhere. But what made them abandon the poor ignorant Legislators? They came here to instruct and became instructed. They came to take Kentucky out, and took out themselves." The Southern Rights men "gave us one comforting glimpse of their red heads, and then seceded. The great question now is, where is the convention of pedagogues, which 'Like an angel's wing through an opening cloud, Was seen and then withdrawn.'"[11]

In any event, the secessionists surely knew that they were still a minority in the General Assembly. When the legislature reconvened, the Southern Rights lawmakers joined the Union Party in touting a convention of the border slave states. The General Assembly called the convention to meet in Frankfort on May 27 and set May 4 as Election Day for Kentucky's twelve delegates. On April 4 the legislature adjourned without even taking a vote on a sovereignty convention.[12]

George D. Prentice was no doubt happy that the legislature had spurned disunion again, but he had no patience for equivocators. His *Louisville Journal* zeroed in on the *Bardstown Gazette*. That paper reflected the uncertainty of many Kentuckians, admitting that it did not know whether states had a constitutional right to secede. But the *Gazette* asserted that states did "have a right to revolutionize, and they must be the judges whether their grievances are sufficient for them to resent." Prentice's paper taunted, "So far as the right of revolution is concerned, what is true of a State is equally true of a county, a city, a precinct, or an individual."[13]

On April 12 the *Statesman* reported the news from Washington, which had taken on "a warlike aspect." Lincoln was deliberately provoking the South by not giving up Fort Sumter at Charleston, South Carolina, the *Statesman* charged. It declared, "There seems to be unmistakable evidence that while deceiving the country and quieting apprehensions with perfidious assurances of a conciliatory policy . . . war, civil war, domestic strife, seems thus to be the deliberate, matured purpose of our Federal administration." The paper was unsure what actions the other border states might take, but it was confident that Kentuckians, despite politicians who might "succeed in fettering our State and holding her in unnatural alliance with her enemies," would ultimately "flock by thousands to the aid of the Confederate states."[14]

By the time the *Statesman* hit the streets, the Confederates were bombarding the island fort with long-range cannons. The war of words became a shooting war at 4:30 a.m., Charleston time, on April 12. The brick bastion's commander was Major Robert Anderson, a Kentucky native, who fought back as best he could. On April 15, two days after the outgunned and outnumbered Anderson had little choice but to strike the fort's colors, President Lincoln issued a proclamation calling for 75,000 volunteer soldiers. The free states quickly responded with an outpouring of young men who were eager to fight, but most of the governors of the eight slave states that were still in the Union rebuffed the president. Kentucky was supposed to send four regiments, or about 4,000 citizen-soldiers. None were forthcoming. "I say, *emphatically*, Kentucky will furnish no troops for the wicked purpose of subduing her sister Southern States," an indignant Governor Magoffin replied.[15]

With the war on, Kentucky's pro-Southern press urged the state to quit dallying and side with the Confederates. The secessionist publishers and editors believed that events at Fort Sumter had finally forced the issue; Kentucky would be Confederate. They were confident that the people, though devoted to the Union, would never become brothers-in-arms with Yankee abolitionists against the South.

Although the Confederates fired the first shot, the rebels and their supporters in Kentucky and elsewhere claimed that Lincoln had egged on the conflict. In his inaugural address, Lincoln had vowed to hold Fort Sumter. The *Courier* accused the president of later pretending that he would abandon the bastion, thus lulling the South into a false "sense of security" while his administration got ready to fight the Confederates. The outcome "of the faithlessness and treachery is before us in the shape of civil war. It is but the beginning of the end." Haldeman's paper banged the war drum: "Kentuckians! Men of the South! what is your duty? For whom will you fight—An abolition Administration elected on a platform subversive of your rights, or for your brethren of the South who stand by the Constitution as our fathers made it, and who will fight and die for it?"[16]

The *Yeoman* also blamed the war on Lincoln and the Republicans. Border states like Kentucky were bound to be drawn into the conflict, the paper stated. "With the authors of the 'irrepressible conflict' doctrine at the head of the Government, we of the Border Slave States are being rapidly hurried to destruction." The *Yeoman* foresaw "a long continuing and bloody civil war, in which, in all human probability, the Border Slave States are to be unwillingly the battle fields." It warned that "the doctrine of Abolitionism" and "the equality of the races" would advance through the borderland "with fire and sword into the bosom of the States South of us, and the horrors of a servile insurrection" would accompany "civil strife." The paper wondered, "What is to stay their baleful influence from us?"[17]

Lincoln's call for troops "to subjugate the cotton States" had triggered "from all parts of the North the uprising of the myriad hordes of Abolitiondom, breathing vengeance upon the slaveholding States and rushing to the standard of fanaticism," the *Yeoman* hissed. Kentucky and the other border states must not "fiddle while Rome is burning," because "the myrmidons of Abolitionism are gathering by tens of thousands at the call of a fanatical President—and we verily believe a madman." The border states had to "move immediately if they wish to check this threatening tide. These Northern hosts must find no friendly pathway through our State."[18]

The *Statesman* argued that a united North necessitated a united South. Thus, "it is with emotions of heartfelt pride that we proclaim our people a unit. The hatchet of political war is buried. Party feeling is gone. Dissentions are at an end." Such was hardly the case; Kentucky was still sharply divided, albeit more unionist than secessionist at this point. Evidently, the *Statesman* had not yet heard of Magoffin's refusal to give Lincoln any soldiers, for it expressed no doubt that the governor's reply "will be emphatic and to the point. When impudence reaches the point of gross insult, it becomes amusing." The Lexington paper scoffed, "An Abolition President calls for four thousand Kentuckians to aid in the subjugation of Southern people. The impudence of the Administration quite relieves the call of its offensive character."[19]

From northern Kentucky, the *Covington Journal* chimed in, declaring that "the position of Kentucky" could no longer be doubted. *"She will give no aid to the North in its war upon the South*—NOT A MAN, NOT A DOLLAR." Magoffin's "reply . . . to the requisition of the Black Republican authorities at Washington is heartily endorsed as a fitting response to an insulting demand." Even so, the *Journal* stopped short of demanding secession. Beyond refusing to send troops to Lincoln, Kentucky "is not at present prepared to go."[20]

In another editorial headlined "The Fruits of Abolitionism," the paper quoted an 1839 speech by Henry Clay in which the Great Compromiser supposedly warned, "Abolitionism should no longer be regarded as an imaginary danger. THE ABOLITIONISTS, let me suppose, SUCCEED IN THEIR PRESENT AIM OF UNITING THE INHABITANTS OF THE FREE STATES AS ONE MAN AGAINST THE SLAVE STATES. UNION ON ONE SIDE WILL BEGET UNION ON THE OTHER; and this process of reciprocal consolidation will be attended with all the violent prejudices, embittered passions, and implacable animosities, which ever degraded or deformed human nature." Clay added, "ONE SECTION WILL STAND IN A MENACING AND HOSTILE ARRAY AGAINST THE OTHER. —THE COLLISION OF OPINION WILL BE FOLLOWED BY THE CLASH OF ARMS." He gloomily predicted, "ABOLITIONISTS THEMSELVES WOULD SHRINK BACK IN DISMAY AND HORROR AT THE CONTEMPLATION OF DESOLATED FIELDS, CONFLAGRATED CITIES, MURDERED INHABITANTS, AND THE OVERTHROW OF THE FAIREST FABRIC OF HUMAN GOVERNMENT THAT EVER ROSE TO ANIMATE THE HOPES OF CIVILIZED MAN."[21]

The *Paris Flag, Georgetown Journal,* and *Cynthiana News* joined the anti-Lincoln chorus. The *News*, said the *Covington Journal*, had been "an ultra Union sheet" but was "now owned and edited by Mr. Tucker, late Assistant Bell-Everett Elector." Tucker succeeded A. J. Morey. The *Flag* gloried in Magoffin's "reply to Lincoln's impudence." The *Journal* had "not room for comment upon the villainous policy pursued by Lincoln and his Administration." In his valedictory editorial, Morey thundered, "We would just as soon expect to see Kentuckians rallying under the Stars and Stripes, if raised by the King of Dahomey, in Africa, as to hear that they were taking up arms to support the policy now being pursued by Lincoln." Morey was "now in favor of a Union of the South" because "Lincoln has driven us to the wall, and Union men must choose whether they will fight the Northern Abolitionists or their home folks."[22]

Lincoln's call for troops also frustrated Kentucky's unionist publishers and editors, who feared it might drive the state into the Confederacy. Prentice's *Louisville Journal* was "struck with mingled amazement and indignation," arguing that "the policy announced in the Proclamation deserves the unqualified condemnation of every American citizen." The *Journal* declaimed the president's action as "unworthy not merely of a statesman but of a man" and called it "utterly hair-brained [*sic*] and ruinous." The president could not have it both ways, it argued. "If Mr. Lincoln contemplated this policy in the inaugural address, he is a guilty dissembler; if he has conceived it under the excitement raised by the seizure of Fort Sumpter [*sic*], he is a guilty hotspur." In any event, Lincoln was "miserably unfit for the exalted position in which the enemies of the country have placed him," claimed the *Journal.* Its editorial concluded with a call for the people to "instantly take him and his Administration into their own hands if they would rescue the land from bloodshed and the Union from sudden and irretrievable destruction."[23]

The *Yeoman* was happy to reprint the *Journal*'s editorial, praising it as "the first manifestation of Southern feeling that we have yet seen in that sheet." But the Frankfort paper wondered, "Is it a mere fitful gleam, soon to be obscured in the fog of sickly Unionism? Are we to have a recantation to-day, or is the ability and influence of the Journal to be devoted henceforward to the noble, philanthropic, and truly patriotic aim of uniting all the Southern people in defense of their hearth-stones and altars?" The *Journal* stuck to its unionist guns.[24]

The *Maysville Eagle* stayed pro-Union, too. But the *Covington Journal* delighted in quoting its denunciation of Lincoln's call for troops. The order deserved "the unqualified condemnation of every American citizen," the paper declared. "It is unworthy of a President of the United States; it is utterly disgraceful to the man." The *Eagle* reproached the president in what sounded like a paraphrasing of the *Louisville Journal*'s editorial: "If any such policy was contemplated in his inaugural address, he is a guilty dissembler, but if he has determined upon it in the heat of passion, upon receiving the news of the attack on Fort Sumter, he is a passionate fool, or a madman, totally unfit for a position so trying as the one he occupies." The *Eagle* vowed never to support the Lincoln administration "while the sun shines. Will we obey his summons to take up arms against any portion of the people of the United States? Never while life is in us."[25]

The *Louisville Democrat* pleaded for calm. "Beware of precipitation! Rash counsels are indiscreet. It is easy to get into war by haste; not so easy to get out." Despite Lincoln's call for soldiers, "there is no danger of coercion now." Besides, the *Democrat* suggested, the Confederates at Fort Sumter "showed [an] ability to resist all that Lincoln can do." Kentucky's interest was in peace, and the paper suspected that "this fighting is a means employed to precipitate the Border States into the Southern Confederacy." Kentucky should stay put and allow "those who began the fight to take care of themselves, which they seem abundantly able to do, until there is necessity for other events."[26]

Kentucky unionists echoed the *Democrat*'s warning against rushing off to fight. In a Lexington speech on April 17, Crittenden begged the people to stay out of the "fratricidal war" and pleaded with them to act "as a peaceful mediator" instead. The next night, James Guthrie, Archibald Dixon, and Judge William F. Bullock, all well-known Union men, spoke to a large gathering at the Jefferson County courthouse in Louisville. They promised that Kentucky would not fight for the North or the South, and they warned both sides to keep their soldiers out of the state. Shortly after the meeting, the Union State Central Committee, whose members included George Prentice and John Harney, composed an "Address to the People of the Commonwealth of Kentucky" that embraced neutrality.[27]

The pro-Southern press denounced neutrality in no uncertain terms. The *Courier* castigated the Union men who were pushing neutrality, calling them feckless "Submissionists" who were foolishly estranging Kentucky from both the North and the South. The paper argued that by endorsing Magoffin's refusal to furnish troops, they made the North an enemy. By opposing secession, they "cut themselves off from the sympathy, friendship, and assistance" of the South. The *Courier* also argued that the state militia, called the Kentucky State Guard, was in no position to enforce neutrality against either side because the legislature had blocked appropriations to arm the soldiers adequately. The pro-Union lawmakers believed they had good reason to be chary with the militia, which was largely pro-Southern, from its commander, Inspector General Simon Bolivar Buckner of Hart County, down through the ranks. Union men suspected that Magoffin might use the State Guard to force Kentucky into the Confederacy at bayonet point, perhaps in conjunction with an invading rebel army.[28]

At any rate, the *Courier* found it impossible for anyone to believe that Lincoln's call for troops was not aimed at "the overrunning and subjugation of the seceded States." Yet the Union State Central Committee "advised delay and inaction while the North were arming for the conflict." The panel opposed putting "the State in a defensive condition" and "cried out against 'precipitation' when it was suggested that the whole question be submitted to the people for decision" by means of a sovereignty convention. The state's supreme secessionist sheet was on a roll: "While the Free States are collecting their legions, burnishing their guns, sharpening their swords, molding bullets, and organizing vast armies with which to attempt to 'overrun and subjugate' the South, and after hostilities have actually commenced, still insult the intelligence and spirit of the people by crying peace, peace, and advise 'a little more slumber, a little more folding of the arms to sleep!'" The *Courier* exclaimed, "Great God! Is there to be no end to this folly? Is this madness still to rule where reason should reign?"[29]

The next day, Haldeman's sheet satirized the big Union meeting in Louisville. The paper conceded that the crowd was large, but it claimed there was doubt about whether the gathering had approved the resolutions put to it. Nevertheless, the chairman had ruled that they were adopted. In the same issue, the *Courier* went after the state's "Submission" papers, claiming they were "lost to every feeling of patriotism." Their editors and publishers wanted Kentucky "to stand still, to make no alliance and to form no connection with the States South of us." The South's "interests are identical with ours," and its "safety depends as ours does on a successful resistance to the usurpations of a Government which has risen on the ruins of the Constitution and of the Republican system which our fathers erected on that compact between sovereign States." The North was united for war, the paper said. Yet "these men among us seek, for what purpose may be well guessed, to divide the South!" These same men who had left Kentucky "unarmed and defenseless" were standing idle "while seventy-five thousand Abolition mercenaries, *armed and provisioned and paid out of a common fund to which we will have to contribute not less than five millions of dollars a year for Heaven only knows how long*," were warring against "our brethren of the South with all the means known to military science." The *Courier* maintained that "armed neutrality" was a "pretext" by which "they would have us really give powerful aid to the North in their unhallowed enterprise."[30]

The *Courier* singled out the *Journal* for special scorn as "An Administration Organ." Prentice's sheet had vigorously attacked Lincoln's call for 75,000 volunteers "in order to secure the ear of the people of the South." Since then, the *Journal* had been "rushing to the defense of the Administration; and even now, while deprecating in strong terms the policy of Mr. Lincoln, it constantly argues and asserts to justify the course he has pursued." The *Journal*'s "acts contradict its words—its arguments, if arguments they may be called, are in behalf of what it ostensibly attacks: it is supporting the Administration, while seemingly opposing it. Beware of it, Kentuckians!"[31]

On the surface, it seems unlikely that any president would permit a supposedly loyal state to opt out of helping to quell an armed rebellion against the government he was sworn to protect and defend. A president less prudent than Lincoln might have forced Kentucky to provide its share of soldiers, sending in federal troops if need be. But Lincoln showed remarkable wisdom and forbearance toward his native state. Like the state's unionists, he was patient. He, too, had faith that the longer the state stayed in the Union, even as a neutral territory in a widening war, the less likely it was that Kentucky would join the Confederacy. He was correct.

Meanwhile, down the Ohio at Paducah, editor John C. Noble, Haldeman's faithful ally, was unsurprisingly unimpressed by the Louisville Union meeting. The *Herald* sneered that the conclave called "to take into consideration the war declared by Northern Abolitionism against the South" had resolved only "that it was foolish to risk Dixon's one hundred and fifty negroes and Guthrie's houses in Louisville for such things as the property, rights, liberty and lives of the Southern people; and that they did not care who went under, so that *their* dumplings boiled peacefully in the pot." Noble likened the secessionists to the patriots of the Revolutionary War, a comparison that became common throughout the Confederate states. He quoted Patrick Henry's "reply to the dumpling men of that day. . . . 'Give me Liberty or give me death!'"[32]

Kentucky's "dumpling men" were anxious to discover Lincoln's intentions toward the state. Would he really countenance neutrality? Would he make Kentucky join the fight? On April 26 Garrett Davis of Paris, a leading Union supporter, conferred with the president in Washington. Davis reported Lincoln's assurances that "he contemplated no military operations that would require him to march troops into or across Kentucky." The next day the president told Warner L. Underwood of Bowling Green, another Union man, that he hoped Kentucky "would stand by the government, in the present difficulties; but, if she would not do that, let her stand still and take no part against it; and that no hostile step would tread her soil." Lincoln's words greatly reassured Kentuckians who wanted to keep the state in the Union but out of the war.[33]

Naturally, the secessionist press vilified Davis, Underwood, and likeminded unionists. The *Statesman* of April 26 dismissed them as frauds. "There are men in Kentucky who still cry Union! Union! to the people with the hope of deluding them into an alliance with the North in a war of Southern invasion and subjugation." The unionists "would take advantage of the potent spell that clings to that rallying cry, to betray Kentucky into the hands of Northern traitors and fanatics. There is no 'Union' such as Kentucky once loved to recognize." The new Union consisted of "Abolition States now combined to invade Southern soil and murder the people of the slave States," the *Statesman* claimed. After listing the seven original Confederate states plus the newly seceded Virginia, the paper predicted that Maryland, Tennessee, and Arkansas would soon leave. North Carolina, too, was virtually out of the Union, the *Statesman* said. "Then what remains? *Kentucky* and *Missouri,* with the free States, engaged in a war of subjugation against the Southern whites, and of extermination of the institution of slavery!" The paper thundered, "Kentuckians, blush for your native State! Mourn that your own Kentucky should ever be reduced to so questionable an attitude! Let the people rise in their might and redeem the State from the impending disgrace." The *States-man* was wrong about Maryland; it stayed in the Union, as did slave-state Delaware.[34]

Even though almost no Kentucky unionists were abolitionists, the April 26 *Statesman* also claimed that "the old Emancipation party" was reviving and would soon form the core of a powerful organization. Early on, there was some opposition to slavery in the state. More than a few whites, Henry Clay among them, embraced the racist notion of colonization. But as slavery grew in the state—and abolitionism rose in the North—opposition to slavery waned in Kentucky. Nonetheless, the *Statesman* maintained that "already men have avowed themselves the champion of 'freedom' and the movement is on foot to lead them to large accessions of voters now being rallied under the 'Neutrality' flag." The paper was sure "that when Kentuckians understand the issue, and raise their voices, the old Commonwealth will be righted." Yet it confessed impatience: "But how long; oh, how long are we to hold this humiliating, dishonest and contemptible attitude of neutrality?" At the same time, the paper again urged a sovereignty convention to put the state in the Confederacy.[35]

Such a conclave would never meet. But the election of delegates to the border-state convention was still on for May 4. After the war began, most Kentucky secessionists considered the convention futile and ignored it. The *Russellville Herald*, which had endorsed the Union ticket, said the vote should be called off, arguing that it would divide people "and increase excitement in Kentucky." The paper noted that the nation had been at peace when the convention was called. Thus, it proposed, "*instead of wrangling over an election, which, when over, will amount to no practical good, we should be taking steps to arm the State and put ourselves in a position to maintain our rights and resist invasion or oppression at any moment the occasion may demand.*" But the *Herald* predicted the election would go on anyway. On April 26 the *Courier* stopped running the list of secessionist candidates; the same day, the *Statesman* announced that the Southern Rights slate had been officially withdrawn.[36]

On April 27 the *Covington Journal* reported that rabidly secessionist congressman Henry C. Burnett of Cadiz, an erstwhile Breckinridge Democrat and the First District's Southern Rights candidate for the convention, had informed the *Paducah Herald* that he was bowing out. With the secession of Virginia and the imminent secession of Arkansas, and with no delegates named from Delaware, North Carolina, Maryland, or Tennessee, the *Journal* concluded, "it is hardly worthwhile to make a contest over the election of delegates in Kentucky." The paper trusted that "the Southern Rights ticket will be withdrawn from the field." Below the story, the *Journal* noted that, "since the foregoing was put in type," it had heard that the ticket had indeed been pulled.[37]

On the day of the election, the *Courier* argued that going to the polls was pointless. "There will be no differing opinions, no wrangling and quarreling, no taking up of hats to leave the room because insulting propositions are made; and their proposition, whatever it may be, will, we suppose, be presented to the Administration or to Congress." It added, "When they cannot submit any plan or proposition which the usurpers at Washington will accept, we trust their friends will be brought to confess that the enslavement of the South is the purpose of the Northern people." Thus, the paper concluded, "the people of Kentucky may be united by this means, if the thunder of the enemies' guns along our border shall not have made them one in thought, determination, and action before that time."[38]

On the same page, the *Courier* derided Garrett Davis's visit with Lincoln. It dismissed "the little president of Bourbon county" as a "self-constituted commissioner from Kentucky." The paper suggested that Davis had probably "consulted with some of the fossil leaders of those with whom he acts here before going" and speculated that he had gone "to Washington to see about getting arms with which to fight in the Union." The paper doubted "the bellicose little giant wants anything on the peace establishment from the Administration." The *Courier* noted that the *Journal* had been pleased to print Davis's account of his meeting with the president. (The *Courier* had also published it.) "The Journal certainly agrees with Mr. Davis; and the left-wingers will all cry amen! to the conclusions of the Journal." By "left-wingers," the *Courier* meant staunch unionists. (The term originated during the French Revolution; the radical Jacobins sat on the left side of the hall where the republican legislature met.)[39]

The dozen Union candidates for the border-state convention won on a platform supporting the Crittenden Compromise and neutrality. Even if the secessionists had stayed in the race, the Union Party almost certainly would have carried every region except the Purchase. Statewide, the Union candidates received more than 107,000 votes, or almost three-fourths of the total ballots cast in the 1860 presidential election. The Union total in the border-state convention balloting bested the Bell, Douglas, and Lincoln vote total by nearly 14,300.[40]

In the final analysis, the election of delegates to the border-state convention proved that Fort Sumter had a decidedly different effect on Kentucky than it had on Virginia, Arkansas, North Carolina, and Tennessee. Those states seceded. Kentucky adopted neutrality, but neutrality within the Union.

The *Courier* cried fraud because it claimed the total vote in Louisville exceeded the city vote for president by 735. "We suppose the election . . . was regarded as a huge joke by the Submissionists, who felt privileged to enjoy it to any extent they pleased; and accordingly they amused themselves with such freaks as we would scarcely expect from those who profess to have so much regard for the 'Constitution and the enforcement of the laws.'" The paper also accused the Union side of cheating and inflating their vote in Maysville and elsewhere. The *Courier* did not know who was "responsible for this shameful and criminal proceeding," but it believed the guilty parties should be punished. Meanwhile, the paper claimed that by overdoing the fraud, the managers had deprived themselves "of any advantage they might otherwise have reaped" and exposed "the unscrupulous tactics of these conspirators against the State."[41]

Despite the election results, the *Paducah Herald* believed unionism was on the wane statewide. "It is our solemn conviction that if the vote could be taken to-day as to whether Kentucky would join the Southern Confederacy, it would carry by fifty thousand majority," it editorialized. Noble was whistling in the dark. Union power was holding firm everywhere except in his region, where the events at Fort Sumter had greatly reduced the Purchase's small Union minority.[42]

Meanwhile, Lincoln called a special session of Congress to convene on July 4. Magoffin named June 20 as Election Day in Kentucky; the terms of the state's congressmen had expired on March 4. "We presume there will be no contest, and probably no candidates at this election," the *Courier* speculated. The paper painted a bloody—and patently false—picture of Washington. "Southern men have been shot down in sight of the President's house for treason, without a trial by jury of their peers, or even the formalities of a court martial." It reported that citizens of slave states who were still in the capital city were fast fleeing a prevailing "reign of terror" (another allusion to the radical phase of the French Revolution, during which the Jacobins dispatched thousands of their enemies, real or suspected, via the guillotine). A Kentucky lawmaker who might "stand up in Congress and arraign the conduct of the Administration and justify the South, would be at once arrested and executed for treason." The *Courier* concluded, "If in any district in this State, there is one man whose submissionism is so abject, or whose ambition is so great, as to lead him to desire an election to the Congress at Washington, we trust our friends will let him make the canvass undisturbed, and be elected unopposed." The paper noted that regardless of such a man's willingness "to sacrifice his manly feelings and patriotic impulses and State pride for a Union that no longer exists, he will soon be driven home cured of his respect for the North and of his love for the Administration."[43]

On May 8 the *Courier* put Cassius Clay at the top of its list of Kentucky abolitionist administration "lovers." Others included Robert Breckinridge, Warner Underwood, court of appeals justice Samuel S. Nicholas of Louisville, and court of appeals chief justice George Robertson of Lancaster. Clay and the rest were "leading spirits in this struggle to separate Kentucky from the other slave States." The *Courier* asserted that "the abolition of slavery is a portion of the price Kentucky is expected to pay for permission to disunite herself from the other slave States and remain with those who hate her institutions and have no regard for her interests." If Kentucky stayed in the Union, "the emancipation of her slaves will follow as a necessary and inevitable consequence." Haldeman's paper again pandered to racism, predicting that "at once her two hundred thousand negroes, not sold South, nor sent to Liberia, would become the political equals of the whites; negroes would crowd the free white man at the voting places, black children would take their places in our common schools; free negro labor would be brought into competition with our white mechanics and laboring men; and in the jury box, on the witness stand, and in all political privileges, those now slaves would be the peers of the whitest." Thus, the *Courier* concluded, "If the slaveholders want to be robbed of their property, if the non-slaveholders want to have two hundred thousand negroes made their political equals and brought into direct competition with them in the ordinary pursuits of life, let all join Lincoln and Seward in maintaining the Union—let all join Clay, Underwood & Co. in keeping Kentucky with the Free States."[44]

Meanwhile, Fort Sumter prompted Magoffin to call the legislature back to Frankfort on May 6. In his opening message he urged a convention and called for the arming of the state. The *Commonwealth* denounced the governor's words as "warlike" and said he offered "no ground of hope for the peace-loving citizens of Kentucky." The paper found nothing in Magoffin's message that it could approve. "There is not a recommendation therein contained that every Union man will not oppose. It is unreasonable, inflammatory, and altogether foreign to the sentiment of Kentucky as expressed" in the border-state convention election.[45]

The Union Party was still dead set against a sovereignty convention, and it was determined to make neutrality the official state policy. The *Yeoman*, still in favor of a convention, again raised the core argument of the secession press: Kentucky had to secede because Lincoln aimed to end slavery. The paper trotted out Old Testament imagery, unflatteringly comparing Lincoln to Rehoboam, the ancient king of Israel whose allegedly unwise policies led the ten northern tribes to rebel and start their own kingdom. "Mr. Lincoln—the Rehoboam of the American Israel—will be known in all coming time as the *Perjured President.* History will so indict him, posterity will so convict him, and eternity will so infamize him." The real purpose of the war was "to bring about compulsory abolition of slavery in the Southern States, and to drive out of the Union every slave State resisting the achievement of that object." Rehoboam, the *Yeoman* noted, had been agreeable to keeping "any of the tribes under his rule willing to pay him tribute and submit to his hated government." The *Yeoman* acidly observed that the president "will graciously permit Kentucky to continue a member of the Federal Union, if we will continue to pay our proportion of the Federal revenue, to be expended in conquering our Southern brethren, fight our brethren under the desecrated banner he bears—and submit also to the inauguration of the 'irrepressible conflict' policy in our very midst of abolishing slavery; *but he will recognize us on no other terms.*"[46]

On May 10 the *Yeoman* detected "two stripes of neutrality" in Kentucky. One was sincere; after all, the state had done nothing to bring on the war. Although the paper was inclined toward neutrality, it rejected the idea because it was "a legal and logical absurdity, which will be respected by neither belligerent, and which, therefore, will prove an impracticable attitude." Besides, was not "virtual war" already at Kentucky's borders? Had not the Union military established "camps of observation along the Ohio, pointing their guns upon Kentucky, overhauling vessels engaged in peaceful commerce," and had not "an embargo or a blockade—one or other as Mr. Lincoln deems us in or out of the Union—[been] ordered to be enforced at Louisville?" The other stripe was duplicitous, "a political stepping stone to Lincolnism." Advocates of that form of neutrality "will soon be for joining Kentucky in Lincoln's mad raid against the South. Mark the prediction." The Confederate press repeatedly warned that neutrality would be followed by Kentucky's siding with the North against the South.[47]

Meanwhile, the General Assembly's rejection of a sovereignty convention had led the secessionist *Columbus Crescent* to charge that the legislature did not reflect the true sentiment in the state. The unionist *Frankfort Commonwealth* took the same position, but from the opposite perspective. Albert Hodge's paper complained that "many of the strongest Union counties are being misrepresented by the most rabid disunionists in the Legislature." They were "a queer set to be talking about the will of the people," according to the *Commonwealth.* Undoubtedly, editor Hodge was pleased when these Southern Rights men who were up for reelection in August lost or, facing almost certain defeat, chose not to run.[48]

On May 16 the Kentucky house approved a neutrality resolution and, at the same time, endorsed Magoffin's refusal to send troops to Lincoln. Four days later, the governor issued a proclamation of armed neutrality, warning both sides to keep their soldiers out of Kentucky. The legislature adjourned on May 24, but not before the senate passed neutrality resolutions of its own and lawmakers created a Union Home Guard as a counterweight to the State Guard. Magoffin was, constitutionally, the commander in chief of the state's armed forces. To break his power, the legislature put the Home Guard and the State Guard under a five-member military board. Magoffin was a member of the board, but he was just one of five. To help arm the Home Guard, President Lincoln, at the behest of navy lieutenant William O. Nelson of Maysville, agreed to furnish 5,000 muskets, dubbed the "Lincoln guns."[49]

Perhaps because Haldeman sensed that a large majority of Kentuckians approved neutrality, the secessionist *Courier* acquiesced in the legislature's action, thereby baffling the *Journal*. "We confess that we do not think it at all strange," the *Courier* replied to its enemy's skepticism. "We think yet the policy we denounced is all we said of it. But the people of Kentucky, bound hand and foot by their faithless representatives, and denied the privilege of determining the future position of the State, have indicated their wish to occupy for the present a neutral position." The *Courier* still favored a sovereignty convention but pledged to abide by majority rule. At the same time, the *Courier* doubted that neutrality would work. Thus, the paper looked forward to a time when "the voters of Kentucky will have an opportunity of formally declaring whether their State shall make one of the Northern Confederacy; one of the Southern Confederacy; or be an independent nation; and when they shall have spoken, their will be obeyed." Of course, the *Courier* was certain that the people would elect a secessionist majority to a convention that would, in turn, put Kentucky out of the Union and into the Confederacy.[50]

The *Courier* also charged that the Lincoln guns were part of a plot hatched by Kentucky's "tory leaders," in league "with the usurpers at Washington," to force the state to stay in the Union. The paper declared that many Kentuckians were on to the scheme, noting that in several places, men "will not even touch the guns," while in others, the firearms have been quietly and safely stored "subject to the order of the Governor." Still other men "will use them to maintain the armed neutrality which they have been taught to believe is the proper policy for the State, by driving all invaders, from whatever quarter, from our soil." Naturally, the *Courier* expected the invasion to come from the North. In any event, the paper maintained that the muskets had "aroused the people to a full appreciation of the damnable purposes of those who would light up the flame of civil war to aid them to work out their ends." It concluded, "Thus good is brought out of evil—thus an over-ruling Providence defeats this hellish conspiracy against the peace of the Commonwealth and the safety of its people."[51]

Predictably, the *Statesman* issued a double-barreled denouncement of neutrality and the Lincoln guns. It argued that neutrality was untenable. "Can Kentucky, while continuing a member of the Federal Union, enjoying the common protection of that Union and sending its representatives to Congress legally refuse to bear the burdens of the Government and decline to recognize as enemies those against whom the Government is waging war?" The *Statesman* answered, "Most assuredly not." Monroe's paper argued that the "strict neutrality" adopted by the Union-majority legislature was one-sided. The pro-Union lawmakers really meant that only Confederate soldiers must be kept out of the state. Too, the unionists "assert the right of the Federal Government to occupy Kentucky and carry on [Lincoln's] . . . war from this State against the South, and that Kentucky must pay her quota for the expenses of this war."[52]

The *Statesman* charged that the Lincoln guns represented a dangerous and illegal introduction of weapons into Kentucky. The paper claimed to know of "convincing evidence" that Garrett Davis and some "other Administration men" in Kentucky had sought the muskets for *such private citizens of Kentucky as will subscribe an obligation to use them in obedience to the order of the President of the United States.*" The *Statesman* challenged, "If citizens in this State are arming for civil war, let it not be done stealthily and secretly. Kentuckians, whatever their differences, should never resort to secret measures of domestic strife. In a word, if we are to be plunged into fratricidal war, let all understand it and prepare for it."[53]

The *Yeoman* ridiculed claims that these weapons were private property bought and paid for by the men who received them. The muskets could be had for half a dollar, the paper reported. It asked, "Fifty cents a-piece for muskets that cost twenty-five dollars each! Who does not see the fraud and imposture of this ridiculous pretense? Is Abe Lincoln enacting the part of peddler of United States muskets at fifty cents each!" The *Yeoman* lowered the boom: "This attempt of the bloody-minded tyrant and usurper to arm one-half the people of Kentucky against the other half is one of the most stupendous acts of cold-blooded ferocity and lawlessness ever heard in Christendom. Thank God, however, the attempt of this infuriate madman will be frustrated by the good sense, the loyalty, and fraternity of the great mass of men who have received these arms." The *Yeoman* predicted, "Very far the largest number of the muskets will be pointed at the breasts of the invader's forces, rather than at the Kentucky brethren of those who may ever pull their triggers." Naturally, the Frankfort paper expected the invaders to be wearing blue uniforms.[54]

Joseph Holt. (Library of Congress)

John Bell. (Library of Congress)

Henry C. Burnett. (Library of Congress)

Henry Watterson. (Library of Congress)

Beriah Magoffin. (Library of Congress)

John C. Breckinridge. (Library of Congress)

Abraham Lincoln. (Library of Congress)

John J. Crittenden. (Library of Congress)

Robert Anderson. (Library of Congress)

Reuben T. Durrett. (Filson Historical Society)

Durrett family grave marker, Cave Hill Cemetery, Louisville.

George D. Prentice. (Filson Historical Society)

Haldeman family grave marker, Cave Hill Cemetery, Louisville.

Walter N. Haldeman. (Filson Historical Society)

Walter N. Haldeman's footstone, Cave Hill Cemetery, Louisville.

John H. Harney. (University of Louisville)

Albert Gallatin Hodges. (Filson Historical Society)

S. I. M. Major. (Filson Historical Society)

Thomas B. Monroe. (From Ed Porter
Thompson, *History of the Orphan
Brigade*.)

George D. Prentice statue, Louisville Free Public Library.

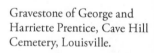

Gravestone of George and Harriette Prentice, Cave Hill Cemetery, Louisville.

5

Neutrality Summer

The secessionists and their allies in the press chafed under neutrality. They charged that the unionists were using neutrality as a cover to build support for entering the war on the Union side. The secessionists suffered another hard blow at the polls on June 20, when unionist candidates won nine of Kentucky's ten seats in the congressional elections. The Southern sympathizers and their journalist friends pinned their last hopes on the August elections for the state legislature, in which all 100 house seats and half the senate seats were on the line. Meanwhile, as chances for a Confederate Kentucky melted in the summer heat, some Confederate papers cooled their secessionist ardor and seemed to acquiesce in neutrality, at least for the time being. Neutrality, they reasoned, was better than fighting for the North. But the secessionists stuck to their argument that the "Black Republicans" would destroy slavery and make African Americans and whites equal in Kentucky. When the Union Party won its biggest victory yet in the state elections, it was emboldened. The unionists supported a recruiting camp for Union army volunteers in central Kentucky. The state was on the verge of abandoning neutrality and fully embracing the Union war effort.

Dutifully, the border-state convention assembled in the state senate chamber on May 27. The turnout was tiny, and nothing came of the convention. "Marshall," the *Louisville Courier*'s less than impartial correspondent, reported that the delegates knew the hour was too late "for making empty speeches and issuing paper bullets." Tennessee was about to secede, and Virginia was already in the Confederacy. The scribe concluded that "the proper time for this Convention, unfortunately, has past and gone. The whole country is now in arms, and not to prepare to meet the coming storm would but be to 'fiddle and dance while Rome burns.'"[1]

Before May was out, Haldeman had changed his mind about the congressional election and decided the Southern Rights side should jump in. Hence, the *Courier* began running a list of the secessionist candidates. At the same time, the paper leaped at the chance to make some money off the election. The daily *Courier* was doing fine, but Haldeman wanted at least 20,000 more subscribers for his weekly edition sold in Kentucky, Tennessee, and Missouri. New subscribers were "necessary to the success of the great cause of Southern Rights." By reading the paper, the citizenry could keep up with "current events in out of the state," including "the illegal and unconstitutional acts of the present Administration." In addition, they could find out about "the purposes, plots, intrigues, and acts of those among us who sympathize with the usurpers in Washington."[2]

Of course, the Reverend Robert Breckinridge disagreed with Haldeman's description of current events. He blamed the South for starting the war. The Confederate government had been mad to bomb Fort Sumter instead of waiting for "its peaceful surrender, in three days, through starvation," he wrote in the *Danville Quarterly Review.* Breckinridge conceded that it was possible for the country to divide "*peaceably,* into two or more nations, by the consent of the American people, and the change of the Federal Constitution." But it was impossible "to rend it by a military revolt." The pastor-publisher stressed, "We are not partizans of the present National Administration," but he recognized the federal government as "the true and only lawful representation of the nation itself." He believed that most citizens, whether Northern, border state, or Southern—the latter group "cruelly oppressed and silenced"—agreed "that the American people are a nation—that the Constitution and laws of the United States are supreme in this nation—that the Federal Government is the true and only legal representative of this nation."[3]

Unionists like Breckinridge must have been looking forward to the congressional elections. Their party had swept the balloting for border-state convention delegates and would have won even if the Southern Rights side had not withdrawn. Neutrality seemed to be popular and holding; both armies had steered clear of Kentucky. But on June 5 a small party of Yankees from the big Union base in Cairo, at the southern tip of Illinois, crossed the Ohio River into deeply Confederate Ballard County to disperse a dozen or so armed secessionists from nearby Columbus. The Cairo commander said some local unionists, fearing the intruders, had invited his troops over. In any event, the blue-clad soldiers departed after discovering that the men had abandoned their camp and gone home.[4]

Although the incursion had been minor and brief, the *Courier* claimed it was a major breach of neutrality. "As offensive, as inexcusable, as irritating as well calculated to provoke resistance and bring on a bloody fight as was this act, the excuse offered for the violation of the sovereignty of Kentucky is still more insulting and still more indicative of the disposition of the Administration to set aside the Constitution and the laws and to subject us all to the iron rule of an irresponsible and unlimited military despotism," the paper declared. "If it were true, as it is not, that men in that part of Kentucky have been threatened with violence or menaced in any way by Southern Rights men, or by any body whatever, have we not laws for their protection, and courts to see that justice is done and the laws administered, and power to execute the decrees of the courts?" The *Courier* trusted that Governor Magoffin would "have this whole thing investigated, promptly and thoroughly, and that steps will be taken to prevent such descents in future."[5]

Word of the little foray also made big news in the *Covington Journal.* The paper admitted it had no information about the Columbus campers but grumbled, "Federal officials class as 'Secessionists' all who do not throw up their caps for Lincoln and endorse his policy." The *Journal* argued that even if the camp "was formed for an unlawful purpose," the federal incursion onto neutral soil was illegal.[6]

On June 12 the Yankees returned to the Purchase, this time by river, and visited the campers' hometown. Union troops from Cairo boarded the steamer *City of Alton* and traveled to nearby Columbus, a small but bustling Mississippi River port in Hickman County. The Yankee soldiers scrambled ashore, gleefully grabbed the town's big Confederate flag, and hauled the banner back to Cairo as a war trophy. After the *Alton* departed, editor Len Faxon of the *Columbus Crescent* sharpened his poison pen and stabbed at the flag snatchers and their commander. Apparently, Faxon was already in the Confederate army; in any event, his blast amazed the "world's first and greatest" war correspondent, Sir William Howard Russell of the *Times of London.* The Briton preserved Faxon's fulmination in *My Diary North and South,* his book about the American Civil War. If not for Russell, Faxon's fusillade probably would have been lost because, evidently, no copies of the 1861 *Crescent* survived. Russell, who covered the Indian mutiny and the Crimean War for his paper, was visiting the Union camp at Cairo on June 20 when he picked up a copy of the *Crescent* containing Faxon's account of the *Alton's* unwelcome visit.[7]

As editor of the *Times and Delta,* Faxon had been famous for poking fun at the locals, including editor Mose Harrell, who was now in charge at the *Cairo Gazette.* "Len Faxon, formerly a squatty little editor at Cairo, has been appointed a Colonel in the Confederate army," Harrell wrote. He claimed that, while helping to guard Clarksville, Tennessee, Faxon had waylaid a suspicious Cumberland River skiff with a shotgun blast across its bow. The colonel "threatened to wade out and upset her unless the 'sturdy knight of the oar' pulled in." He complied, and Faxon dutifully searched the man, discovering on his person "one pair of shoe-strings; two bridle buckles; four ten-cent pieces; some unpressed tobacco; one twine-string; receipt for the Columbus *Crescent* which had never been sent; a spoon-handle; a hame string; a few seed-oats, and a letter of introduction to Jeff. Davis." Faxon, according to Harrell, declared "the articles contraband, and confiscated them."[8]

Harrell also reported a "prevalent" rumor that Faxon, purportedly promoted to one-star general, had been in Cairo spying on the Yankee army. He was "disguised as a female and engaged in peddling radishes," the *Gazette* reported. "We saw the female in question, and she was partially sober—proof positive that it could not have been Faxon." Harrell continued to lampoon his old friend, revealing, "On Monday, at midnight, we climbed the Bell and Everett pole, and by the aid of a double back action rotary-motion spyglass discovered Gen. Beauregard and Brig. Gen. Faxon on the Missouri side, looking up at the heights of Cairo." The duo "appeared to be gazing through the bottoms of green glass tumblers. This is entirely reliable."[9]

Harrell reported that "Colonel Len" was "said now to be bitterly hostile toward Cairo, and threatens to wipe it off the map." The *Gazette* chief could understand the source "of this 'burning feeling of revenge,'" claiming that "the last time we saw him, he had been three months trying to drink up all the whisky in Cairo, and was hopping mad because he couldn't do it." Thus, Faxon "intimated that if he could not thus destroy all the rot-gut in town, he would on the first occasion annihilate the town itself." Harrell had "left him still at the good work, and from his present attitude infer his laudable exertions 'on the first part' signally failed."[10]

In any event, Faxon, whom Russell identified as "Colonel L. G. Faxon of the Tennessee Tigers," missed the *Alton's* foray into Columbus. Back in his editor's chair, Faxon opened fire in the June 19 *Crescent*. Russell recounted that Faxon apologized "for the non-appearance of the journal for several weeks" and explained that before departing, evidently to join the rebel forces, he had "engaged the services of a competent editor, and left a printer here to issue the paper regularly." Even though Faxon's hiatus was lengthier than expected, the editor insisted that "the aforesaid printer promised faithfully to perform his duties, but he left the same day we did, and consequently there was no one to get out the paper." Faxon charitably surmised "that fear and bad whiskey had nothing to do with his evacuation of Columbus."[11]

Russell quoted Faxon's bluster, claiming that "the Irish are for us, and they will knock Bologna sausages out of the Dutch, and we will knock wooden nutmegs out of the Yankees." The editor wished the folds of the purloined flag "had contained 1000 asps to sting 1000 Dutchmen to eternity unshriven." But the Yankees likely would have been too drunk to feel anything, Faxon derided: "The mosquitoes of Cairo have been sucking the lager-bier out of the dirty soldiers there so long, they are bloated and swelled up as large as spring 'possums. An assortment of Columbus mosquitoes went up there the other day to suck some, but as they have not returned, the probability is they went off with *delirium tremens;* in fact, the blood of these Hessians would poison the most degraded tumble bug in creation." Faxon reloaded, aimed, and fired anew: "When the bow-legged wooden-shoed, sour craut stinking, Bologna sausage eating, hen roost robbing Dutch sons of — had accomplished the brilliant feat of taking down the Secession flag on the river bank, they were pointed to another flag of the same sort which their guns did not cover, flying gloriously and defiantly, and dared yea! double big black dog-dared—dared, as we used to say at school, to take that flag down." The Yankees demurred, Faxon reported. "The cowardly pups, the thieving sheep dogs, the sneaking skunks dare not do so, because their twelve pieces of artillery were not bearing on it." After flaying the federal soldiers, Faxon lambasted their leader, Brigadier General Benjamin Prentiss, who would become a Union hero at the Battle of Shiloh in April 1862. Faxon sloughed him off as "a miserable hound, a dirty dog, a sociable fellow, a treacherous villain, a notorious thief, a lying blackguard, who has served his regular five years in the Penitentiary and keeps his hide continually full of Cincinnati whiskey, which he buys by the barrel in order to save his money—in him are embodied the leprous rascalities of the world, and in this living score, the gallows is cheated of its own."[12]

Finally, Faxon tossed down the gauntlet: "Prentiss wants our scalp; we propose a plan by which he may get that valuable article." Prentiss could pick 150 of his best fighters "or 250 of his lager-bier Dutchmen." Faxon would line up 100 Columbus worthies. "Then let both parties meet where there will be no interruption at the scalping business, and the longest pole will knock the persimmon," he challenged. "If he does not accept this proposal, he is a coward." Prentiss ignored Faxon. But Russell suspected that the soldier-editor had ruffled Prentiss's feathers more than the general wished to admit.[13]

Clearly, the Southern Rights Party and its allies in the press figured the two breaches of Kentucky's neutrality in the Jackson Purchase, small as they were, were big enough to boost their chances at the polls on June 20. After all, their gray-clad friends were content to stay south of the Bluegrass State's border. Yet at the same time, political realities had moved some Southern Rights papers to tone down their secessionist editorializing and at least purport to go along with peace and neutrality—for the present, anyway.

The unionists were not about to let the secessionists off the hook. They claimed the Southern Rights candidates really wanted to be in the Confederate Congress. That charge got a rise out of the *Courier*, which was in high dudgeon over such "Lincolnite" trickery. "All the candidates on the Southern Rights ticket, are before the people in good faith; and such each of them as may be elected will go to Washington, [and] take their seats in the House of Representatives," the paper declared. If nothing else, they could "enter their solemn protests against the violations of the Constitution by the President and other officers of the Government, and against the war policy of the Administration which is bringing ruin and want and suffering upon our people." The paper conceded that it may have erred in opposing the election at first. Likewise, the Southern Rights candidates might be wrong in bothering to run. "But neither of these questions concern the people, who have to choose between the candidates before them."[14]

First District secessionists nominated Congressman Henry Burnett for reelection on the Southern Rights ticket at a late May convention held in Mayfield. He was as stubbornly secessionist as ever. So were his constituents. Indeed, the delegates considered a military alliance with soon-to-be-Confederate Tennessee, which would have been tantamount to secession. Ultimately, the western Kentuckians rejected the plan, fearing it would harm the secessionist cause statewide. They believed the Southern Rights Party would flip the Kentucky house and senate in August, summon a sovereignty convention, and make Kentucky Confederate. Burnett was unsure that he could swear allegiance to Uncle Sam, according the *Statesman*. "If he could take his seat with honor to his constituency, and if he could be useful, he would enter the walls of Congress in July next." At any rate, should Burnett go back, "it was his firm determination to arraign the traitor Lincoln before the bar of his country for treason, and if, in his endeavors to bring the usurper to justice, he should lose his life, he expected that Kentuckians would avenge his death."[15]

Meanwhile, the *Covington Journal* reminded the unionist congressional candidates of Kentucky's official noncombatant status. "The Legislature of Kentucky, by nearly an unanimous vote, has declared the position of the State in the unhappy war between the North and the South, to be that of strict neutrality. A vast majority of the people of Kentucky have endorsed the action of the Legislature." Likewise, Magoffin's refusal to supply troops to Lincoln to fight the South "has been heartily approved by the Legislature and the people of the State." Thus, "if the Kentucky members of Congress act in harmony with the deliberate and unequivocal declarations of the authorities and people of the State, they will refuse to vote a man or a dollar for the prosecution of the war." The paper claimed that Aaron Harding of Greensburg, the Fourth District Union Party hopeful, had pledged to "*vote men and money to carry on the war with the South, and that he was willing to see blood shed for seven years to coerce the Secessionists.*"[16]

Unionist Seventh District congressman Robert Mallory of New Castle backed the war, the *Courier* claimed on Election Day. "*This is no war of subjugation, but a war of defense; and as long as the Government is defending its rights, I will vote men and money to carry it on,*" Mallory had purportedly announced at an election eve rally in Louisville (the newspaper's italics indicating the congressman's emphasis). "He assumes a position as insulting to the intelligence of the people as it is disgraceful to his understanding, admitting that he is honest in the assertion that this is a war of defense," the paper maintained.[17]

That same day, the *Courier* pleaded that "the solemn, the imperative, the binding duty of the voters of Kentucky" was to prove "that they desire peace, that they will not sanction the violations of the Constitution by the President, that they will not take up arms to aid in the fool-hardy and suicidal attempts to subjugate their friends, customers and brethren of the South, and that they will not pay any portion of the vast sums which this useless and ruinous conflict is costing." The paper proposed that the issue was "not Union or disunion—secession or anti-secession"—it was "the indorsement or condemnation of the unconstitutional and illegal acts of the President—peace or war—the maintenance of the Constitution or its destruction—the perpetuation of a constitutional government or the erection in its stead of a military despotism."[18]

A hefty majority of voters ignored the *Courier*'s entreaties. Unionist candidates won nine of the state's ten congressional districts by wide margins. Mallory mauled secessionist Horatio W. Bruce of Louisville by a vote of 11,035 to 2,862. Burnett was the only secessionist winner, but he would have lost, too, had it not been for his huge landslide in the Jackson Purchase. Beyond "the South Carolina of Kentucky," he won only Trigg, his home county, and by only 20 votes. Some secessionists apparently boycotted the election because the total Southern Rights vote was only 37,700, compared with 53,143 for Breckinridge in 1860. But it is also possible that some Breckinridge voters turned out to be unionists. At any rate, the total unionist vote of 92,540 was only 513 fewer than the 1860 totals for Bell, Douglas, and Lincoln. Clearly, the Union tide was strong.[19]

Naturally, the secessionist press was quick to offer postelection alibis. The *Paducah Herald* claimed that everybody but Burnett lost because "our friends in every portion of the State except below the Tennessee river [the Purchase]" blundered and campaigned on "false policy," meaning neutrality and peace. The paper bragged on itself and its region: "In the 'Purchase,' where the Herald boldly threw out the banner of secession, and where the contest was distinctly made upon that issue, we have triumphed gloriously and by thousands." Editor Noble claimed that in the First District counties east of the Purchase, "where the voice of Burnett . . . and others could have been potent with a bold issue, we are defeated, because the dodge game proved to be really an aid to the Unionists instead of a weapon of destruction." The *Herald* claimed that, like Burnett, other Southern Rights leaders such as Magoffin and Breckinridge were really secessionists but chose not to make "a bold, manly, honest, open fight for Secession." The paper argued, "They acted upon a mistaken policy, and we have lost the State, and would have lost even the First District had not a few bold men below the Tennessee river forced the true issue and won the district by the innate power and truth of Secession." In any event, Noble proposed to make the August 5 election for the state legislature a "fight . . . *in favor of Secession and the Southern Confederacy.*" The *Herald* thus begged the Southern Rights Party to campaign "upon the fair issue of Secession or no Secession—to remain with the abolition North or join the South—to remain a Slave state or abolish slavery." He concluded with a warning that the idea of the Purchase separating from the rest of state was still alive: "Kentucky *must* leave the abolition Union. The Kentucky Purchase, at least, *will* do it."[20]

The *Herald* was almost certainly wrong about why the secessionists lost. Had the Southern Rights candidates campaigned harder "upon the fair issue of Secession," they likely would have attracted even fewer votes. Noble wrote with the certainty of the most doctrinaire of secessionists and with the knowledge that the great majority of his readers—and of Purchase citizens—were with him. But Noble was blind to—or unwilling to accept—public opinion everywhere else in Kentucky. The state elections would prove him dead wrong.

In its postmortem, the *Courier* said the Union side "may have succeeded in deceiving and cheating those whose honesty of purpose is such that they little dream of the arts and machinations of men who want office, place, executive favors, or Administration gold." Somehow, though, the paper asserted that "day by day, and hour by hour, for weeks, have the people been more fully realizing the nature and extent of their danger; and with each development of the 'hair-brained [*sic*] and ruinous' policy of the Administration, the inevitable tendency of which is to drench the land in blood, and separate still wider the States comprising the two Confederacies now existing within the limits of the old Union, the cause of the Constitution, the rights of the States, and the liberty of the people has been strengthened." Like Noble, Haldeman was deluding himself; secessionism was anything but on the rise in the Bluegrass State.[21]

Nonetheless, the *Courier* kept after the unionists, repeating the charge that they were using neutrality as a ploy to drag Kentucky into the war on the Yankee side. The paper claimed that "a prominent member of the Union-Submission-Lincoln party in Louisville, recently told a responsible citizen that his party never intended to stand by neutrality; and as far as the leaders are concerned he was unquestionably correct." Like the *Herald,* the *Courier* urged Southern Rights men to focus on the state elections. "Let candidates be announced at once in every county and district . . . let the oldest, wisest, ablest, best man everywhere be put in the field—and no matter how hopeless apparently the prospect is, let each candidate be supported as if the fate of an empire depended on his success." Couching the election in hopeless terms suggested that Haldeman was less than sanguine about its outcome. Nonetheless, the *Courier* challenged, "To arms; then, freemen of Kentucky! And may the right win!"[22]

On June 22 the *Frankfort Yeoman* also tried to be upbeat about the Southern Rightists' shellacking. The capital city's paper had "no fancy for lumbering our columns with the imperfect details. They will doubtless be sickening enough when reported in full; but although we are apparently defeated for the present, we say cheerily to our friends, that we are not conquered and can not be subjugated." The *Yeoman* hearkened to the dreary days of the War of Independence, when Thomas Paine fired flagging patriot ardor with *The Crisis,* his famous pamphlet. "This is a time to try men's souls, just such a time as tried the souls of our fathers of the Revolution. We have the same cause to fight for—the right of self-government—resistance to lawless tyranny and despotism."[23]

The *Yeoman's* tack was hardly unique. Secessionists in Kentucky and elsewhere often compared themselves to America's fighting founders. But as historian James M. McPherson pointed out, the rebels of 1776 and 1861 were warring for decidedly different "rights and liberties." The Confederates were contending for "the right to own slaves; the liberty to take this property into the territories." Thus, he concluded, the Confederates were really counterrevolutionaries.[24]

The *Yeoman* also tried to boost secessionist morale with the hoary notion that good can result from bad. "From this very reverse, we can foresee deliverance from this untoward present evil." The Union congressmen-elect will go to the capital and be forced to support Lincoln's agenda. By backing the president, "they will betray and undo their own people. If they do not, they will be spotted by the Usurper, and what will be worse, they will return to their betrayed and undone constituents shorn of all recognition for their statesmanship." Major's paper mused, "Will they still submit to the Usurper, or resist? . . . We shall see." Like the other secessionist sheets, the *Yeoman* pinned its hopes on the state races. "Before the ides of August, the people of Kentucky will appreciate their true position and relations, and they will be prepared to assume and maintain them."[25]

The *Covington Journal* assured its readers that they had nothing to fear from Congressman-elect J. W. Menzies of Covington. The Union candidate had received 8,373 votes, to 4,526 for state senator Overton P. Hogan of Grant County, the Southern Rights hopeful. "Mr. Menzies stands pledged to vote against men and money for the subjugation of the South," the paper promised. "He is a conservative man, and will neither propose nor vote for extreme measures."[26]

In contrast, the *Statesman* had no such faith in Congressman-elect John J. Crittenden and found it hard "to conceal the surprise, regret and mortification with which Southern Rights men watched the progress of yesterday's election." Crittenden had defeated the Democrat–turned–Southern Rightist incumbent Simms by a comfortable margin—8,272 to 5,706. The spread "was not only unexpected to us, but utterly beyond the calculations of the opposition. We confess our inability to account for the vote of the people and our loss to know what construction it ought to bear." The paper rationalized that the campaign had been "short and the true issues greatly obscured by partizan rallying cries and deceptive appeals." The *Statesman* also moaned that Crittenden's campaign had been better organized and succeeded in buying "the whole floating or purchasable vote," whereas Simms, naturally, had run a clean race. Too, Crittenden had won over almost all the German and Irish voters, and "the absence of the usual violence and intimidation heretofore practiced toward that class, tended to swell the vote beyond its past strength."[27]

The *Statesman* also emphasized that the August elections were critical. "The issues of this struggle, unlike those of past contests, can not be revolved in the public mind year after year, until shorn of all deceptive coloring. . . . The people have to pass upon them in a few weeks, once for all, and if they permit themselves to be deceived by politicians, they will reap the fruits." Thus, in the congressional balloting, the paper took little solace "from the fact that the true questions were not understood and the legitimate inference of the election were not contemplated by those who swelled the majority." Unlike the *Herald,* the *Statesman* insisted that Union or disunion was not the issue. Paducah may have been "the Charleston of Kentucky," but Lexington was no secessionist hotbed, and Monroe knew it. Like Noble, however, he understood that the race card was the secessionists' ace in the hole everywhere in Kentucky. So he played it again, proposing that since "two Governments now exist within the old limits of the United States," Kentucky had to choose one or the other. "If she cast her destiny with the North let her prepare to surrender her slaves and support a quarter of a million free negroes," he warned. "If she follows the dictates of sympathy, honor and interest, she has only, at the proper moment, to unsheath her sword and make the common cause with the South."[28]

In the same issue, the *Statesman* ridiculed Kentucky's neutrality. Monroe could not fathom "how a member of the Union could be neutral in a war wherein the Federal Government is a party belligerent." Nonetheless, Kentucky unionists "planted themselves upon the platform, and the Federal authorities seem inclined temporarily at least, to recognize the anomalous position." As untenable as neutrality seemed to the *Statesman,* it seemed logical to most Kentuckians. To the majority, neutrality meant that Kentucky was still under the Stars and Stripes and at peace, while armies fought bloody battles beyond the state's borders.[29]

As Independence Day neared, the *Courier* waxed nostalgic, recalling how much Kentuckians revered the Union of their forebears and how they had voted for peace and neutrality in the border-state convention and the congressional elections. But Lincoln and his allies had "chosen to interpret these demonstrations for the Union, those demands for peace, as indications of fear," the paper declared. Lincoln and the Republicans believed Kentuckians were "ready to be reduced to subjection, to give up their rights and liberties, to surrender the Constitution and the Government." Yet the *Courier* was certain, "as surely as to-morrow's sun shall rise, as surely as God reigneth, so surely will the hour come when the people of Kentucky will assert all their rights, and make the assertion good by deeds of valor, if need be, that shall be sung by future bards, and coupled in future ages with the story of Thermopylae."[30]

On July 3 the constitutional definition of treason appeared on the *Courier*'s front page, and the paper all but accused Lincoln of that crime for sending muskets to the Home Guard. The paper asserted that the shippers and receivers of the "Lincoln guns" were "traitors in spirit if not in fact" and demanded an investigation. "It cannot be possible that there is no law to reach those criminals whose atrocious acts, involving the peace, happiness, and security of the people, and the safety of the Commonwealth, deserve the execration of mankind." Murderers suffered the death penalty, the *Courier* pointed out, and it asked, "Does no crime attach to those who put the weapons of murder in the hands of men who have no use for them but to take the lives of their neighbors?"[31]

In addition, the *Courier* accused the *Journal* of taking liberties, if not lives, by repeatedly flip-flopping on the war. It published a laundry list of the *Journal's* alleged transgressions: Prentice's paper insisted that "Abolitionism, if it should obtain control of the Government, would destroy the Union," yet it was supporting Lincoln's war against the Confederates. Haldeman's paper maintained that the *Journal,* after declaring "a Union held together by the sword was not worth preserving," was "now in favor of forcing the seceded States back into the Union at the point of the bayonet." On the accusations rolled.[32]

On Independence Day—the same day Congress convened—the *Courier* eagerly compared "the Revolution of 1776" to "the Revolution of 1861," arguing that "the men of the Revolution did not take up arms against the British Constitution, but in defense of their rights under that Constitution." The current "Revolution" was "more grand in its proportions, and not less vital to the cause of human liberty, than that of 1776." The paper praised the Declaration of Independence as the work of "a Southern man and a slave holder," a document that "enunciates the great principles of free government on which our Government was founded, and that lie at the very bottom of that adopted by the Confederate States." The free states, charged the *Courier,* disregarded those principles, thus making "a dissolution of the Union the only alternative of a total destruction of the Government itself." The states of the Confederacy "asserted their independence on the same grounds in almost the same words that the colonies did," the paper declared. "They are fighting as the colonies fought, for the right of self-government; and on their success depends the last best hope of Republican government on earth."[33]

During the Revolution, Dr. Samuel Johnson, the celebrated Tory and man of letters, famously wondered, "How is it that we hear the loudest yelps for liberty among the drivers of negroes?" Johnson's comment was, in effect, echoed by many Northern opponents of slavery during the Civil War. The *Courier's* stand was an example of what McPherson called an "Orwellian definition of liberty as slavery" that provoked derision in the free states. For secessionists to liken themselves to the American revolutionaries was "a libel upon the whole character and conduct of the men of '76," the historian noted, quoting William Cullen Bryant's abolitionist *New York Evening Post.* The revolutionaries had battled Britain "to establish the right of man . . . and principles of universal liberty." The eleven slave states were in rebellion "'not in the interests of general humanity, but of a domestic despotism. . . . Their motto is not liberty, but slavery.'" McPherson added that, according to Greeley's *New-York Tribune,* Jefferson's Declaration of Independence championed "'Natural Rights against Established Institutions.'" Greeley's paper maintained that "Mr. Jeff. Davis's caricature thereof is made in the interest of an unjust, outgrown, decaying Institution against the apprehended encroachments of Natural Human Rights." The Confederates were fighting not for liberty but for "reversing the wheels of progress . . . to hurl everything back into deepest darkness . . . despotism and oppression," the *Tribune* argued.[34]

Also on July 4, the *Courier* published President George Washington's farewell address. The next day, the paper noted that he had counseled against "the formation of sectional parties, of political organizations bounded by geographical lines." The paper bent more history toward the Southern side:

> A party characterized by a geographical discrimination, built upon the idea of hostility to a portion of the States and their institutions, gained a foothold at the North, and grew and became stronger day by day, until, with the active support of the schoolmaster, the preacher, the politician, and the essayist, it obtained control of the free States, demoralized with the Higher Law doctrines which it asserted and the madness it disseminated [in] the public mind . . . , and finally triumphed over the friends of the Constitution and the rights of the States in a contest for the control of the Republic, and with the power so obtained destroyed the Constitution and subverted the Government.

The paper was confident that if the venerated Washington came back to earth, he would applaud "the heroic men" of the Confederacy. Never mind that Washington was a staunch nationalist and a defender of federal power. Forget that, in his will, Washington freed his slaves upon his wife's death—the only slaveholding founder to provide for manumission in his will. Dead men, of course, cannot defend themselves against future generations. The Confederates put an equestrian image of Washington the federalist and the emancipator of slaves on their official national seal, even though they invoked the ultimate principle of sectional partisanship and state-over-federal authority by leaving the Union for fear of losing their slaves.[35]

The *Covington Journal* also kept fanning the flames against Bluegrass State unionists. "The telegraph informs the public that at a meeting of Kentuckians (not members of Congress) at Washington city, it was resolved that the government must be sustained in its war policy," the paper reported. The *Journal* suspected the meeting had been attended by selfish men "seeking appointments from the Federal administration in the civil service or in the army, or sharpers on the lookout for fat contracts." At the same time, the paper claimed the president had said that neutrality was "disunion completed." The *Journal* jumped on the phrase, implying that it meant Lincoln was getting ready to invade Kentucky. The paper recalled that when Davis and Underwood had met with Lincoln, he had promised to respect Kentucky's neutrality. "What have these gentlemen to say now?" The *Journal* also chided the Union State Central Committee's widely publicized neutrality stance, singling out Prentice and Harney for disapprobation. "Do you stand by your deliberate declaration made in April last, or do you surrender that position and give your assent to the dictum of A. Lincoln, that neutrality is disunion completed?"[36]

On July 16 the *Yeoman* returned to race-baiting. It ran a long editorial denouncing the Reverend Henry Ward Beecher's anti-slavery newspaper, the *Independent*. Hated in the South, Beecher was an outspoken abolitionist and pastor at a church in Brooklyn, New York. Major's paper quoted from the *Independent* to show its readers how the "wicked, bloody and brutal programme" of "Beecher, the Pious," was influencing Lincoln and the Republicans. The *Yeoman* claimed the issue it cited had been "published but a short time before the meeting of Congress, as if for the very purpose of strengthening the policy of Abe Lincoln, the Usurper." Thus, the president's message to lawmakers "plainly avowed the policy of elevating the negro race to the rank of equality with the white race, as indispensable to the very existence of the government." Put another way, Lincoln was saying that "the government would be destroyed unless slavery should be abolished and the blacks placed on a footing of equality with the whites." The *Yeoman* insisted, "We have demonstrated this . . . by the clearest evidence." According to the Frankfort paper, the *Independent* had declared, "The grand result—the only solution of the question—is fast coming up: the *emancipation of the slaves by the nation.*" The *Yeoman* added that if the federal army, "as a 'military necessity' and strategical act," freed all the slaves, 4 million people would immediately become Union allies.[37]

The *Yeoman* was in high dudgeon. "'*The emancipation of slaves by the nation!*' Not by the free will of the people of the slave States, but '*by the nation.*' Not by moral suasion, but by force. Not by the ballot-box, but by the sword." Of course, the South had no intention of voting slavery out of existence. The anti-slavery Republicans were a free-state party. Lincoln was so detested in the South that he had not even been on the ballot in ten of the eleven future Confederate states. Virginia had given Lincoln only 1,929 votes, all but 527 in the western counties that became the Union state of

West Virginia in 1863. At any rate, the *Yeoman* was aghast at the prospect of "Southern lands desolated by the allied arms of Black Republicans and Black Africans." The horror at the thought of African Americans in blue uniforms would not be confined to secessionists. When the Union army made soldiers of slaves later in the war, almost all white Kentuckians, even devout unionists, exploded in fury.[38]

Elsewhere, the *Yeoman* charged that Lincoln was plotting a "reign of Terror" in the state and that Prentice's *Journal* was feigning fear of secessionist violence to smooth the way for the president's purported military machinations. The *Yeoman* compared Prentice to "the guilty Macbeth," who, in "his distorted vision," saw "daggers pointed at his own throat." Shakespeare's Thane of Cawdor had merely "been looking at the filthy witness of his own red hands. It was all this that peopled the gloom of his guilty sanctum with visions of terrible secessionists, and made him dread a peril near at hand." The *Yeoman* assured Prentice "that the ghosts of Banquo that so affright his soul, are only ghosts of his own conjuring; or, in other words, that the charges which he makes of terrible designs entertained by Kentucky secessionists, are groundless, and cannot be supported by any reliable evidence." The paper claimed not to know of a single Kentuckian who was for secession "in the sense of the Journal—not one." The *Yeoman* conceded that there might be some Kentuckians who supported secession in theory but added, "The States rights men . . . are not madmen." They believed in majority rule, according to the *Yeoman*. The paper was, of course, stretching the truth. Several Kentuckians had enlisted in the rebel army. And the *Yeoman* had published an account of the Mayfield convention, where separation from Kentucky had been seriously discussed and Confederate volunteers sought.[39]

If the *Journal*'s worry was fake, was secessionist confidence in the August elections genuine? Surely the Southern Rights men saw the tide steadily ebbing away from them. Fort Sumter had convinced Virginia, North Carolina, Arkansas, and Tennessee to exit the Union. Kentucky chose neutrality—within the Union—with the full support of the Union Party. The party, standing foursquare for neutrality and against secession, had won big in the elections for the border-state convention delegates and for Congress. What if the Union men enhanced their state house and senate majorities at the polls in August? Would neutrality give way to outright support for the Union and the war against the South?

Support for secession was waning in the rebel press, which desperately embraced neutrality as eminently preferable to siding with the North against the South. On July 20 the *Covington Journal* conceded that neutrality had kept Kentucky out of the fighting, "and if adhered to may" prevent "the belligerents from bringing the war within our borders." By remaining neutral, Kentucky could also act as a mediator between the belligerents. The paper acknowledged, however, that some Kentuckians had joined one or the other army. "But it must be remembered that these were movements of *individuals,* and that the State has had nothing to do with them." The paper quoted the *Carrollton Signs of the Times,* which similarly editorialized, "We don't belong to Jeff. Davis' Confederacy, and are not advocating its claims. We do belong to Kentucky, however, and, as Old Abe has assailed the position of our State, we are disposed to oppose him and his abolition cohorts and sympathizers, whether in Kentucky or Massachusetts."[40]

Meanwhile, the war was widening elsewhere—notably, in Virginia, Kentucky's parent state. In July a Union army marched from Washington, aiming to end the war by capturing Richmond, just ninety miles south. But on July 21 the Union forces collided with a Confederate army in the Battle of Bull Run in northern Virginia. The Union army was routed in the war's first large clash of arms since Fort Sumter. The *Courier* reacted to the news of the Yankee defeat "with mingled feelings of joy and sorrow, with mingled smiles and tears." The paper called the clash, named for a creek near Manassas, Virginia, "the first great battle . . . in the second War of Independence." The South had not sought war, claimed the *Courier;* the conflict had been "madly and wickedly thrust upon the Confederate States by the Administration and its friends—it was the legitimate and inevitable result of the 'hair-brained [*sic*] and ruinous policy' adopted by Mr. Lincoln and sustained and upheld by 'the enemies of the country' who elected him; and upon his head and upon their heads will rest the responsibility, and against them will be the blood of the slaughtered thousands who sleep the sleep of death at Manassas cry out forever." The rebel dead were part of an army that had no choice but to fight; "they could not be slaves." The *Courier,* like the rest of the secessionist press, failed to see—or ignored—the irony of characterizing the war as white men fighting to keep themselves from becoming "slaves" and to keep millions of African Americans in bondage. Haldeman's paper posited that "the great God who ruleth and guideth in all things" had enabled the rebels to smite the Yankees "and blessed them with a great victory." While relishing the Confederate victory, the *Courier* prayed "most sincerely" that the Northern defeat "may open the eyes of our mad rulers, may convince them of the impossibility of subjugating free peoples, and may lead them to recognize the independence of the new Republic, and so to restore peace to our unhappy country."[41]

Doubtless, the *Courier* still hoped Kentucky might join the Confederacy and share the glory of the Southern battlefield. But neutrality was the best the secessionist press could hope for, so the paper challenged, "Now is the time to speak for peace, if you want it!" Voting the Southern Rights ticket was the only way to preserve the peace, according to the *Courier*. It reminded Kentuckians, "You have voted, fellow-citizens, for Union men for everything from the beginning of these troubles." Shifting into lecture mode, the *Courier* continued, "We told you the policy of those you have elected to office would lead to war. Claiming to be 'Union' men and peace men, they have not prevented the dissolution of the Union nor averted the evils of war." To keep the peace in Kentucky, the voters had to elect legislators "who are brave enough to look the situation of the country full in the face, honest enough to tell you the truth, and have sense enough to deal with it as becomes practical men with great interests at stake." The paper argued, "You have had enough spread eagleisms and buncombe:—they are ruining you."[42]

The next day the *Courier* again appealed to white supremacy: "If the North shall succeed in their effort to conquer the Slave States, whatever else may happen, it is absolutely certain that slavery will be exterminated." The president and his party, "those who now have control of the Federal Government believe slavery is a national sin, . . . they believe it ought to be abolished wherever it exists, and . . . they intend to lift the burden from the backs of all men." Kentucky and Missouri would be the first to feel the effects of the Republicans' anti-slavery crusade, the paper maintained. It directly pandered to less well-heeled whites, small-scale farmers, and town laborers. "Have the non-slaveholders of Kentucky ever thought of the consequences of the success of this policy?" the *Courier* asked. "Have they ever thought of the effect of the emancipation of all the slaves in the country? Do they wish to send their children to schools in which the negro children of the vicinity are taught?" The rapid-fire questions continued: "Do they wish to give the negro the right to appear in the witness box to testify against them? Do they wish to see the negro privileged to serve on juries sitting on their property, liberty, or life? Do they wish to be met at the polls, and have their votes neutralized, by the suffrage of the freed negroes? Do they wish to have the emancipated slave brought into competition with them in the field, in the workshop, in all the pursuits of life?" These were all "very serious" and "practical questions," the *Courier* maintained. It argued that if the North forced abolition on the Confederate states, slavery "could not last a day in Missouri, Maryland, and Kentucky." It added, "The negroes are among us. They cannot be annihilated. They must remain either bond or free. If the North shall succeed in this contest, they will not be permitted to remain as slaves. They must then be freed and elevated to the level of the white race as they are now in Massachusetts and other Abolition States."[43]

On August 1 the *Courier* trotted out another standby charge: the Lincoln administration was subverting the federal and Kentucky constitutions. "Now a new theory prevails in the councils of the nation: the consent and support of the people are to be enforced at the point of the bayonet, with lead and steel, with fire and sword; and to sustain this theory, the people are to be ruined by commercial regulations that beggar them, and then ground to the earth by oppressive taxes!" The paper urged, "Let the people answer on their consciences and before God!"—and at the ballot box.[44]

The next day the *Courier* warned voters to beware of candidates who were out for personal gain, such as cushy government jobs. It claimed that Kentuckians' interests, happiness, honor, safety, and liberty were on the line. Thus, voters must look out for "politicians who would ruin you forever to earn a share of the hundreds of new offices being created and placed at the disposal of the President." Patronage grabbing aside, the old partisan politics had to be forsaken, the paper declared. If war came and neutrality went, "the original Union man and the original Secessionist will suffer equally and fatally. The same torch which envelopes in flames the house of the one, may leave the residence of the other but a mouldering heap of ashes. A common destiny, whatever it may be, awaits the people of Kentucky."[45]

On Election Day the *Courier* made a final plea for the Southern Rights candidates, again invoking the Divine: "God forbid that a record shall be made to-day which will humble us as a State in the eyes of the world and stand as a deed of transfer of ourselves and our children to the dominion of a master!" The paper listed thirty actions by Lincoln that were "in violation of the Constitution of the United States, or without authority of law." Number thirty was "prosecuting a war looking to the abolition of the slaves and the equalization of the races in the South."[46]

Despite its usual bluster, the *Courier* conceded that in many parts of the state, the Southern Rights ticket would likely lose. Nonetheless, the paper urged a strong Southern Rights turnout "against the candidates of the Lincoln party, and in favor of the Constitutional rights of the States and the people." It challenged, "If there is any district or precinct in the State in which there are but one dozen freemen who have not bowed the knee to Baal, they should not fail to enter their protest against the overthrow of their Government, trusting that by the next election others may join them in battling for Constitutional liberty." The *Courier* wanted the entire Southern Rights vote in the state "polled—to the last man; and we trust no one who has had the courage and patriotism to espouse and stand by the good cause will prove careless or recreant now."[47]

The race-baiting, the demonizing of the Union Party, and every entreaty by the secessionist press went for naught. The other side scored their greatest victory yet, as the Union Party captured 76 of 100 house seats and swelled its senate majority to 27 versus 11. At the same time, state treasurer James H. Garrard, a Union man, was reelected, easily defeating Southern Rightist James R. Barrick. Secessionist Gobias Terry withdrew before the election but still received 12,160 votes. Garrard attracted 83,151 votes to 3,845 for Barrick.[48]

The voters had spoken, and decisively. But the rebel press, led by Haldeman's *Courier,* lost no time in trying to spin the results, even before all the votes had been tallied. The state's chief secessionist organ tried to hand readers the we-lost-but-not-as-badly-this-time line, predicting that the Southern Rightists would better their vote from the congressional elections. "As the knowledge of the President's usurpations and tyranny extends among the people, the spirit of resistance grows and expands and assumes proportions more consistent with the real magnitude of the controversy; and this should inspire them to continue the noble work they have undertaken in favor of peace, the Constitution and free government," the *Courier* whistled past the graveyard. The paper quoted from Percy B. Shelley's famous poem "Queen Mab": "Falsehood now triumphs; deadly power / Has fixed its seal upon the lip of truth." Nonetheless, the *Courier* urged, "let us be encouraged to hope, the full knowledge of what is being done and what is contemplated will break that seal." It then served up another helping of Shelley:

Kingly glare
Will lose its power to dazzle; its authority
Will silently pass by; the gorgeous throne
Will stand unnoticed in the regal hall,
Fast falling to decay; whilst falsehood's trade
Will be as hateful and unprofitable
As that of truth is now.

The *Courier,* in full literary mode, called on Kentuckians to remember words from "The Battle-Field," a well-known poem by William Cullen Bryant: "Truth, though crushed to earth shall rise again." Shifting to the Bible (Philippians 3:14), the *Courier* admonished, "With stronger faith and brighter hopes and an unconquerable spirit 'press forward to the mark of the prize.'" Finally, "when victory, glorious victory, shall perch upon our standards, the people of the State, 'redeemed, regenerated, and disenthralled,' will crown us with laurels, and our children will rise up and call us blessed." There was irony aplenty in the *Courier's* clarion call; abolitionist Bryant often quoted scripture to condemn slavery as un-Christian.[49]

Naturally, the *Courier* also accused the unionists of cheating. "The secret oath-bound party, under the guise of the Union . . . committed more infamy than ever was known in Louisville. They certainly cast 2,000 illegal votes, in addition to compelling their members to vote against their will. In various precincts in the county, all kinds of threats and intimidations were used." Further, the paper claimed that hordes of soldiers from Camp Joe Holt, a Union recruiting center in Indiana, across the Ohio River from Louisville, "were stationed at various precincts in the county to intimidate legal voters." The *Courier* offered no proof to back up its charges of fraud.[50]

The Union side won in Frankfort, too. The *Yeoman*, like the *Courier*, grasped at straws, claiming that the local Union vote had dipped by 1,200 compared with the congressional elections. Statewide, "a large number of men who would have voted for the Southern Rights ticket have left the State for service in the Confederate Army since June last." The paper also maintained "that in several of the counties the Union candidates were compelled to take position in opposition to the war measures adopted by Congress, and for which the Union delegation from Kentucky voted." The *Yeoman* argued, "Had more time elapsed between the June and August elections, this reaction would have developed itself in the triumph of the States Rights ticket." But it conceded that "the complexion of the coming Legislature appears now the same as though the majority had been elected by the vote of June last, but we believe that the next thirty days will strengthen the sentiment against the unwise, aggressive, and unconstitutional acts of the administration, and its Congress, that the majority in the Legislature will not dare to act in opposition to what will then be the unmistakable will of the people of Kentucky in reference to the policy of the State in this unhappy contest."[51]

The *Statesman,* too, was in full damage-control mode and pointed to a reduced Union vote in August. It cited its house candidate James B. Clay, Henry Clay's son, who lost to unionist James B. Buckner by 667 votes. "Six weeks ago, Mr. Crittenden received a majority of 1030 votes in this county," it stated. Although the paper hesitated to "express the opinion that Lincoln will not have a majority of adherents in the next Legislature, . . . we do mean to assert that, unless we greatly misconstrue the voice of this election that majority will be so overwhelmed by public sentiment as to forestall their contemplated surrender of our State to the North." The *Statesman* wanted more anti-Lincoln public meetings. "Under the inspiration of yesterday's vote let our Southern friends redouble their exertions and the people will, by spontaneous action, uprise in their majesty and themselves take into hand the great destinies of Kentucky."[52]

The *Statesman* further declared that the unionists were out-and-out Lin-

coln men, a common charge in the rebel papers. Almost all Kentucky unionists vehemently denied that they were pro-Lincoln. But the paper vowed that
on Election Day, Lexington unionists had cried, "'Hurrah for Lincoln!' 'Hurrah for Old Abe!' 'I'm a Lincoln man all over!' These and a hundred kindred
shouts went up. . . . It was not 'hurrah for the Union!' but 'Lincoln,' 'Lincoln,'
was the rallying cry, and it came not from the lips of the rabble alone; gentlemen of intelligence and standing, political leaders joined in the unnatural
outcry." Given that virtually every Kentucky unionist was also pro-slavery, it
seems likely that the *Statesman* twisted the truth about the popular clamor
for Lincoln. Nonetheless, the paper pummeled the president and hoisted its
familiar flag of white supremacy: "Lincoln the perjured despot, Lincoln, the
violator of the Constitution, Lincoln, the author of the irrepressible conflict,
Lincoln, the enemy of slavery and the hater of the South, Lincoln, the advocate of the equality of the white and black races, Lincoln, the invader of old
Virginia, was the name around which the *Union* men . . . rallied."[53]

Three days later the *Statesman,* still full of fight, declared, "The time is
near at hand when the masses will throw off the political leaders who have
so long controlled their action. The *Union* party can not now escape a position which the people will repudiate." The state had been moved away from
"*neutrality* into an attitude of *position and active support of* the U.S. *Government.* The *Union* party as a political organization is irretrievably committed
to the support of the Government." In anger and frustration, it blurted, "We
have again and again warned the people that this must be and would be the
ultimate position of the Union party, but we could not convince them. Time
has developed the truth of our prediction." Yet the citizenry "seemed to sus-
pect the truth, and the result was a large falling off of the Union vote in the
last election." Even so, Lexington was not buying what the *Statesman* was
selling.[54]

Indeed, the final vote totals showed that the Southern Rights Party had
been drubbed in every region of Kentucky except the Jackson Purchase,
which elected five secessionists to the house, at least three (or possibly four) of
them unopposed. The *Paducah Herald,* the region's leading paper, had urged,
"Let us make the fight for the Legislature. Let it be done upon the fair issue
of Secession or no Secession—to remain with the abolition North or join the
South—to remain a Slave state or abolish slavery." On August 10 the *New
York Times* mocked the *Herald,* hooting, "We hope the Herald is satisfied
with the response of the people."[55]

The *Journal* could not resist poking fun at editor Robert McKee of the
Courier, claiming that he went fishing after hearing the election results.
"When the twelve disciples were in great trouble and perplexity as to what

they should or could do next, Simon Peter, with his usual facility of recourse, said, 'I go a fishing,' and Bob said so too." McKee was "so appalled by the popular vote, that he at once bounded from poll to pole. Finding that in political conflict he was out of his element, he went to see if he couldn't haul a few pike, bass and catfish out of theirs." When McKee figured out "he could no longer cheat the people, he lowered his pretentions materially and undertook to retrieve his self-esteem by fooling the poor simple fishes." The *Journal* also fired on the *Statesman*. That secessionist paper, "remarking upon the overwhelming defeat of James B. Clay as a candidate in Fayette for the Lower House of the Legislature, thinks that he is entitled to extraordinary credit in not having been beaten more than he was." The *Journal* pointed out that "the majority against him in Fayette as a candidate for the House was several hundreds greater than the majority against [James B.] Beck as a candidate for the Senate. If there is any honor to him in such a result, let him enjoy it with whatever appetite he may." The *Journal* called Clay "the most odious thing in Fayette county, except secession—and perhaps the more odious of the two. The secession that Fayette would like best would be his secession from her borders."[56]

The *Journal*'s lampooning of Clay reflected the postelection surge of Union confidence. Yet even before the election, some unionists set in motion a plan to recruit, arm, and train Union volunteers in the state. Such a step was as risky as it was bold. Even friends of the Union might regard a training camp as a blatant violation of the state's neutrality. Then what? Would Kentucky openly support the war? Would it provoke a Confederate invasion from Tennessee? One thing was certain—the secession press would be appalled to see "abolition hordes" being trained to fight the South on Kentucky soil. From the start of the war, Kentuckians had to go beyond the state's borders to enlist in either army. Union volunteers crossed over to Camp Holt or to Camp Clay, opposite Covington. Men who preferred rebel gray need only step across the Todd County border to Camp Boone, near Clarksville, Tennessee. Would most Kentuckians welcome, or at least tolerate, a Union camp in the state?

6

The Twilight of the Rebel Press

After the August elections in which the Union Party enhanced its majorities in the Kentucky house and senate, almost all of the state's Confederate press gave up on secession and fully embraced neutrality and peace. Earlier, the rebel editors had scorned neutrality as craven. Now they saw it as their last hope to keep Kentucky from fighting the Confederacy. The rebel editors and publishers denounced the establishment of Camp Dick Robinson, a training center for Union volunteers in Garrard County, as a blatant violation of neutrality. But it stayed open and symbolized Kentucky's growing unionism. In September, Confederate and then Union armies invaded Kentucky. The legislature, over Governor Magoffin's veto, ordered only the Confederates to leave and fully embraced the Union war effort.

After Kentucky declared its neutrality in May, volunteers had to leave the state to don Yankee blue or rebel gray. But as the state's unionism deepened in the summer, some leading unionists decided it was time to start a training camp on Kentucky soil. The Union men were confident their side would do well in the August elections, but they decided to wait until the votes had been counted and the great Union victory confirmed. The training center was named Camp Dick Robinson, after the owner of the farm where it was sited.

Magoffin denounced the camp as a violation of Kentucky's neutrality, and on August 19 he sent a pair of commissioners to see Lincoln. He also complained about the camp in a letter to the president. Magoffin wrote that Kentucky had been at peace before Union army officers arrived to arm and school soldiers. Lincoln, doubtless emboldened by the election results, replied that the troops were Kentuckians and were not harming good citizens. The president also told Magoffin that Kentuckians wanted the camp and that the governor and his commissioners were the only ones asking him to close it. Thus, Lincoln held firm and ended his letter by observing, "It is with regret that I search and cannot find in your not very short letter, any declaration or intimation that you entertain any desire for the preservation of the Federal Union."[1]

Naturally, the *Louisville Courier* agreed with Magoffin about the camp. The paper claimed that some "renegade Tennesseans," in league with "the Lincolnites of Kentucky," were poised to invade the Volunteer State "with torch and brands" and destroy "the now quiet and peaceful homes of their own brethren." The paper also alleged that a Military District of Kentucky and Tennessee had been created under the command of now Brigadier General Robert Anderson. Even though the Confederates had fired the first shots against the Kentuckian and his garrison at Fort Sumter, the *Courier* castigated Anderson as "the man who bears the awful responsibility of having begun this most unrighteous war."[2]

The *Courier* also reported that Garrett Davis had gone to the camp in an attempt to get the troops dispersed, but with no success. The paper noted "that considerable feeling was manifested among the troops against Mr. Davis, and some denounced such Union men as he is no better than Secessionists." The *Courier* repeated its charge that soldiers from the camp and elsewhere in Kentucky were gathering to attack Tennessee and suppress Southern Rights men in the Bluegrass State. It stated that the new legislature, backed by the troops at the camp, would "disband and disarm the State Guard and perhaps . . . depose our patriotic Governor." In doing so, the Union men hoped to prevent "the true patriots of Kentucky" from stopping "this horrible attempt to plunge Kentucky into this war for the subjugation and destruction of the Southern States, whose only fault is that they, like Kentucky, have slavery incorporated in their social system." The *Courier* warned, "Woe to the Lincolnites, when the honest Union men of Kentucky find out their real game."[3]

The *Frankfort Yeoman* was happy to hear that Davis had gone to Washington, supposedly to urge Lincoln to shut the camp. It was also gladdened to learn "that many leading Union men of Kentucky" viewed the camp "with emphatic disapprobation, as a practical violation of our neutrality, and as menacing the peace of the State." The *Yeoman* did not say which unionists had denounced the camp. Meanwhile, the paper took a swipe at the *Louisville Journal,* which mused that Magoffin might issue a proclamation to close the camp via an executive order. Kentuckians had appealed to the governor to order the camp's closure, said the *Yeoman,* but he preferred to leave it to the troops' "own sense of duty" to go home. Meanwhile, Magoffin was "faithfully co-operating with Union men in making this appeal for their voluntary action." The paper suggested that if nothing came of his efforts, there would be "time enough to consider what steps the Governor should take."[4]

On August 9 the *Kentucky Statesman* reported that it, too, had learned that Camp Dick Robinson was a staging area for a Yankee attack on Tennessee. "Manifestly, the certain result of a consummation of these movements will be the bloodiest war ever witnessed," the paper warned. It wanted all to know that "we have had no hand in it. The Southern Rights men of this State are guiltless. . . . Let the people note these movements and hold guilty those who shall first violate Kentucky neutrality."[5]

Nonetheless, the *Covington Journal* was pleased to find out that Congressman Crittenden had purportedly joined Davis in trying to get rid of the camp. It fervently prayed they would succeed but feared they had "come too late." The paper claimed the Union Party's pro-neutrality stand had been based on duplicity all along. "Three times—on the 4th of May, on the 20th of June, and again on the 5th of August—the leaders of the Union party presented themselves to the people of the State, and claiming to be the especial friends and advocates of neutrality, demanded on that ground their support and confidence. They succeeded. They have secured the offices, and control of the Legislation of the State." The paper quoted a dispatch from Washington exulting that the great Union victory at the polls "will be followed immediately by a physical one not less magnificent." The communiqué revealed the presence of "10,000 organized Union men in Kentucky only awaiting the accomplishment of this victory at the ballot-box to take the field and drive the rebel forces out of Kentucky and Tennessee." The dispatch claimed that a "Kentucky Legion" was being organized, and its men were "burning with a desire to aid their Union neighbors of Tennessee to free themselves from the despotism of the Davis mobocracy." The *Journal* also reported that former congressman Green Adams of Barbourville was home advising unionists "to lay aside neutrality, and prepare to take up arms and fight for the Government." Nonetheless, it remained convinced that the great majority of Kentuckians still clung to neutrality and predicted, "Their indignation will yet reach the men who have deliberately deceived them."[6]

In a subsequent issue, the *Covington Journal* argued that the fate of neutrality "RESTS WITH THE LEADERS OF THE UNION PARTY." It added that, according to Magoffin's emissaries to Lincoln, the president's policy toward Kentucky would be based on "THE WISHES OF THE UNION MEMBERS OF THE LEGISLATURE AND THE UNION DELEGATION IN CONGRESS." The paper also quoted the *Paris Flag*'s August 28 edition, which claimed that "prominent friends" of Garrett Davis, who had spoken with him after his return from the capital city, "state that he says the authorities at Washington ARE WILLING TO

LEAVE THE QUESTION OF THE REMOVAL OF THE CAMP ENTIRELY WITH THE
UNION PARTY OF KENTUCKY." The *Flag* reported that, according to Davis's
friends, he was now in favor of the camp and had declared that it should stay
even if it caused civil war in the state. In addition, the Covington paper, quoting the *Louisville Journal,* said that Jeremiah T. Boyle of Danville, another
leading Union man, had essentially echoed Davis's position in a speech in
Garrard County. "Without doubt a vast majority of the people of Kentucky
are in favor of maintaining the neutrality of the State," the *Journal* argued.
"They have been voting for it all the time. They elected Union-party members of the Legislature only because they claimed to be better friends of neutrality than the State Rights men." The paper concluded, "The people of
Kentucky, still anxious to preserve the peace of the State, and shun the horrors of war, will await with intense anxiety the action of the Legislature."[7]

The *Courier* claimed that nobody had done more to bring war to the
state than Davis. It predicted, "When fire and steel shall have become the
only arbiters between brothers and friends and neighbors arrayed in hostile
armies around their own homes and firesides, with every death-shot, with
every shriek of his murdered countrymen, will ascend a prayer to the God of
justice for vengeance on Garrett Davis." The paper likened him to Benedict
Arnold, sneering that he might "find in some Yankee State refuge from the
vengeance of the people he is so grievously wronging, but he can never escape
the tortures of his conscience, nor regain the place he once held in the estimation of his fellow men." The *Courier* linked Davis with a trio of "miscreants
and tories"—Congressman Emerson Etheridge and Andrew Johnson, both of
Tennessee, and "Carlisle," evidently referring to state representative John G.
Carlisle, a unionist from Covington. All four "will go down to future generations loaded with the curses and execrations of all good men." The paper compared them with the trio synonymous with the French Revolution's "reign of
terror": "Robespierre, and Danton, and Marat guided the Revolution . . . for
a while, and reveled in its most atrocious and fiendish excesses, but the time
came when their power passed away, and then they fell victims to the fury of
their own friends." The *Courier* warned, "Let those who are sweeping away all
safeguards of life, and liberty, and property, and law, and order, learn ere it is
too late the fate they are preparing for themselves."[8]

On August 19 the *Louisville Journal* again defended Camp Dick Robinson, firing a salvo at the *Cynthiana News.* The paper said that many of
the men at the camp were Ohioans and Pennsylvanians who had disguised
themselves as civilians so they could sneak into Kentucky. These Northerners
were "committing outrages known only in countries where civil war has broken out," the paper charged. "We are told that these *unhung scoundrels enter*

the homes of unoffending citizens and insult their wives and daughters, maltreat the old men, and appropriate provisions, &c, to their own use, without remuneration, and if remonstrance is offered the lives of the people are threatened." The *Journal* yanked the cannon lanyard. Prentice's paper claimed that editor A. J. Morey, who had supposedly left the *News,* was evidently back and "has caught the disease which prevails amongst the secession leaders." Morey "received no such information as he pretends to have received. He got the idea from his own secession brain; there is not a particle of truth in the charge he prefers against the Union troops in Garrard." The *Journal* claimed the soldiers were Kentuckians—to a man "honest, hard-working, industrious, sober." It sneered, "The Editor of the Cynthiana News would no more call one of them to his face, 'an unhung scoundrel,' than he would dip his head in molten iron." Thus, "the object of the News is very apparent. The Editor desires to arouse against those Union troops wide-spread prejudice and hereby damage the cause in which they are enlisted."[9]

The *Journal* also quoted the Cynthiana paper's hope that Magoffin would sign off on a proclamation ordering the camp closed. If the troops would not disperse, Morey wanted the governor to invite "the people of the State, and any *other State,*" to help Kentuckians "drive these violators of law from the State at the point of the bayonet." The *Journal* cautioned, "Let those beware who would forcibly interfere with" the camp, adding that it was "a fixed fact, which no Magoffin proclamation, however backed, can unfix."[10]

The *Yeoman* fired back at the *Journal* for denying that Magoffin had the power to order Camp Dick Robinson dismantled. "The frighted vision of the Journal has conjured up merely ideal ghosts." Quoting from *Hamlet,* the paper soothed, "Rest, perturbed spirit." Magoffin, according to the Frankfort paper, preferred to let the unionist legislature decide the camp's fate. However, the paper predicted that if the camp stayed open, "The public will naturally accept the facts as conclusive, that the so-called Union party means to renounce neutrality at the hazard of civil war in the state."[11]

Meanwhile, the *Courier* fell back on its stock charge that Lincoln was leading "a war against the institution of slavery" and that "hostility to slavery is the predominant feeling in the North." The *Courier* claimed the country would be at "peace in less than sixty days if the ultra-Republicans did not believe that [with] the further prosecution of the war, in some way or other, slavery in the Southern States would be abolished." The *Courier* quoted the August 5 issue of an Ohio anti-slavery paper, the *Ashtabula Sentinel,* which proposed that there were only two ways to settle the war: "One is acknowledging secession, and recognizing the 'Southern Confederacy' as an independent nation. This cannot be done. The other is abolishing slavery. This must be done." The *Courier* commended its readers to the story's last sentence: "Emancipation must be our watchword—our battle cry—the inspirer of courage and our hope."[12]

On August 30, just three days before the legislature was scheduled to convene, an unexpected event in Missouri portended trouble for Kentucky unionists. From his headquarters in St. Louis, Major General John C. Fremont, commander of federal forces in Missouri, issued a proclamation confiscating the property of secessionists and freeing their slaves. The abolitionist Fremont had been the Republican Party's first presidential candidate in 1856. His order played straight into the Kentucky secessionists' hands. They shrieked that it proved the war was indeed an anti-slavery crusade. The secessionist press flogged the proclamation for all it was worth. Was this the break the reeling secessionists had long hoped and prayed for?

On September 2 the *Courier* excoriated Fremont as a "petty creature of a bastard Nero" who imagined himself king of Missouri. The paper warned Kentuckians to "*be ready, we repeat, for like a thief in the night, the spoiler comes, and to-day or to-morrow or next day he may be in our midst, our presses may be silenced, and our citizens sent off to share the fate of hundreds of prisoners who now fill the cells of Fort Lafayette* [a fortress and prison in New York harbor]."[13]

The next day the *Courier* reloaded and fired anew on Fremont. "The President claims absolute and uncontrolled power; he claims the right to declare States in rebellion whenever his prejudices or caprices may prompt; and he arrogates the right to delegate his subordinates the power to treat every slaveholder in the district as a Rebel, and to liberate the slaves of such by proclamation." Lincoln could thus deem Kentucky to be in rebellion at any time. The president's military commander would be empowered to "abrogate the civil law by proclamation, substitute for our Courts of Justice Courts Martial, define crimes and affix the punishment, and confiscate the property, real and personal, of our people, and doom them to speedy and certain death." The *Courier* concluded that such matters "*demand* the consideration of the freemen of Kentucky. —What was done in Missouri may soon be attempted here." Lincoln grasped the fearful effect of Fremont's action, especially on the border states. He immediately asked the general to withdraw his proclamation, arguing that it would disconcert unionists in the South and possibly "ruin our rather fair prospects for Kentucky." Fremont balked. So on September 11 Lincoln countermanded the general's emancipation order, a move that greatly relieved Kentucky unionists.[14]

Between the August election and the convening of the legislature, the Southern Rights Party took a last stab at preserving Kentucky's teetering neutrality. In desperation, they organized peace meetings across the state and called for a peace convention in Frankfort on September 10. Peace advocates were supposed to sport white rosettes or ribbons and fly white flags with "Peace" written on them. They were also instructed to coax local officials into joining the movement. In turn, these officials would encourage everybody to hoist peace banners over their homes and fly them from trains and wagons and steamboats.[15]

The *Journal* lampooned a peace meeting at the Jefferson County courthouse on the night of August 17. Before the conclave, the Southern Rightists "made themselves very busy . . . in importuning Union men to be at the meeting, holding out as an inducement that the Hon. Judge [Henry] Pirtle would be Chairman; and that the Hon. James Guthrie would act on one of the Committees." E. S. Worthington, lugging a bundle of small white handkerchiefs, was the first to show up. As the crowd filed in, he busied himself hanging the hankies on and around the dais. When the meeting started, a Colonel Boone—probably W. P. Boone—moved that James Speed, a well-known unionist, chair the meeting. Worthington, flummoxed, warned Boone, "If the Union men should have the organization of the meeting, they would have to hold it over his dead body." The colonel responded in pretended protest. "'Oh, no,' replied Boone, 'we didn't come for anything of that sort; this is a *peace* meeting—we are all for *peace.*'" Unfazed, Worthington proposed secessionist James Trabue as chair and gave a speech in which he argued "that the getters up of the meeting were entitled to the organization." After he concluded his remarks—reportedly all the while waving a white flag in his right hand and supporting the remains of the bundle of handkerchiefs under his left arm—somebody in the crowd demanded, "But how are we to know who are the getters up?" Worthington nonetheless called for a vote, and according to the *Journal*, his nominee was not the people's choice. "A few said 'aye,'" it reported, "but a large number said 'no' without waiting for the noes to be called." Worthington then announced that the ayes had it, and a skeptical Speed proposed a recount of sorts. He suggested that everybody "in favor of himself as Chairman should go to the right hand and those in favor of Mr. Trabue to the left. Almost the whole meeting rushed to the right, only a few scattering individuals remaining on the left." Conceding defeat, Trabue "proposed that all the SECESSIONISTS—the word was distinctly heard—should adjourn with him to Concert Hall. A few followed him—so few that they were not missed—Mr. Worthington taking his body out, having probably relinquished the laudable ambition of having the Union men hold their meeting over it."[16] The *Journal*, in feigned grief, was sorry "to say that Mr. Worthington took off with him all the little white cotton handkerchiefs, with which he was laudably and usefully ornamenting the stand, when Colonel Boone's motion for a Chairman arrested his useful labors. We wish all the handkerchiefs could have been hung upon the stand. They would have made an *imposing* array." Apparently, a peace parade had been planned for the following Saturday, and the handkerchief display would "have given us a foretaste of that splendid procession of secessionism . . . with white rosettes, cotton handkerchiefs, and lambskin aprons. If any of them are without handkerchiefs, have they not shirts?" After the secessionists decamped, the unionists heard speeches from Speed and other unionist leaders and passed resolutions denouncing disunion and calling for peace and restoration of the Union.[17]

Naturally, the *Courier* praised the Louisville peace conclave. "We were not present at the opening of the meeting . . . but understand that so soon as the hall opened, the meeting was at once packed by a crowd of Lincoln men, who proceeded to its organization by the selection of the supporters of the Administration as officers of the meeting," the paper reported. "Upon this interference those who called the meeting immediately adjourned, and assembled in large numbers at Concert Hall." The *Courier* said the action "of the so-called Union men" proved that "there should be no free expression of popular sentiment; that, if an unbridled and irresponsible mob can silence free speech, that it shall be silenced in this city." The paper singled out speech maker Nathaniel Wolfe, who had just been reelected a state representative. It characterized him as a turncoat, claiming that in the last legislature, he had promised "in the event of war against the South," he would "unite his destiny with his brethren of the South, and that he would resist the North at every hazard and to the last extremity." Wolfe "now openly advocates the Lincoln war" and "will be the most ready and active supporter of Lincoln" in the new legislature, the paper predicted. The *Courier* also published a series of resolutions approved at the Concert Hall gathering. The measures proposed peace, but on decidedly Southern terms.[18]

Soon after the *Journal* ridiculed the peace meeting, the paper zeroed in on one of its favorite targets: Congressman Henry Burnett. Prentice's paper charged him with "PREACHING TREASON." On August 29 he gave a lengthy speech to a crowd in southern Christian County, orating from a stand adorned with two big Confederate flags. Burnett hailed "South Carolina as a bright pattern of heroism, and denounced Union men as Abe Lincoln's dogs." The congressman counseled armed resistance to the war tax "if necessary," scorched Kentucky's Union leaders as hypocrites and traitors of the worst sort, "abused the United States Government in the most ferocious terms," pledged his fealty to Jeff Davis, and deeply regretted that the Union army had not been annihilated at Bull Run. The paper laid into the lawmaker:

"Now is it not passing strange that this Congressman, who blusters and raves like a bedlamite against the Lincoln Government, as he calls it, should go to the Lincoln Congress and pocket Lincoln gold?" The *Journal* found it odd "that this flaming secessionist has no scruples whatever of making his living off Lincoln's treasury." It characterized Burnett as "a standing monument of the astonishing clemency and tolerance of the American government." It observed that Uncle Sam should not tolerate the traitor's "monstrous conduct" and invited Burnett to decamp "to the Confederacy, which he extols as the most humane and free [country] upon the earth, and which the unanimous voice of the world brands as the most tyrannical in the history of despotism." Among the rebels, the paper scoffed, "he may console himself with the reflection that no one can retort by calling him a dog, for he is 'A creature / Whom 'twere base flattery to call a dog.'" Likewise, Burnett could "pride himself in the consciousness that although he may not wear a dog's collar he has brass enough in his impudent forehead to furnish a brace of collars for all the dogs in creation." The *Journal* wrapped up by branding Burnett a "Kentucky Thersites" who was "admirably qualified for the office of Blackguard Extraordinary and Scullion Plenipotentiary to the Court of Jeff Davis, for his brain is as feeble as his lungs are forcible and his mouth is as dirty as a den of skunks."[19]

The *Yeoman* rushed to Burnett's defense, denouncing "the unscrupulous press employed in the interest of Lincoln, the Usurper." The paper insisted that the congressman was not a secessionist, though he was "certainly opposed to the prosecution of Lincoln's coercive war, for he believes its prosecution will prove ruinous not only to the prosperity of the country, but destructive of our republican institutions." The *Yeoman* quoted from Burnett's remarks recorded in the *Congressional Globe*. The lawmaker said he was for peace, not secession. He argued, "*There was no warrant in the Constitution for the doctrine of secession . . . I do not believe in it as a Constitutional doctrine.*" Yet within weeks, Burnett would be in Russellville, behind Confederate lines, helping to establish Kentucky's bogus Confederate government, and he would wind up as one of the state's two senators in the Confederate Congress.[20]

While the *Yeoman* was defending Burnett against his detractors in the unionist press, the *Louisville Democrat* was also castigating the congressman. "Who does not know him to be a rank Secessionist and fierce Disunionist?" the paper challenged. "Burnett, demagogue as he is—unscrupulous and treacherous—is chief among the traitors in the country, and more responsible than any other for the reign of terror in his district." The paper ridiculed Burnett as "the pet of the Frankfort Yeoman," claiming, "He went to Washington, to the recent session of Congress, principally to draw his mileage and per diem, and abuse the Government he had sworn to support. This has commended him in the eyes of *Secessia,* and the Yeoman is in ecstasies over him."[21]

Meanwhile, the war raged east and west of Kentucky, and both sides massed troops along its borders. In all war, strategy is based on political and military considerations; from April through August 1861, the former outweighed the latter in both Union and Confederate policy toward Kentucky. Yet both sides coveted the Bluegrass State. "I think to lose Kentucky is nearly the same as to lose the whole game," Lincoln fretted. "Kentucky gone, we cannot hold Missouri, nor, as I think, Maryland. These all against us, and the job on our hands is too large for us. We would as well consent to separation at once, including the surrender of the capital." The Confederates were just as eager to woo Kentucky. With the Bluegrass State in the Confederacy, the Ohio River would divide North and South. From Newport or Covington at the northern tip of Kentucky, a Confederate army would need to drive no more than 250 miles to Lake Erie to cut the Union in two. But when Kentucky declared its neutrality, both sides stayed out. President Lincoln knew that if he sent troops into Kentucky, he might propel the state into the Confederacy. Likewise, President Davis understood that if he invaded Kentucky, the state might forsake neutrality and join the war on the Union side.[22]

In early September the scales finally tipped toward the military side of the strategy equation. On September 2 a small Union force moved to Belmont, Missouri, opposite Columbus, Kentucky. The rebels in Tennessee suspected that the Yankees planned to seize Columbus. On the night of September 3, Major General Gideon J. Pillow led a Confederate army from the Volunteer State to Hickman, Kentucky, where he stopped in deference to the Union troops at Belmont. The blue-clad soldiers withdrew on September 4, and Pillow arrived at Columbus the same day. Suspecting that the Confederates planned to capture Paducah at the confluence of the Ohio and Tennessee Rivers, General Ulysses Grant advanced up the Ohio from Cairo, Illinois, and bagged "the Charleston of Kentucky" early on September 6. He also sent forces to take Smithland, where the Ohio and Cumberland Rivers join.[23]

Meanwhile, not all Confederate authorities blessed Pillow's move. Secretary of War Leroy Pope Walker commanded Pillow's superior, Major General Leonidas Polk, to order his subordinate to pull his army back to Tennessee. Magoffin sent a protest letter to Tennessee governor Isham G. Harris, who agreed the troops should be withdrawn. But President Davis backed his generals, and the rebels stayed put in Kentucky.[24]

The *Journal* was glad that Magoffin had protested to Harris, but it faulted the governor and his allies for encouraging the Confederates. "We may say to Gov. Magoffin that he and his organs and immediate political friends must be regarded on all hands as responsible in an exceedingly great measure for the outrage perpetrated upon Kentucky's honor and her rights," the paper declared. "The whole of the secession organs in Kentucky without a single exception have been proclaiming every week, and some of them every day, for many months, that the Southern Government had a perfect right to send an army into Kentucky whenever it pleased."[25]

Conversely, the *Journal* claimed that Grant had been right to seize Paducah. "If it had been delayed a little longer, the town would have been in the hands of the Confederate troops." Instead of demanding that Grant's forces withdraw, the paper called on the legislature and the people to respond with like "promptitude and an energy suited to the exigency." State pride, chivalry, and patriotism "must be roused to action, to instant and resolute and resistless action by the knowledge of the startling fact that Kentucky is invaded, that her soil is trodden by the armed enemies of her country," the *Journal* trumpeted.[26]

In light of their recent pro-neutrality stand, the secessionist papers had little choice but to insist that both armies leave the state. The *Courier* led the way. Although the rebel army had been the first to arrive, Haldeman's paper blamed the Lincoln administration for provoking the Confederate incursion. "They determined in their wicked counsels to force the war in Kentucky. They are now carrying out their plans. The bloody consequences will be on their heads." The *Courier* claimed that Kentuckians "want peace, but it is denied them. They will determine whether they will fight for despotism or freedom; for consolidation and tyranny, or State Rights and independence; for chains and slavery, or for liberty. They have to choose now."[27]

The next day the *Courier* claimed the Confederates had advanced into Kentucky to stop Union troops from seizing Hickman and Columbus, thereby threatening Memphis. "Whether Tennessee acted wisely or well is another question," the paper suggested. It conceded that both sides "may have acted wrong or hastily" in invading Kentucky, but it argued that "the practical question is, Can the *status quo* be restored, and peace maintained?" Still, the paper believed bloodshed could be avoided if everybody would "rise above party or selfish considerations and act like men not totally demented." It urged the legislature to order both armies out of the state, predicting that both sides would agree to leave. But "if either or both shall refuse, then let the people of the State be united against either or both as the case may be; and thus, at least, our own citizens will not be compelled to cut each other's throats in fratricidal war."[28]

On September 9 the *Yeoman* reminded its readers that the peace convention would open the next day. "It has been insinuated in some inflammatory newspapers that the Convention has been called with a view to violence. The insinuation is utterly unfounded; and the character of the delegates, as well as their action, will rebuke the calumny." The paper believed the convention would be productive in terms of maintaining peace and neutrality, and it could not "conceive that any opposition to it can exist except among those who wish to embark Kentucky in war."[29]

Not surprisingly, the peace convention was a failure. The *Democrat* dismissed it as a "Jeff. Davis pow-wow." Nonetheless, representatives from seventy counties congregated in Frankfort and urged Kentuckians to stick with a policy of strict neutrality. The convention called on both armies to vacate the state, and if they refused, state troops should drive them out. At the same time, delegates blamed the war on Lincoln and denounced Fremont's proclamation in Missouri. The *Courier* claimed the convention was "the largest and most respectable that ever met in the State, notwithstanding hundreds of delegates were detained at home by fears of interruption of travel and apprehensions of danger in Louisville, many having returned to their homes from this city." The paper added, "The proceedings were orderly and harmonious, and the resolutions adopted are conservative and must prove satisfactory to every friend of peace in the State."[30]

The *Frankfort Commonwealth* was decidedly less charitable in its account of the conclave. "It was a meeting to promote the interest of the Southern Confederacy—a peace meeting for the promotion of war and rebellion," Hodges's paper scoffed. The *Commonwealth* judged the meeting "a miserable failure," adding that "the attendance of delegates was by no means as large as usual in State conventions." The paper growled, "They were eloquent in denouncing Lincoln for *violating* the Constitution, but had nothing to say about Jeff. Davis' attempt to *destroy* that sacred instrument."[31]

The *Yeoman* argued that as the first violation of Kentucky neutrality, Camp Dick Robinson had forced the Confederates to invade Kentucky. Who could not realize that its establishment "by one of the belligerent powers, would necessarily lead to the seizure of strategic positions by the other?" Major's paper asked. "Are we to ignore human nature in the presence of this fratricidal war?" The *Yeoman* argued that if the state "suffers one of the belligerents to occupy our soil, she cannot expect the other to keep off." In congressional and state elections, Kentuckians had voted for neutrality and against war, the paper maintained. The legislature could still save neutrality and stave off war if lawmakers declared "that it is the will of the sovereign people of Kentucky that neither belligerent shall occupy or march over her sacred soil." The *Yeoman* correctly reported that on September 8, General Polk had written to Governor Magoffin, promising to give up Hickman and Columbus if Grant vacated Paducah and Smithland at the same time. The *Yeoman* endorsed Polk's offer.[32]

Harney's *Democrat* vehemently denied that Camp Dick Robinson represented the first breach of neutrality and claimed it had nothing to do with the rebel invasion of Kentucky. "The impertinence and insolence of such a plea is infinite," the *Democrat* harrumphed. "The whole northern border of Tennessee has long been dotted with hostile camps of armed and equipped soldiers, ready to be thrown upon the State at the first signal." There had been no pledge that Kentucky "would not be assailed by these troops; on the contrary, threats of invasion have been made constantly for many months." Worse, according to the *Democrat*, "ruffians from these camps have invaded this State, seized our citizens and robbed us of property." Thus, the camp had sprouted from farmer Robinson's fields. The *Democrat* claimed that Polk said "he occupied Columbus from a military necessity; not because the neutrality of Kentucky was violated by the existence of Camp Dick Robinson." Thus, "It is left for the Disunionists of Kentucky to hunt up shallow excuses, which even the authors of the concern are ashamed to urge in their own behalf."[33]

The *Statesman,* too, called for peace and neutrality. "Let Kentucky resolve as with one acclaim all of her sons, that she will not participate in the war. Let her proclaim to the belligerents with unbroken voice, Kentucky will take no part in your unnatural hostilities." But if both armies refused to leave, the paper was in favor of fighting them both. "Better, far better, that the men of Kentucky, standing shoulder to shoulder, as a band of brothers, should bare their breasts to the combined hosts of both governments, than they should with fiendish spirit, plunge the dagger into each other's hearts." Of course, Polk had offered to remove his men if Grant did likewise.[34]

On September 9 a resolution was introduced in the state senate calling on the Confederates to leave. The measure also sought aid from the federal government. Two days later, the legislature approved a resolution requiring Magoffin to issue a proclamation ordering the rebels to withdraw immediately and unconditionally. Magoffin vetoed it, claiming that both armies should go. A substitute resolution containing the governor's demand lost decisively, and the original proposal was passed over his veto. He acquiesced, though reluctantly. On September 18 the legislature officially declared that neutrality was over and that Kentucky was at war against the South. Anderson was appointed commander of Kentucky volunteers, which he was authorized to recruit. Already commander of the Department of Kentucky, he shifted his headquarters to Louisville, his hometown. At the same time, Thomas L. Crittenden, a son of the senator, was named commander of state troops (Simon Buckner had resigned to become a Confederate general). Again to no avail,

Magoffin wielded his veto pen on the grounds that under the state constitution, he was commander in chief of the militia.[35]

The unionist press was overjoyed. "The Legislature has with promptness responded to the demands made upon it," the *Democrat* exulted. It praised lawmakers for choosing Anderson and Crittenden and denounced Tennessee, from which Polk and Pillow's soldiers had come. The *Democrat* waxed biblical, noting that the Volunteer State had "sown the wind and will reap the whirlwind." Tennessee "has aroused the lion State of the border, and must pay the penalty, and under such a commander as we have, and the enthusiasm that will cluster around him, we are sure, not only of victory, but of a triumphant annihilation of this base insulter who has attacked us." The *Journal* was overjoyed when it heard that the house and senate had voted to add Kentucky to the states fighting to put down the rebellion. "Well, thank God, we have at last weighed anchor, and set out for the haven of safety and honor. Now, let all possible sail be spread, and the noble ship of state be driven into the lines of her insolent foe with the whole might of the valor and devotion of her true men."[36]

The *Commonwealth* was certain the General Assembly would continue to chart the proper course for Kentucky. "It is composed of *leaders* who thoroughly understand and appreciate the great responsibility resting upon them." The paper predicted that the Union lawmakers "will prove equal to the emergency. Refusing to be hurried either by friends or foes, they will advance slowly and surely but will take no step backwards." The *Commonwealth* could not resist another slap at the peace convention: "The fidgety and wormy individuals, who congregated here upon the 10th of this month, and declared 'eternal war upon this Legislature' in certain contingencies, have dispersed, the Lord knows where." The paper claimed, "They bullied, and prayed, and cursed around here for forty-eight hours, with no effect save what was produced upon the whisky market and their own lungs. They are gone. As a foul miasmatic vapor is rendered inoctious [*sic*] by the clear rays of the morning sun, so was the treasonable odor of the 'Peace convention' annihilated by the first action of our noble Legislature."[37]

7

The Death of the Rebel Press

Kentucky's Union occupiers suppressed the state's secessionist papers as treasonous. A few editors were arrested, but most were soon released. Walter Haldeman fled to the Confederates at Bowling Green when federal authorities shut down the *Louisville Courier*. He resurrected the *Courier* in the Warren County seat but retreated from Kentucky with the Confederate army. Thomas Bell Monroe suspended the *Kentucky Statesman*, joined the rebel army, and was fatally wounded at Shiloh. The *Paducah Herald* and *Hickman Courier* also ceased when their editors donned rebel gray. The *Frankfort Yeoman* and other papers toned down their secessionism, but the *Yeoman's* presses were ultimately silenced, too. Other rebel papers faded away and ceased to exist for the war's duration.

As Louisville rapidly became crowded with Yankee soldiers, Haldeman surely must have suspected that the *Courier's* days were numbered and that a jail cell awaited him. Yet if the publisher feared suppression and arrest, his paper did not show it. The *Courier* shouted for disunion as loudly and defiantly as ever.

Haldeman obviously had many enemies in Kentucky, but a Hoosier helped start the *Courier's* downfall. On September 9 Charles Fishback of Indianapolis forwarded Secretary of State William Seward several clippings from the *Courier* with a note asking, "Is [it] not about time the editor were an occupant of Fort Lafayette or some other suitable place for traitors?" Fishback fumed, "The people are getting tired of sending their sons to fight rebels while such as this editor, more mischievous by far than if armed with muskets, are allowed to furnish aid and comfort to the enemy unmolested."[1]

Silencing the *Courier* was General Anderson's call, and he made it on September 18. There was much to find objectionable in that day's paper. For

the umpteenth time, the *Courier* had abused Joe Holt, now an Anderson ally.
"His name is a synonym for base cowardice and pernicious meanness. —The
people here have not forgotten the fact that [court of appeals justice Joshua
F.] Bullitt threw a quid of tobacco in his face, at the Louisville bar, which
he was too cowardly to resent, and that a few years ago, in order to avoid the
payment of city taxes, he formally published in a Louisville newspaper his
renunciation of his citizenship." Soon enough, Holt would be in position to
get even with the *Courier.* He was about to become judge advocate general
of the army.[2]

Hammering Holt was typical *Courier* boilerplate. So was criticism of the
General Assembly for voting to forsake neutrality and make war on the Confederates. "The people, if they can be heard, are no more willing to fight their
Southern brethren to-day than they were last April," the paper claimed. "The
Legislature may be bamboozled in this way, but when the people are called
upon to draw the sword they will draw it on the side of the South. Already
the notes of preparation are being heard, and for every man who enlists in the
Abolition ranks, there will be ten to meet him on the other side." The *Courier* was wrong again. All told, some 25,000 to 40,000 Kentuckians joined
the Confederate army, and approximately 90,000 to 100,000 served in the
Union forces.[3]

In any event, the *Courier* charged onward, and Haldeman was heedless
of the consequences. The Union vote in the August election had been "misunderstood," it claimed. Knowing "it would be," the paper had "so warned
our people at the time." According to the *Courier,* those "thousands and thousands" of Kentuckians who had voted for Union candidates "did so as a re-
endorsement of the neutrality position assumed by the State. If the question
had been honestly put to them, as it should have been, 'will you fight for the
North or the South?' what well informed man but knows there would have
been at least a five to one in favor of the South?" Based on the number of
Kentuckians who eventually donned a uniform, the *Courier* was once again
way off the mark.[4]

Heaping scorn on Holt and questioning election results did not get the
Courier shut down. Nor did another editorial castigating "atrocious formulas
of Lincoln & Co.," most notably the "ruling idea of the liberty of the negro."
The president and the Republican Congress had "destroyed all other kinds
of liberties"—infringing on freedom of speech and of the press; establishing
martial law and "police boards"; enacting high tariffs, blockades, and embargoes; and suspending the writ of habeas corpus. An editorial allegedly from
Reuben Durrett's pen led to the paper's demise. Despite his retirement in
1859, Durrett evidently authored editorials from time to time. At any rate,

this one, headlined "Once More," was the last straw for Anderson. It charged that neutrality was a failure; the unionist majority had subjected Kentucky "to insult and invasion, and now leaves her on the verge of civil war." The writer knew "of but one way to avert this dire calamity now, if it be not now too late, and that is, to adopt an honest and manly neutrality, without any more sneaking and shuffling and contradictory conditions and reservations." Then the writer let fly: "But this can be done only by separating from the Northern Union. By this alone can Kentucky be duly exempted from contributions of men and money; from implication in embargoes, and all other belligerent measures. And we say she is under no obligation to remain in that Union, but under many to leave it." The editorialist seemed to be proposing that Kentucky become a sort of Switzerland, an independent nation between two warring countries.[5]

Continuing its theme of "one might as well be hanged for a sheep as for a lamb," the *Courier* claimed that "the 'United States of America' no longer exist, in law or in fact; and the Constitutional Compact can be no longer executed. Kentucky does not, and cannot belong to 'the Union' according to the cant of the Lincoln men. She may, by express compact, unite herself to the Northern States, but we beg leave to assure Messieurs, the members of the present Legislature, that they cannot do it by acts of commission or omission. It can only be done by the people of Kentucky in their primary capacity or by delegates in sovereign convention assembled." The paper defiantly declared, "the assumption of any authority over Kentucky by the Lincoln Government or by the present Legislature under it" would be "a usurpation, and revolutionary." Thus, "no citizen of Kentucky is bound to obey" state or federal authority.[6]

The next day, under the headline "The Courier Throws Off the Mask," the *Louisville Journal* reprinted the most damning parts of the editorial—not to refute or stigmatize "the treasonable stuff" but to show "where the Courier stands in the struggle that is now upon us." The excerpts were enough to prove that Haldeman's paper was in "open rebellion against the nation and the State." The *Journal* presently had "no remarks to offer touching the position; we leave the army and the judiciary to deal with it." But it warned, "The mission of the pen in this contest with rebellion in Kentucky is at any rate well nigh fulfilled; what remains belongs especially to the sword and the hangman's rope."[7]

The *Courier* was already under suspicion, and not just for editorials that were deemed disloyal. On September 13 the paper's wagon hauled five bundles marked "Louisville Courier" to the Louisville & Nashville Railroad depot. The packages were bound for Confederate cities—Memphis and Nashville.

Detectives opened the parcels and discovered copies of *Hardee's Tactics* and other military publications, as well as two letters connected to smuggling.[8]

Meanwhile, Seward, having read the editorial, told Postmaster General Montgomery Blair that the *Courier* should be banned from the mail because it advocated "treasonable hostility to the Government and authorities of the United States." The next morning, US marshal A. H. Sneed took over the *Courier* and cast a dragnet for traitors that snared Durrett, ex-governor Charles S. Morehead, and Martin W. Barr, the telegraphic news reporter for the New Orleans press. The trio was charged with treason or complicity with treason and ended up imprisoned at Fort Lafayette in New York City and Fort Warren in Boston Harbor.[9]

The *Frankfort Commonwealth* cheered the demise of the *Courier* and the reputed arrest of "Mr. Haldeman and a few of the miscellaneous editors." Albert Hodges's paper pulled no punches. "This pestiferous sheet which has for months been a sewer for conveying to the public the treasonable ravings of the few secessionists who infest Louisville, is at length abated." The *Commonwealth* denounced the editorial as "rank treason to the State" and maintained that "it was written for the express purpose of exciting resistance to the laws and authority of this Commonwealth, and to encourage mobs." It declared, "The United States authorities very properly abated the nuisance."[10]

In contrast, the *Louisville Democrat*'s Frankfort correspondent stuck up for the "pestiferous sheet." In a page-two story published on September 20, the scribe pleaded for free speech and a free press, even for an enemy newspaper in wartime. He wrote that the suppression might have been justified "as a question of policy," but "on that ground only." He added, "That policy can only be based on the idea that they would give publicity to plans of the commanding officer which should necessarily be kept quiet." The reporter asserted that "freedom of the press must never be violated, unless it be that they abuse that freedom to the detriment of the public welfare, which may be the grounds on which the suppression was affected." The writer could not "justify the act, and does not believe the report."[11]

On page one, the *Democrat* reported that the authorities had closed the *Courier* "for publishing incendiary articles, and giving aid and comfort to the enemy." But because the paper could cite "no particulars [that were] reliable," it would not traffic in rumors. Yet elsewhere on the front page, the *Democrat* reported, "There was a movement on foot yesterday to allow the Louisville Courier to be continued, providing it should publish nothing but news." Another front-page short had Haldeman aboard a train bound for Louisville from his home in Peewee on September 19. "At O'Bannon's Station it was announced that the Courier was suppressed and some of its editors arrested, and at the next station (Hobbs') he [Haldeman] very wisely got off. The State Marshal and other officers were prepared." The *Democrat* also reported that authorities put Morehead, Durrett, and Barr in a skiff, took them across the river to Jeffersonville, Indiana, and lodged them in Browning's Hotel. "Some of them [were] very much frightened; others cool and easy." Morehead, according to the paper, objected to being transported in the skiff because it was so small. "The Governor has had an idea that he is such a great man that we suppose the Great Eastern is the kind of 'vessel' he would like to travel in," the *Democrat* derided, referring to the famous British ocean liner that was, in its day, the largest ship on earth. "Our oleaginous friend can rest assured that as certain as oil floats on the water he was safe in crossing the Ohio." Without mentioning the arrestees, Haldeman, or the *Courier,* the paper barbed, "Treason is drying up in Louisville. The noisy, intolerant braggarts, who denounce their country and the Government in the same breath, are growing quite submissive under the rigor of the law. We are in favor of coercing obedience to the laws of the country."[12]

At the same time, the *Journal* was more conciliatory toward the common foe. "The suppression of the Courier has given us sincere and deep pain," the paper declared on September 20. "Personally and professionally our sympathies are with all who have been recently connected with that paper; and, although we do not doubt the interference of the authorities with its publication was a stern duty, the fact that circumstances existed rendering it a duty makes us realize painfully and poignantly the dreadful character of the crisis in our public affairs."[13]

The next day, the *Democrat* chortled that the arrests (it did not mention Durrett, Morehead, and Barr by name) had "raised a flutter in the bosoms of some of the Secessionists of the city, and we hear much about the disregard of law." The paper understood the men had been apprehended "under a regular indictment from the Federal court" and were charged "with corresponding with, and giving information to, the enemy, of the movements of the forces of the Union. Under such a charge, if it is correctly reported to us, no other step could possibly be taken." The Confederate army had advanced to Bowling Green and was threatening Louisville. "We find men calling themselves Kentuckians who are willing to give all the information necessary to introduce the enemy into our midst, and involve the whole city in one common ruin." The paper claimed that every man arrested "was known to be . . . giving aid and comfort" to the Confederates, but the *Democrat* still rued the arrests. "As gentlemen, there are none whom we respect more; but the cause they have been engaged in involves such penalties. If they are guilty of what is charged upon them, they ought to expect no other result, and doubtless, they had prepared themselves for it."[14]

When Haldeman heard that Durrett was in custody, he must have assumed his fate would be a Yankee dungeon. He dashed off a message to Anderson, agreeing to publish a paper shorn of political commentary if the general would kindly lift the *Courier*'s suspension. Anderson agreed. Haldeman also sent a notice to the *Journal* promising to repent. The paper printed his "card" on September 21. Haldeman tried to wiggle off the hook, admitting he had been the major stockholder in the *Courier* since December 1860, but adding that he was "exclusively the business manager of the office." Haldeman's implication, of course, was that he had nothing to do with the treasonous editorial. In any event, he explained that from now on, he would run the whole paper. The reborn and repentant *Courier* would "entirely ignore politics and be devoted exclusively to the publication of local and general news and miscellany." Haldeman swore he would "studiously avoid the publication of any matter that will either directly or indirectly be prejudicial to the Federal Government or the interests which are placed in Gen. Anderson's keeping here; and as long as Kentucky is a member of the Federal Union I will be loyal to her and to the Union." He stated that while arrangements were being made to restart the *Courier,* he would entrust the paper to faithful subordinates. Haldeman had no intention of running a nonpolitical paper. His proposal was a ruse designed to buy time to escape to the Confederate army at Bowling Green, where he planned to resurrect the *Courier* as unrepentantly rebel as ever. Naturally, the *Journal* scorned Haldeman's flight: "Where is W. N. Haldeman now? *He joined Jack Allen's Cavalry and has gone to Bowling-Green and taken service under Gen. S. B. Buckner in the invasion of Kentucky!* There's human nature for you in one of its innumerable phases."[15]

Though he condemned Haldeman for running away, George Prentice pleaded the case of Durrett, Morehead, and Barr all the way to the president. On September 24 the *Journal* chief wrote to Lincoln seeking their release. Prentice had no illusions about Durrett, with whom he had shot it out on a Louisville street in 1857. "Mr. Durrett has been and I presume still is a bitter personal enemy of mine but I am extremely anxious for his release. He is a secessionist, but he has never done any harm in our community. He couldn't do any harm if he would." Yet Prentice's main reason for wanting Durrett freed was that otherwise, "his wife, a most estimable woman . . . will go utterly and hopelessly mad." Prentice and Morehead, an old Whig who had been elected governor on the Know-Nothing ticket in 1855, had been close friends for almost thirty years. He acknowledged that Morehead was a Southern sympathizer but doubted that the ex-governor's "arrest was necessary or expedient." As for poor Barr, he simply "telegraphed what he thought would be most agreeable to his employers." If Barr were released, Prentice assured

Lincoln, "he will be sure to do no such work again." In addition, Louisville postmaster J. T. D. Osborne telegraphed the president asking for Durrett's release "on his poor wife's account, who is in a very bad way."[16]

Holt, however, was understandably delighted that Durrett had been incarcerated. On September 25 he sent a copy of the offending editorial to Lincoln. Durrett's "arrest has rejoiced the hearts of Union men, and his discharge [from prison] under the circumstances in which the State is placed would in my judgment be a fatal mistake," Holt wrote. "He will no doubt offer to take the oath of allegiance, but I express only the convictions of those who know him best when I say that he would take the oath if necessary on his knees, and would stab the Government the moment he rose to his feet." The *Courier* had stabbed Holt verbally time and time again. Who could blame him for wanting Durrett to cool his heels behind bars?[17]

Seward wrote to Prentice that because the military authorities in Kentucky had sent the trio to Fort Lafayette in New York, he could not properly "intervene, especially without further knowledge of their cases than I now possess." Lincoln told Morehead's son-in-law that he was willing to release any of the captives with the assent of James Guthrie and James Speed.[18]

Guthrie, Prentice, and seven other leading Louisville unionists petitioned the president on Durrett's behalf. "We are assured that he had not been the editor of the paper for about two years," they pleaded. "He wrote some articles at the request of the editor who was absent which are certainly not such as we could justify in any manner; but the most objectionable and which were thought to be written by him we are assured by the affidavit of W. H. W. Randal, an employe[e] in the printing office, were not written by him, and we are satisfied that this is true." Durrett, as far as the petitioners knew, "behaved himself well and rather modestly during the excited time of the spring and summer. He is not a man who is calculated to do such harm to the State as could require in any sense a military imprisonment." They said that Durrett's wife and mother-in-law (the latter lived in Cincinnati) were pro-Union. "The worth of this family is well known to Mr. [Treasury] Secretary [Salmon P.] Chase." Chase was also from Cincinnati.[19]

In his affidavit, Randal said he believed "another editorial assistant" had authored the offending editorial, but he did not name which one. On October 10 W. D. Gallagher, head of the US customs office in Louisville, wrote to Chase on Durrett's behalf. Gallagher had twice visited Durrett's wife and mother-in-law and reported that Lizzie Durrett "is in a truly pitiable condition," and her mother's state "is not much better." He declared that both women were patriotic and greatly deplored "the writing of the editorials in The Courier which caused Mr. Durrett's arrest." Gallagher was convinced that while Durrett "was acting as one of the editors of The Courier he was more imprudent than wicked, and acted worse than he thought." He explained, "I am of this opinion from a conversation I had with him a few days before he undertook temporarily to assist in the editorship of the paper. He then expressed much regret at the condition of the country; said he hardly knew which side he was on, and declared that so far as fighting was concerned he didn't intend to fight for either." Gallagher believed that freeing Durrett, once he had taken the oath, "would do good rather than harm to the Union cause in this part of the country." He noted that the writer of the September 18 editorial was still "at large." He added that "if anything of the sort is treasonable this certainly is," and "Mr. Randal knows who wrote it."[20]

On September 30 Randal's old boss penned a card for the *Nashville Union and American* in which he promised to go home and reestablish the *Courier* "when Louisville is again free, . . . with the aid tendered by gallant and glorious Tennessee and the chivalric South to the freemen of Kentucky." Haldeman trusted that liberation day would come soon. He advised that the resurrected *Courier* would be nothing like the paper described in the *Journal* card. It "will be resumed under its former auspices, and its labors will be consecrated to the triumph of the great principle of civil and religious liberty it has so long advocated."[21]

Haldeman visited the *Union and American* on October 1, and the paper published his card the next day. It introduced him as a brave Kentuckian "who has been exiled from Louisville on account of his political opinions, and because he had the manhood to publish an independent journal, which fearlessly and ably exposed the usurpations of the tyrant and usurper, who has filled with terror and fears every Southern State which has not resisted his despotism." The *Union and American* found its new friend "as cheerful and spirited as though he were going to a festival instead of being an exile from his family and friends, and having his property confiscated, his business broken up and his habitation changed by the blood hounds of Lincoln." Haldeman understood "that he has suffered sacrifice and persecution on account of a glorious and noble cause, and he is now ready to endure all that is necessary to see Kentucky released from the domination of the vulgar tyrant and his purchased minions." Thus, the *Union and American* invited "attention to the card of Mr. Haldeman, in another column, which corrects some misapprehensions relative to the card, in the Louisville *Journal*, over his signature."[22]

In the *Union and American* card, Haldeman said he had expected the Union military to suppress the *Courier*. So he had decided to evade arrest and escape to the Confederacy, "where I could still breathe and think as a freeman; and from that determination I never wavered for a moment." Haldeman had been at his home in the country on the morning of September 19, when he heard that Anderson had shut down the *Courier.* The publisher had steered clear of Louisville but kept himself "sufficiently near to communicate with my friends, and through them transact some business important to me." Haldeman claimed his political friends had entreated him to devise some plan by which Anderson might permit the *Courier* to continue, even "as a *newspaper* strictly, politics being ignored in its editorial columns." His allies "reasoned that the facts are now the strongest arguments against the Administration" and pleaded that "the entire suspension of the only daily Southern rights paper in the State would make the people of Kentucky dependent upon the tory papers of Louisville for information of current events." Thus, Haldeman concluded, "it would be better to print the *Courier* upon almost any terms involving no sacrifice of principle, than to thus leave the public mind entirely at the mercy of these unscrupulous mouth-pieces of tyranny, which have systematically perverted or entirely suppressed facts necessary to a correct understanding of the condition of public affairs."[23]

Mindful that "some fifteen or twenty" Southern sympathizers had been arrested—he did not mention anyone by name—Haldeman started negotiations, through friends, with Anderson. The publisher proposed to swear off political commentary and print only "local and general news and miscellaneous matter"—nothing that might tip off the Confederates to Union military moves. Anderson replied that Haldeman must first write an article for the *Courier,* subject to the general's approval, "expressing regret for its past course, and as a States-rights paper, pledge it to conform to and support the action and policy of the Kentucky (Lincoln) Legislature." Haldeman naturally turned Anderson down and told the general that he would rather "lose property, liberty and life itself."[24]

The *Union and American* also reprinted the *Journal* card, which, Haldeman insisted, had been published without his permission and was "not the one written by me." His statement had been "altered in some unimportant particulars, and important explanatory remarks were entirely omitted." He speculated that perhaps "friends acting doubtless from the best of motives" had changed the card. In any event, Haldeman "had not the slightest expectation" that the general would accept anything he might put on paper. He believed the parley and "the unwarranted publication of my card" had been a scheme to lure him into town and grab him. "The pretended assent to my proposition and the publication of the paper (which under the arrangement would have been carried on by employees of the office), was at once withdrawn when it was ascertained that I would not trust myself in Louisville until Gen. Buckner and the strong right arms of thousands of brave Kentuckians would open the way for me to do so as a freeman."[25]

Haldeman said that Anderson and his subordinates had promised he would not be arrested during talks about the *Courier*. But he mistrusted "the pledges of men who had sold themselves to a faithless and perfidious administration, and, as the result proved, wisely kept out of their power." Anderson not only suppressed the *Courier* but also "took and still holds possession of the entire printing establishment, and of the books, papers, and money in the iron safe in the counting room at the time it was seized." The general would not even permit "any of our clerks or attaches . . . to enter the building to procure articles of clothing, &c., in it and belonging to them."[26]

On September 24 Anderson sought to calm secessionist fears about wholesale arrests. He issued a proclamation promising that nobody would be arrested who did not, by word or deed, oppose the federal or state government. When Anderson learned of numerous arbitrary arrests in some parts of Kentucky, he followed up on October 7 with General Orders No. 5. He deeply regretted "that arrests are being made in some parts of the State upon the slightest and most trivial of grounds," and he ordered his soldiers to stop arresting people unless they were "attempting to join the rebels, or are engaged in giving aid or information to them." Anderson urged civilian authorities and the Home Guard to do the same. In every case, the proof had to be strong enough to convict such individuals in a civil court. The general said that because many Southern sympathizers wanted to be loyal again, "a conciliatory, fair course pursued towards such persons will join them to our cause," whereas "the reverse may force them into the ranks of the enemy," Anderson argued.[27]

In any event, the *Journal* was livid over Haldeman's card in the *Union and American*, blasting it as "a thing most disgraceful to him in all respects." His old rival added, "There is certainly good reason to think he will not come back to raise the Courier from the dead or to do anything else here until the U.S. Government shall cease to have any operation among us." His creditors had seized "his printing materials." Worse, while he was surveyor of the customhouse, Haldeman had "confiscated at least ten or twelve thousand dollars of the public money to his own use," a crime punishable by up to twelve years in prison. Hence, "he will unquestionably give Louisville a wide berth so long as the authority of the United States shall exist here." The *Journal* protested that it took no pleasure in exposing Haldeman's multiple misdeeds. "We bear him no personal ill-will. When we learned that he proposed to revive the dead Courier, making it a mere newspaper, we, without consultation with any one, immediately wrote an earnest letter to Gen. Anderson, urging him to give his consent to the proposition." The *Journal* had done so "from a sense of duty, and without the slightest thought or expectation, that, if our well-meant interference should be successful, Mr. H. would thank us for it. We knew that he would not."[28]

To prove Haldeman's perfidy, the *Journal* published a long letter from Dr. T. S. Bell in which he disputed Haldeman's *Union and American* notice, point by point. The physician began with a note from Noble Butler and William H. Walker, who, on the morning of September 19, had left Peewee Valley Station on a train bound for Louisville; also on the train was Haldeman, who lived nearby. The publisher told the two men that the *Courier* had been shut down and he wanted to restart it "as a mere newspaper" under the direction "of some person or persons" of General Anderson's choosing. "Feeling great regard for Mr. H. as a neighbor, we offered to call on Gen. A. and present his proposition." When Butler and Walker pressed him for details, Haldeman reiterated "that he wished merely to publish the current news, abstaining entirely from political discussions, and that if the publication of any particular item of news should be regarded as injurious to the Government, it might be suppressed by the person or persons under whose supervision the paper might be placed." Butler and Walker agreed to telegraph Haldeman the result of their interview with Anderson. Haldeman then detrained at Hobbs's Station, claiming he intended to seek support from E. D. Hobbs.[29]

After Haldeman's traveling companions reached Louisville, they went to Dr. Bell and asked him to accompany them to see Anderson. The general listened to Haldeman's proposal via his three emissaries and agreed to it. Walker telegraphed the news to Haldeman, while Bell and Butler arranged with Anderson's subordinates to ensure that Haldeman would not be arrested. Bell also sent Haldeman a letter from Butler, setting out the general's terms. At that point, everybody believed Haldeman planned to return to Louisville. Bell wrote: "I could not and would not have had anything whatever to do with it if I supposed that Mr. Haldeman's object was to gain time to slip away from the officers, and I feel sure that neither Mr. Walker nor Mr. Butler would have done anything in the matter, had they suspected anything of the kind." After meeting with Anderson, Bell presumed his job was done. It was not.[30]

Between 9:00 and 10:00 that night, two men arrived at Bell's office with a letter from Haldeman. Bell said the missive begged him to find out from Anderson "his conditions for the resumption of the publication of the Courier, although he had already received the conditions." Haldeman's letter stated that Butler had advised him of the meeting with the general and that Judge Joshua Bullitt and others had spoken with General Anderson as well. Parts of Haldeman's letter sounded like the notices published in the *Journal* and *Union and American*. He acknowledged that he was the largest stockholder in the *Courier* company and had been the business manager since December, again implying that others had written the editorials. "The good will of the office I regard as of more value than the machinery and material in it, and a suspension for any length of time would entirely destroy the value of that good will," he pleaded. Haldeman repeated his pledge to publish a paper filled only with news and devoid of political commentary. He offered "to submit such news &c., before publication to such supervision and censorship as Gen. Anderson might suggest or require." Haldeman also agreed "to permit the publication of nothing that would be detrimental to the cause Gen. Anderson represents." He hoped that Bell could meet with Anderson that night "and write me the result of the interview by the train to-morrow morning." Meanwhile, Haldeman would "endeavor to see and advise with some friends to-night." If Bell thought "it advisable and safe," Haldeman would catch a train for Louisville in the morning.[31]

The arrival of the two messengers must have perplexed Bell, who evidently thought everything had already been settled. He told them it was too late to call on the general and that such a visit was unnecessary because "the identical propositions of the letter had been verbally submitted to General Anderson, and General Anderson's response had been sent to him in Mr. Butler's letter, written in my office, and concurred in by me, as a faithful report of the result of our interview." Nonetheless, Haldeman's men begged Bell to write to Haldeman, sketching "what I supposed would meet General Anderson's approval, as a guide to Mr. Haldeman in preparing his card for publication." Bell relented. But the doctor advised the men not to wait for the morning train to deliver the message to Haldeman. He recommended that they "get a horse and buggy then, about midnight," and leave "immediately so as to give Haldeman time to think upon his action before starting to the city." The duo departed at the suggested hour, promising Bell they would return by 8:00 the next morning. The doctor awaited their return until 10:00 a.m., even though shortly after 8:00 "a gentleman from Peewee Valley called . . . and stated that Mr. Haldeman had fled." Bell refused to believe the news but admitted, "if true, it looked as though he had 'inveigled' Messrs. Walker, Butler, and myself into the business of deluding Gen. Anderson and the officers, while he slipped away." The men returned sometime between 3:00 and 4:00 p.m. with Haldeman's "card." They said they had not been able to locate the publisher until 7:00 a.m.[32]

Bell read the card and took exception to the opening sentence because it expressed "a humiliation and degradation, which General Anderson had not demanded, and which I thought he would not approve." Haldeman's messengers were still in Bell's office when W. D. Gallagher arrived and asked whether he had "heard from the country." Bell showed him Haldeman's card. Gallagher "also strongly objected to the first sentence and said it ought not appear in a form so injurious as that to Mr. Haldeman." Bell "felt authorized" to change it, as the "sentence had nothing whatever to do with the terms of settlement contained in the rest of the card." As it turned out, Haldeman did not appreciate the favor.[33]

Accompanying the card was a letter thanking Bell. "I wanted to come to the city and attend to this matter in person, but Butler, Walker, Hobbs, and other friends advised me to remain in the country and not place myself in the way of arrest," Haldeman explained. "I would even now come down could I think there was no danger." However, the publisher's understanding of what Anderson required of him differed from the doctor's. "He seems inclined to make no offer not coupled with terms of humiliation," Haldeman wrote. "Rather than accept such I would prefer to lose every dollar I had in the world and liberty, or even life itself." Haldeman believed his card would satisfy the general, and he asked Bell to send him a message, via train the next morning, advising him of Anderson's decision. He would be at home awaiting word. Bell took the card to Anderson, who "objected to the first sentence as expressing a serfdom which he had not required of Mr. Haldeman, and which he did not desire him to express." The sentence read: "Having received permission from the Government authorities of the United States to resume the publication of the Courier, I make the following statement." Anderson wanted "*a sentence more favorable to Haldeman*," so Bell proposed this substitute: "The interdiction against the publication of the Courier having been modified, I proceed to make the following statement." The rest of the card was printed exactly as Haldeman wrote it, according to the doctor.[34]

Meanwhile, Bell, via another Haldeman confidant, sent Anderson's approval to the *Courier* chief by the 6:00 a.m. train. Marshal Sneed was aboard to assure Haldeman personally that he would not be arrested and that he was free to reopen the *Courier*. The lawman found Haldeman gone. In the *Union and American*, Haldeman denied authorship of the *Journal* card, but Bell insisted that, with the exception of the first sentence, Haldeman had written every word. Bell also denied that Anderson required Haldeman to apologize for his secessionist views and to promise "to conform and support" the Kentucky legislature in the resurrected nonpolitical *Courier*.[35]

Bell's communiqué also included statements from Gallagher, Prentice, and Oliver Lucas, the latter evidently a member of the *Journal* staff. All of them vowed that Haldeman had written what the *Journal* published. Gallagher, who had worked with Haldeman at the customs office, swore that Haldeman's card "was unquestionably that gentleman's own writing. His writing is as familiar to me as any other man's." Likewise, Prentice and Lucas said the *Journal* card "was an exact copy of the manuscript card of Mr. Haldeman, with the single exception of the first sentence." Both said they knew Haldeman's handwriting and that "this card was in the handwriting of that gentleman." Bell mocked, "Let the friends of the Courier rest in hope. The Greek Kalends, thought rolling slowly, if rolling at all, through cycles of time, may be along after a while."[36]

Haldeman's initial response came on October 14 in the *Courier*'s first Bowling Green edition, which Cincinnati papers castigated as "twice as reckless as the concern published in Louisville." Haldeman had not seen Bell's letter in the *Journal,* but he understood the paper had made "an infamous and liebellous [*sic*] assault upon us." Haldeman declared that Kentuckians knew the *Journal* was given to "fiercely defaming all the prominent, honored and pure men of the State who have espoused the cause of Southern independence." He claimed that Prentice, "reeking with infamy and corruption, attempts to blast private character by making charges which he could have if he been so disposed, easily have satisfied himself were entirely destitute of the shadow of foundation." Haldeman was referring to the *Journal*'s allegation—on the same page as Bell's letter—that he had stolen at least $10,000 to $12,000 of government funds from the customhouse. He maintained that records in the customhouse and in the US treasury in Washington would prove his innocence. But Haldeman confessed that he did have "some sixteen or eighteen hundred dollars of Government money subject to draft," which, he hoped, it would "soon be our pleasing duty to" hand over to the Confederate treasury. Haldeman "only wished the amount was of some consequence."[37]

Haldeman said that he and Robert McKee, his editor in Louisville, had restarted the *Courier*-in-exile "to meet the necessities of the hour." The newspaper would be published daily in Bowling Green, providing its readers, "to the best of our ability, a full, fair, and impartial account of whatever events may be worth recording, and through which we will support those principles and advocate that policy, the maintenance of which brought down on the Courier the weight of the displeasure of the government of Mr. Lincoln." The publication would remain in Bowling Green "until such time as the occupation of Louisville by the brave men who have taken up arms, or are doing so, against the despot and his government and for constitutional liberty and the inalienable and indefensible right of self-government, shall restore to its people the privileges which have been wrested from them and make good therein the guarantees of the State and Federal Constitutions in favor of freedom of speech and of the press." Meanwhile, Haldeman would "send our Courier out on the wings of the wind to greet our friends everywhere." The *Courier* left Bowling Green in February 1862, but not for Louisville. Haldeman and McKee headed south with the retreating Confederate army.[38]

Perusing the Bowling Green edition of the *Courier,* one could make a good case that the Cincinnati organs were right about the rebel paper-in-exile. The *Courier* seemed even more venomous and vitriolic, and it heaped more scorn on a familiar target: Joe Holt. The paper reported that he was on "the 'grand tour' of the North," giving speeches "denouncing the Southern people and everything else that is Southern, and encouraging and stimulating the North to a bloody war upon us." The *Courier* asserted that Holt was in the running for secretary of war or perhaps a seat on the Supreme Court. "He is now in Washington, where he has also been making a speech, advertising his claims for office before the very face of his imperial master, Abraham the First." Because the Kentucky-born Holt was "indebted to the South for all that he has of fame or fortune," it was fitting that his "name should be held up for the scorn and detestation of the people whom he has so basely betrayed." Accompanying the *Courier's* peroration was a Holt hit piece by the *New Orleans Crescent:* "The Renegade," the headline read. Not to be outdone, Haldeman, McKee, or a subordinate editor headlined the *Courier's* story, "A Southern Apostate."[39]

Perhaps Haldeman was "twice as reckless" in Bowling Green because he knew he was a prophet without honor in his own country; Kentucky had resoundingly rejected secession. Louisville, Haldeman's home for most of his life, had rebuked him and his paper. Back home, his old foes Prentice and Harney were triumphant; the Yankees had beaten the rebels to Louisville. Presses at the *Journal* and the *Democrat* were humming daily.

No sooner did he restart the *Courier* in the Warren County seat than Haldeman found himself vexed again, this time by price-gouging paper carriers. On October 16 and in several subsequent issues, he warned customers that purveyors of the *Courier* in Bowling Green and Nashville were not supposed to be selling copies for more than a nickel apiece. "We will be obliged if any deviations from this rule be reported to us, and the transgressors will not be allowed to have any more papers."[40]

At the same time, Haldeman and General Buckner were anxious to increase *Courier* readership in Kentucky, thereby countering their common foe, Prentice. On October 19 Haldeman wrote to Brigadier General Felix K. Zollicoffer of Nashville, informing him that, per Buckner's order, he was sending him "by special messenger" a parcel of papers "of different dates, for the week ending to-day." At the time, Zollicoffer was holding Cumberland Gap with a small army. Haldeman told him that Buckner wanted the issues "distributed gratuitously and as widely as possible among the People of Kentucky, hoping that they may serve to some degree to correct the public mind and to post the people in regard to current events." Buckner, according to Haldeman, "wishes me, if possible, to send you as many copies (from one hundred to five hundred) as you can distribute to advantage." The *Courier* chief complained that it was impossible for him to send the papers from Nashville directly to Zollicoffer's headquarters in the field.[41]

Haldeman was obviously reading the *Journal,* which doubtless had mail subscribers in Bowling Green. As he had back home, he scanned copies for ammunition to shoot back at Prentice. He found plenty. On October 17 the *Courier* claimed that under the rule of Prentice's friends—"Northern Goths and Vandals"—Louisville's economy was in a shambles. To hear Haldeman's paper tell it, business after business had failed, and many workers were jobless and in penury. According to the *Courier,* the *Journal,* "having contributed more, perhaps, than any half-dozen men outside of its office, to bring ruin and suffering on the doomed city," dared to encourage unemployed men to join the army to support their families. "The President wants soldiers; he offers good pay and large bounties; if you will turn into the ranks, and risk your lives in behalf of the North, and cut the throats of those upon whom you are dependent for future employment,—the Southern consumers of the products of your labor,—you can obtain the treasury notes issued by his Government with which to buy bread for your babes; you must do this, or perish in the streets like brutes, as you ought to do!"—such was the substance of a recent *Journal* editorial, the paper howled in high dudgeon. "Surely the devil could go no further in audacity. Surely at last it will provoke the vengeance of those it has misguided, betrayed, and now insults."[42]

The next day, the *Courier* returned to a familiar theme: Lincoln's "mercenary soldiers" with their "bristling bayonets" were waging an unconstitutional war against slavery and if the North won, slavery would perish. "The existence of slavery depends on the success of the Southern arms. But without property, without slaves, with nothing but our wives and little ones, and strong arms and stout hearts, we might be contented and happy, with *liberty*—without liberty there can be no happiness." The paper conceded, "All may not be able to see that an invasion of the rights of any one citizen is an invasion of the rights of all—that the non-slaveholder is really as much interested in protecting the property of the slaveholder as the latter is in protecting the right of the former to vote—but the lowest equally with the highest, the most ignorant with the best informed, the poor and the rich, all must see that life and liberty, common to us all, and dear to all, equally with lands and negroes, are dependent on the result of the war between the sections." The *Courier* challenged that any Kentuckian who would not fight for the Confederacy was "fit even now for companionship with the negroes to whose level he would be reduced by the triumph of the Northern arms."[43]

On October 25 Haldeman, having obtained a copy of the *Journal* with Bell's letter, replied at length. He signed his rejoinder, which took up four of the six columns on page two. "While Dr. Bell's card does not refute a single statement made by me, yet its vile spirit, malignant abuse and bald falsehoods demand that I shall expose it and its author as they deserve," he declared. "Most certainly I did not 'importune' him in the slightest degree," Haldeman added. "It was not at my insistence or through any action of mine that he visited Gen. Anderson in my behalf. And it was not until after he had done so, and then at the request of friends, that I wrote him. I consented to do so because of his oft-repeated protestations of friendship, which I always supposed were sincere."[44]

His dander up, Haldeman blasted Bell: "had I been aware then, as I have since been advised by reliable parties at Bowling Green and Nashville, that he had for some time been the writer of many of the most violent, vindictive and infamous editorials of the Louisville *Journal*—articles coined in his own malignant brain, and designed and intended to excite and inflame the public mind and inaugurate the era of bad feeling now existing in Kentucky, he would not have been permitted to act for me in any capacity." But Haldeman conceded that the statement by Butler and Walker was "correct as far as it goes."[45]

Next, he turned his fire on Gallagher, Prentice, and Lucas, claiming their "certificates . . . only go to establish what I charged and complained of, and what Dr. Bell himself admits—that my article was mutilated, the first portion entirely omitted, and a paragraph of which I never wrote a word substituted." Haldeman dismissed "Dr. Bell's tirade" as "very easily explained. He is sore under the belief that I 'used' him in order to make sure of my escape from the tyrant's clutches." Haldeman confessed that he had negotiated "with Gen. Anderson for this purpose" and defended himself:

> The object sought to be attained, would, I think, have justified me or at least made it pardonable, had I also availed myself of the services of so *denoted* a friend as Dr. B. But with a desire to aid the numerous employees in the *Courier* office, and hoping that a continuation of it as a mere *newspaper* (carried on by long-time employees of the office, but without my presence or assistance) would prevent the value of the property from being seriously impaired, I did make an effort to have

its publication continued, and to accomplish it sacrificed much feeling and yielded everything but honor and principle.

He had not gone into Louisville, he claimed, because he "was not willing to trust the half-way promises of a faithless and perfidious administration."[46]

Haldeman again denied Prentice's "wantonly and infamously false charge" that he had purloined "ten or twelve thousand dollars of the public money." The *Courier* boss admitted that the *Journal* had subsequently reduced the amount "to some three thousand dollars" and had promised it "would not do us 'the slightest injustice.'" Yet Prentice's paper had suggested that it was just "as 'discreditable' to 'appropriate' that amount as the larger." Haldeman claimed the *Journal* chief knew "full well that the small sum of our indebtedness was composed of unadjusted balances subject at any moment to the Department's draft." Haldeman gave a little ground on the charge that creditors had taken over his newspaper's equipment back home. "Attachments against the office have been taken out by some of our creditors and by some parties who held us as security on the paper of others. Had we been permitted to have prosecuted our business without the illegal interference of the agents of the Federal Government, no such proceedings would have been necessary." He complained that if he could not "return to Louisville within a reasonable time and give the attention necessary to our affairs, we suppose property worth more than fifty thousand dollars will be sacrificed to pay a few paltry thousands—that is if all is not soon confiscated or destroyed by the Federal authorities."[47]

Haldeman was still not through with Prentice and Gallagher. On November 16 the *Courier* singled out for special scorn that duo plus a number of other Kentucky Union men. Haldeman started his hectoring with Congressman Crittenden, a venerated state legislator, governor, and US senator. The seventy-four-year-old statesman could not help his perfidy, the *Courier* claimed. He had slipped "into his dotage" and was "now but an instrument of worse men in the attempt to enslave the people who have so often honored him far above his merits." Crittenden, merely "a 'driveler and a show,'" would "pass away from life, leaving behind him a name that will become a synonym for weakness and treachery." Next up was Garrett Davis, "a small man of little intellect and violent and ungovernable passions, of no courage and vast ambition," who "was crammed away in a pigeon-hole with other refuse matter by his fellow-citizens for about a score of years." Davis "has now struggled into notice upon the stage of action as a party to the vilest and most inexcusably wicked conspiracy ever planned for the enslavement of a free people"—an apparent reference to his role in bringing the Lincoln guns to Kentucky. The

Bourbon County resident "aspires to distinction as the most cruel, vindictive and bloody-minded of all the enemies to freedom in Kentucky." The *Courier* also assailed wealthy James Guthrie, noting that "avarice is his controlling passion, and selfishness the motive that has influenced every step of his life." His sole friend "was a free negro in Louisville." To preserve his property, the Louisville & Nashville Railroad chief "would see the State laid waste and all who refuse to bow the knee to Lincoln massacred in cold blood by the minions of tyranny."[48]

Prentice, the *Courier* charged, had been dispatched to Kentucky "years ago as an emissary of the abolitionists of his native New England, and every day and every hour of his residence in the State has been devoted, sometimes directly, oftener indirectly, to the accomplishment of his mission—to bring about the abolition of slavery in Kentucky, and have the emancipated negroes turned loose among us, political equals of the white people." Paul R. Shipman, Prentice's associate editor, also had migrated to Kentucky and "busied himself in disseminating doctrines hostile to the institutions and interests of the State that had given him a home and in acquiring an influence which he has used to bring war and devastation and ruin upon the commonwealth in which he had found an asylum."[49]

The "broken fortunes and desperate circumstances" of representative–turned–Yankee colonel James S. Jackson of Hopkinsville had driven "him into the Congress at Washington, as an apologist for the administration." Subsequently, "fat contracts and a . . . Commission, sufficed . . . to transform him into a full-fledged supporter of Lincoln's perfidious and bloody policy." Gallagher, Bell's ally in discrediting Haldeman, was "a graduate in the worst school of abolitionism, and a *protégé* of Salmon P. Chase, from whom he received his present appointment." Gallagher had once been an editor at the *Courier* but had left "humiliated and disgraced by the torrent of abuse and vituperation poured upon him by Prentice of the Journal, whom he was unable to combat with the pen, and too craven to meet with the sword." Gallagher possessed "neither principle nor character, and is cursed with intelligence enough to enable him to do the bidding of his master, Mr. Chase, and to follow at the heels of his old tormentor, Mr. Prentice, of whose notice he now seems proud, as the whipped spaniel will caress the hand that smote it."[50]

The *Courier* then smote another Yankee officer: Colonel Rufus King Williams of Mayfield, who had resigned as a circuit judge to recruit Union soldiers. Williams was "the only man of the slightest prominence whom the administration has been able to buy in the first Congressional district." According to Haldeman's paper, Williams, a New York native, "has deceived every friend he has ever had, and betrayed every man who has trusted him."

The *Courier* called the colonel a thief and a coward who "challenged a gentleman who had denounced his conduct in fitting terms, and ran away from the field, leaving his second to fight his stead." After Williams, the paper promised to "add to the list similar sketches of others of the accomplices of these men."[51]

True to its word, the *Courier* tacked on General Nelson, Haldeman's old school chum. "This Falstaff, this puffing land porpoise in regimentals, this blatant horse marine, this bag of windy lies" was, of course, loyal "to his lord and master, Abe Lincoln." The paper claimed Nelson had boasted of routing the rebels in a great battle, but everybody who knew him in Bowling Green "immediately set it down as one of Nelson's stunning *canards*." The paper noted that "in the bar-room circles of Washington," he was known as "Bull" Nelson. The general, the *Courier* said, was "about thirty-six years of age, six feet two inches in height, [and] weighs three hundred and fifty pounds." He had "bushy, grizzled hair" and "greedy, glassy eyes." His nose was red, his face "brandy flushed," his lips "thick, sensual," and his mouth "wide" and "lascivious." Nelson was "a person of no common talent; energetic, and unscrupulous to the last degree, a good intriguer; an excellent raconteur." By "drawing on his imagination for his facts . . . [he] can discourse learnedly upon the strategical points of every battle that has been fought in ancient or modern times, and has doubtless impressed old Abe that he is one of the greatest captains of the age."[52]

No doubt Durrett, Morehead, and Barr would have enjoyed reading the *Courier's* barbs, but they were still imprisoned up north. Durrett's release order finally came through on December 5. He took the oath of allegiance and was freed four days later. Morehead stayed locked up until January 6, 1862, when he was paroled. Apparently because he refused to take the loyalty oath, he was ordered "not to enter the State of Kentucky or any insurrectionary State nor to do any act or enter into any correspondence adverse to the authority of the United States, and to hold himself at the disposition of the Secretary of State until otherwise directed." Barr would not swear the oath either and asked to be exchanged as a prisoner of war. He stayed locked up until February 15, 1862, after which he presumably was swapped.[53]

Durrett was not the only rebel editor to end up behind bars. On September 30 soldiers, evidently tipped off by local unionists, arrested A. J. Morey of the *Cynthiana News,* along with the Southern-sympathizing Harrison County judge, clerk, and sheriff. The quartet was charged with "affording aid and comfort to the enemies of the government" and hustled off to the US barracks at Newport. Morey, who briefly served as Cynthiana's postmaster in May 1861, had already felt the wrath of Prentice and the Cincinnati editors.

Friends of the Union also fumed at his editorials, notably one in which he argued, "as the dagger had accomplished so much good in the late Italian revolution, it was to be hoped that it would not be neglected in this [Civil War]." Soon after Kentucky declared for the Union, an Ohio regiment camped near Cynthiana. Morey admitted, "How long the Cynthiana *News* will be permitted to wave is very uncertain," in what turned out to be its last issue. "But one thing is certain," he wrote. "If our office is not destroyed, when we are suppressed, the *News* shall come forth as usual as soon as our friend Zollicoffer makes his appearance in this region." Before the war, Confederate general Felix K. Zollicoffer had published the *Nashville Republican Banner,* the Volunteer State's official Whig paper. It is possible that he and Morey had met in newspaper circles.[54]

Ultimately, Morey, judge J. R. Curry, clerk Perry Wherritt, and sheriff William B. Glave were imprisoned at Camp Chase near Columbus, Ohio. Except for Wherritt, who was not turned loose until late November 1862, their incarceration lasted from three to twenty-five days. Meanwhile, Morey claimed he had repented. On October 3 he penned a long letter to the *Daily Ohio State Journal* confessing his secessionist sins and even offering to fight to defend Kentucky against the Confederates. Morey explained that even before his arrest, he had concluded it was his duty "to yield to a ready, willing and faithful adherence to the wishes and desires of a majority of the people of our State—and a determination to sustain the General Government." He said that local secessionists and unionists had met in Cynthiana and signed a declaration promising "they would not do anything to contravene the laws of the State or National Government." As secretary of the gathering, Morey had signed the document and had done all he could to encourage Confederate sympathizers to do likewise. "I then and there determined to abandon 'secesh,' and give myself up to the advancement and success of the National Government, unconditionally."[55]

Morey declared that he had switched to the Union side after hearing state representative Lucius Desha of Cynthiana give a "patriotic and statesmanlike" speech that "scotched secession in our county." (Also suspected of disloyalty, Desha was arrested by Union troops on July 26, 1862.) Morey vowed he had never been in his "heart for secession, but circumstances carried me down into the vortex, and it was almost next to impossible, while remaining at home, to abandon it." He added, "Before I fell in love with this Southern fanaticism, I was strongly in favor of the 'Constitution, the Union, and the enforcement of the laws,' and battled for it, with a large majority in the county, where I resided, against me. I adhered to it up to about the last of April Inst., when our Union Executive Committee got nervous, and fell into neutrality." Convinced that Kentucky "was drifting Palmetto-ward," Morey had done "a grand summersault, and have since been laboring for the advancement of that ruinous rebellion folly, secession." The editor lamented "its withering influence upon every healthy constitutional principle which I ever entertained." He tried "to shake it off, but could not, on account of my surroundings."[56]

Morey claimed that "after the Legislature met and enacted resolutions forgiving past offenses," he agreed to swear the loyalty oath and gave himself up for arrest so that he might prove his fealty. He was ready "to volunteer in the defence of my State, Kentucky, in good faith." Morey promised, "A large majority of the people of our State declare their determination to remain in the Union, and I will adhere to the will of the majority, because, I believe to submit to the majority is right and is the sheet anchor of a Republican government." The editor, a Mexican-American War veteran, promised he had never fought under any flag except "the 'Stars and Stripes.'" Thus, he "never could or would take up arms against it, and sooner than do so, I would exile myself from all those who are most dear to me in this life." He posited, "The fact that the General Government renders up fugitive slaves to their owners, has exploded all cause for rebellion in the South, in my opinion." He assured the *State Journal*'s editor "that such acts are of as much value to the Government, as an hundred soldiers at this time, because it disarms those who have gone to battle on that plea." Morey hoped for understanding from his fellow newspaperman. "I have been an editor and publisher myself, and many things have been said in my paper, which I did not and could not endorse, but as you are aware, an editor is made responsible for every sentiment uttered through his columns, and he often has more people to think for him, than he really wishes to be accountable for. Such has been my lot to a great extent, and for the purpose of relieving myself and disabusing the minds of many others in this and my own State, I put this forth."[57]

The *State Journal* was happy to publish Morey's recantations; it was a scoop, a reformed rebel's *mea culpa*. "We cheerfully give insertion to the well written communication of our Cynthiana friend who has been so unfortunate as to suffer as 'poor tray' suffered—by falling into bad company." Morey "is represented to us as a gentleman worthy of a better position than he just now *enjoys*. From his manly and straight forward statements concerning the influences that led him astray in Kentucky, we may judge how many others there are with less intelligence and prejudices perhaps more intense, who have been likewise deluded to their own and the country's harm." The Columbus paper was sure "that with his eyes opened to the delusion that had come upon him, and with the uprising of the latent loyalty that must live in so manly a heart, he will find the gentlemanly companionship of our officers in Camp Chase altogether to his liking. And he may be assured that the whole mass of our Southern brethren, manifesting a like spirit, would meet with a like reception at the hands of the North."[58]

The Yankee paper had been had. Morey had faked the letter to spring himself from prison. He hoped that what appeared to be a road to Damascus conversion to unionism would convince his jailers to release him temporarily so that he could visit his gravely ill wife. The trick worked, but she died before he reached Cynthiana. Instead of returning to Camp Chase, Morey made a break for the Confederacy, ending up in Memphis. He explained all in a December 11 letter to the *Memphis Avalanche.* Had Haldeman's phony "card" inspired Morey? He did not say so in his letter, but the *Avalanche* editor was surely overjoyed to print it, thereby humbling the *State Journal* with a genuine scoop. In any event, Morey described what he said were brutal conditions at Camp Chase. (Suffering was widespread in prisoner of war camps on both sides; just over 12 percent of captured Northern soldiers died in confinement, compared with 15.5 percent of Southerners.)[59]

Morey also described his arrest and the grueling trip to Camp Chase. He recounted that he and his three companions—Curry, Wherritt, and Glave—were arrested in Cynthiana and jailed at the Newport barracks, where they were locked "in the cells without even a blanket for twenty-four hours" before being taken across the Ohio to Cincinnati. Glave reportedly tried to defend himself with a pistol and a knife, but the soldiers subdued him. The diminutive Morey challenged one of the Yankees to a duel. At six foot two, the fellow was the largest soldier in his regiment. The Yankee, who described the editor as "a pompous little fellow," agreed to fight. Under the *code duello,* the soldier, as the challenged party, got to choose the weapons and the distance. He proposed "knives at one pace," and Morey wisely demurred.[60]

Morey also wrote that the soldiers briefly arrested local lawyer and former Southern Rights state representative William W. Cleary, who tried to free the quartet via a writ of habeas corpus. Afterward, the Kentuckians were "marched at night through the mud and the rain to the Little Miami Railroad depot," but the train had already left. So the soldiers turned their prisoners around and marched them another four miles to the Hamilton and Dayton station, where they boarded a train for Columbus. "During the march Judge Curry who is over seventy years of age being much fatigued came near giving out, but the captain of the guard with oaths gave orders to drive him up and they punched and struck him in the most brutal manner with their guns, kicking him at the same time." Glave, according to Morey, was also feeble and "unable to keep up, the pace being double-quick, was treated in the same savage manner. Our only offense was that we dissented from the measures of Lincoln." Because his letter to the *State Journal* had been so widely publicized, Morey felt compelled "to say something of the circumstances attending my escape from the Federal jailers." He got word that his "wife being in delicate health was taken dangerously ill after my arrest from the effects of the shock," so he "determined if possible to get out to see her before her death." Thus, he "wrote a letter feigning repentance which procured me a release on parole for ten days." When he reached Cynthiana, Morey found that his wife had been dead and buried for four days. "Considering that I was not bound by either law or honor to observe my parole having been dragged to Ohio for my political opinions in violation of the Constitutions of both the United States and Kentucky I embraced the opportunity to escape from my persecutors and after a very circuitous journey attended with many risks and perils I reached this city."[61]

Morey claimed he had visited Union soldiers in captivity in Memphis and found them well looked after. He concluded, "I do not whine nor ask the sympathies of any one. I am loose from Yankee despotism, and with my musket in one hand and the black flag of extermination to the foe in the other, I intend to avenge my own and my country's wrongs; and, if thoughts of a murdered wife and home made desolate, do not nerve my arm to strength and execution I should be an ignoble son of Kentucky."[62]

Back in the Bluegrass State, Prentice had also fallen for Morey's ruse. "The bitterest secession Editor in Kentucky for some time has been Andrew Jackson Morey, of the Cynthiana News," the *Journal* reported on October 8 under the headline "A Secession Editor's Confession." Prentice's paper noted Morey's arrest, reprinted most of his letter, and mused, "How many of the other secession Editors and ex-Editors of our State could possibly make similar confessions?"[63]

In his letter to the *Avalanche*, Morey noted that *Maysville Express* owner and editor George W. Forrest was also at Camp Chase. He and other local secessionists had been arrested by a hometown Yankee general—Nelson. "Bull" was "Lincoln's supple tool in Kentucky," said the *Courier*. "During the last three months," Nelson "has been the means of accomplishing more evil than he could be able to atone for if he lived to the age of Methuselah." He and his troops had also seized several important men in Covington and Newport, the *Courier* claimed, and the paper suspected these arrests had prompted Anderson's October 7 proclamation. Elsewhere, the *Courier* noted Morey's letter to the *State Journal,* giving his "full adhesion to the Lincoln government." The paper was sure he had written it "under compulsion"; otherwise, "it would debase him."[64]

The *Lexington Observer & Reporter* debased Morey on Christmas Day. The unionist paper reprinted the *Avalanche* story and mocked: "The people of Kentucky will be terribly alarmed when they find that Morey has seized his 'musket and raised the black flag.'" The paper jeered, "He is a real-fire eater in *his own* estimation—but a great scoundrel and coward in the *public* estimation." The *Paris Western Citizen* piled on, repeating the *Observer & Reporter*'s cutting commentary. Morey had allegedly joined the Confederate army and supposedly edited an issue of the *Vidette*, John Hunt Morgan's newspaper, when the "Thunderbolt of the Confederacy" and his troopers occupied Lexington. There is no evidence that he did, and "the pompous and theatrical language used by Morey in his newspaper validates the observations of the . . . soldier he had challenged to a duel."[65]

Other Confederate editors also opted for military service, notably Thomas Bell Monroe Jr. of the *Statesman*. The paper's "temporary" suspension was announced in the September 24 issue. "We know the howl of joy with which this announcement will be met," the *Statesman* sneered. "If it gives you joy to see a free paper suppressed . . . by its own voluntary choice, rejoice for such you now see." The paper, which had been losing money "in consequence of the prostration of business generally," alluded to the arrest of Durrett and the closing of the *Courier*. "We know that only a few days is left to us," so the paper ceased operations not out of fear but "in the sternest defiance to the most infamous and damnable tyranny that has existed on the face of the civilized earth in the last two hundred years." The *Statesman* would return "when the time comes that a free man can utter his sentiments without the Bastille in his face."[66]

Either Monroe wrote the suspension announcement at least four days in advance, or somebody else penned it. According to *History of the Orphan Brigade,* Monroe left Lexington for the Confederate lines on about September 20, and in October he became a major in Colonel Robert P. Trabue's Fourth Kentucky Infantry. The regiment was part of the storied Orphan Brigade, which received its baptism of fire at the Battle of Shiloh on April 6–7, 1861.[67]

Before the battle, Trabue was named commander of the brigade, and Monroe assumed command of the Fourth Infantry. He was mortally wounded at about 1:00 on the afternoon of April 7 and was carried to a field hospital. His brother, Captain Ben Monroe of the Fourth Kentucky, had been wounded and was also out of action. When Ben heard that his sibling was near death, soldiers helped him mount a horse, and off he rode to see his brother. "'Ah! old fellow,' said the dying major in a tone of brotherly affection and confidence, which showed too plainly that he had been anxiously looking and hoped to see him once more before his eyes were closed forever, 'I knew you would come!'" The captain remembered that his brother lived another two hours "without much suffering, perfectly sensible, and conversing freely." Ben added, "After expressing himself perfectly resigned to his fate and willing to die—then sending messages of love to his family—he expired quietly, consciously, and with more perfect calmness and serenity than I have ever witnessed in anyone before."[68]

The major was survived by his wife Elizabeth, a small son, and an infant daughter born after he left for the war. Upon Monroe's departure, his family had moved to Philadelphia, where they lived with Elizabeth's father, Supreme Court justice Robert C. Grier. She and her husband had agreed that she should stay there "until the issue should be determined, or until it should be considered prudent for her to visit him in the army." Thus, Monroe "bade them farewell—the beloved wife and idolized little boy—and each took the several way, she to her childhood's home, to endure the withering blight of absence made sickening with suspense; he to brave the diseases and suffering incident to a change of habits, and the dangers of the field." The Confederates left Monroe's body behind when they retreated into Mississippi. Union troops—perhaps Kentuckians—recognized the major and interred "him with the respect due a soldier and a hero." The Yankees carved his name in the trunk of the tree under which they buried him. Ben too succumbed to his wound. After the war, the brothers were exhumed and reburied side by side in the Frankfort Cemetery. Another Shiloh veteran was the *Courier*'s Robert McKee, who had volunteered as a civilian aide. He survived the battle, although his horse was shot from under him.[69]

A pair of Jackson Purchase editors also donned rebel gray. In the fall of 1861 the *Hickman Courier* closed, and editor Ed K. Warren joined the all-Purchase Seventh Kentucky Infantry, where he served as assistant quartermaster. The *Paducah Herald*'s John C. Noble enlisted as a private but was promoted to captain and wound up on the staff of General Abraham Buford, one of General Nathan Bedford Forrest's subordinate commanders. Editor Len Faxon evidently remained in the "Tennessee Tigers," because Edward I. Bullock took over the *Crescent*. After the Confederates occupied Columbus, he renamed it the *Daily Confederate News*, which cheered Warren and the rest of the Seventh Kentucky: "Let the brave Purchase boys rush to the standard and fill up these ranks, remembering, as says Erin's sweet bard: Far dearer the grave or a prison, / Illumed by the patriot's name, / Than thy trophies of all who have risen / On Liberty's ruin to fame!"[70]

Bullock aimed to make his paper "equal to any daily published in the South." He had worked it out so the *Confederate News* would be privy to "the earliest intelligence of every important result that may transpire in other sections, and also one by which we will be enabled to give our readers all the information touching the army in Kentucky and at this place which can be communicated, compatible with the safety of our troops and the success of our arms." In the November 1 issue, Bullock predicted that "this most unnatural war, forced up on the South by a bigoted and insolent party at the North, like all earthly things, must end sooner or later," but he admitted he did not know "when and how." Even so, Bullock was certain the war's termination would leave the South "a united people, under a constitutional government, in which individual and State rights will be fully recognized and protected."[71]

He also believed the border slave states would unite with the Confederacy sooner or later. Elsewhere in the paper, Bullock disdained the president, claiming "duplicity has marked Mr. Lincoln's administration from the time of the delivery of his inaugural to the present time." Yet "the ultra school of Abolitionists are clamorous and fierce in their denunciations of him because he will not openly endorse their Red Republican ideas of liberty, and by proclamation emancipate all the slaves in the Southern States." Bullock was confident that Lincoln, "in his heart of hearts, desires every slave freed, not so much from philanthropic considerations, as deep-seated hatred of Southerners; but then there are Missouri, Kentucky, Maryland, and little Delaware to be looked to, and such an ultra course he fears would effectually crush Unionism in these States." Rolling on, Bullock blasted Kentucky's "Abolition Legislature," sneering that Union lawmakers were "as much under the pay of Lincoln as the soldiers who have crossed the Ohio to invade the state." He decried neutrality as dishonorable, but what came afterward was worse, declared the editor: submission to the Yankees. "The people see and know this, though their legislators will not. —They have been sold like cattle on the hoof." Nonetheless, Bullock believed Kentucky "will come forth from her shroud with a shining countenance. She will pluck her star from the cold and cheerless banner of the frozen North, and set it where the impulses of the people are as warm and as generous as the Southern sun which shines on their escutcheon."[72]

Of course, the *Confederate News* despised all things Yankee. But Bullock's paper was particularly vitriolic toward local unionists, including Rufus Williams of Mayfield. When the judge tried to sign up Union troops in western Kentucky, the *Courier* let him have it. So did the *News*. The former reprinted Bullock's barb: "This gentleman . . . in direct violation of that [state] Constitution which he was sworn to protect, accepted of a Colonel's commission under Lincoln's government, and is endeavoring to raise a regiment." The *News* needled that some years before, Williams had been "utterly bankrupt in fortune and seriously damaged in character" and that "a trusting and confiding people, comprising this judicial district, made him all he is and more than he ever deserved to be." Then came the coup de grace: "With a full knowledge that nine-tenths of the people who elevated him to office, are heart and soul with the Confederate States, holding onto his office as Judge, he is endeavoring to prostitute that high place, to aid him in recruiting Lincoln forces. Whatever may be the issue of our unhappy difficulties, he is doomed. Nothing but curses and execrations will ever greet his ear from his old friends and constituents."[73]

The *Confederate News* fired an even more withering salvo on January 3. This time, Bullock's target was the whole Union army. "The time has come—the hour arrived—the period pregnant—we are determined to rush to the rescue of our country." The *News* claimed it was "ready and willing" to help fend off a Union attack on Columbus, "although we are no volunteer." Then came, arguably, the most bloodthirsty rant published in any rebel paper anywhere: "We want to kill a Yankee—must kill a Yankee—never can sleep sound again until we do kill a Yankee, get his overcoat and scalp. Indian-like, we want a scalp, and must have it. We'd think no more of scalping a dead Yank than cutting the throat of a midnight assassin—not a shade's difference between the murderer and the deceptious Yank."[74]

Discretion is the better part of valor, or so it is said. In any event, Bullock decamped from Columbus with the retreating Confederate army in early 1862. He went to Richmond, Virginia, the Confederate capital, and returned to Columbus in 1864. After settling in, some "deceptious Yanks" of the Second Illinois Cavalry took over the newspaper office and began publishing the *Federal Scout*. The paper lampooned the Confederates in poetry, prose, and artwork, including a cartoon based on advertisements for escaped slaves. The drawing, captioned "Secesh Leaving Columbus," showed a runaway rebel with a long stick resting on his shoulder and his belongings bound in a tiny bundle at the other end. A portly pig was depicted fleeing ahead of him. After the Yankees hit Paducah, the *Herald* was supplanted by the *Federal Union*, which was similar to the *Scout*.[75]

Meanwhile, with the *Courier* exiled to Bowling Green and the *Statesman* shut down, the *Yeoman* was the last of the big three pro-Confederate papers still publishing. At the same time, most of the small county weeklies were barely hanging on, and others ceased publishing for a variety of reasons. "The military authorities laid violent hands on some, and some were denied permission to buy print paper."[76]

One by one, the smaller Confederate papers also ceased publishing. In October 1861 the *Paris Flag* furled. But on September 25 the Bourbon County seat paper reported that the pro-Lincoln press was enjoying a good laugh over the arrest and imprisonment of Governor Morehead and other Kentuckians "run off to Indianapolis or Fort Lafayette." The *Flag* did not know the charge against Morehead but jeered, "for a great Southern Rights statesman of his calibre, it is sufficient for the despotism which now is trampling on all the great bulwarks of personal and political liberty, that he is for peace and neutrality, and opposed men and money to carry on the unnatural war which now desolates our country." The *Flag* was sure that, "to one versed in our law and Constitution," it seemed odd that Morehead was not being tried in federal court in Kentucky. After all, everybody accused had the right to "a speedy and impartial trial by a jury of the State and district in which the offense is committed." Yet "the law and Constitution are cobwebs, when they stand in the way of Lincoln's State necessity, which now overrides all written Constitutions. It does not suit our armed despotism to allow the least chance of the writ of *habeas corpus,* or the trial by a jury of the State or district." The *Flag* was curious "to see how the hearts and minds of the chivalrous freemen of Kentucky will submit to the incarceration of Governor Morehead, and other illustrious citizens."[77]

Also on September 25 the *Flag* claimed that, under Lincoln, "liberty of thought and speech is suppressed; the presses are silenced or destroyed; searches, seizures, and imprisonments, without defined charges or trials are continually perpetrated; the writ of *habeas corpus* suspended, and the supporters of the Government which order all these attacks on the bulwarks of liberty, boldly announce that State necessity is now the rightful and proper Government." The "Lincolnites" had jailed "all the prominent and talented leaders of Southern and States' rights" or threatened them "with dungeons." The paper warned, "We are rapidly running into the horrible condition of Missouri and Maryland. What can be done to avert such a horrid fate?"[78]

As the secessionist press fell silent, the *Observer & Reporter* claimed that all pro-Confederate Kentuckians, including rebel editors and publishers, were frauds and not true states' rights champions because they were disloyal to their state. The paper observed:

Assuming all along to be Simon-pure States' Rights men—to advocate to the fullest extent the doctrine of "State Sovereignty"—a doctrine that assumes the right of a State to regulate its external as well as its internal relations and policy; that, whenever Kentucky so announced her position, no matter what it might be, it was the duty of all good citizens to yield implicit obedience; and Kentucky, by the only power possessed of authority to act in the premises, having assumed that her position should be one of loyalty to the Federal

Union; yet we find these very men now refusing to respect the enactments of her constituted authorities thus officially assumed. This is a fair sample of what Secession will cause its votaries to do. They respect no principle, no matter how long and how strenuously advocated by them; if it offers an obstacle to their designs; and impelled by the one controlling idea—an idea involving treason to the Government—they can become the advocates of any dogma no matter to what it leads or where it ends.[79]

Secessionist politicians, boosted by the secessionist press, failed to pry the Bluegrass State out of the Union. Nonetheless, some die-hard disunionists took one last stab at a Confederate Kentucky. A group of Confederate sympathizers from thirty-two counties—almost all of them pro-Union to one degree or another—managed to get behind rebel lines at Russellville, near Bowling Green. They assembled on October 29, condemned the unionist General Assembly, declared its actions illegal, and begged Magoffin to convene the legislature outside Union lines. The secessionists knew the governor could not comply even if he wanted to, and the Union lawmakers would never leave Frankfort. So they called a sovereignty convention for Russellville on November 18. In the interim, a committee composed of John C. Breckinridge and others was named to carry the program forward.[80]

On October 31 the *Courier* reported on the preliminary Russellville gathering, claiming that "about fifty counties" were "informally represented." This amounted to an admission, however unintentional, that the state was far from fully represented and that the delegates were self-appointed and had simply shown up of their own volition. Nonetheless, the secessionists "assembled, and, for the purpose of preserving order and maintaining decorum in their deliberations, chose George W. Johnson of Scott County to preside." The paper explained, "The object of this conference . . . [is] we understand to be not to establish a provisional or temporary government." Rather, the idea was to discuss what could be done to preserve and protect "the liberties of the people and . . . their property and legal rights as guaranteed by the Constitution of the State." The *Courier* declined to predict what might happen in November. But clearly Haldeman and his paper were in deep denial. Kentuckians' "sympathies, inclinations, and interests are with the Confederate States," the *Courier* maintained. "Their minds revolt at the idea of joining their arms with those of the North in the war now being so ruthlessly waged against the right of the people to govern themselves." Even though Kentuckians had clearly chosen the Union over secession in three free elections, the paper insisted that they were "the victims of a monstrous fraud, perpetuated on them by men in whose honor they confided and to whom they had long looked as political leaders whose guide they could follow with propriety and safety."[81]

In subsequent issues, the paper provided more details about the meeting, which named Congressman Burnett its chairman and editor McKee its secretary. More secessionists showed up at the appointed time—as many as 200 of them from sixty-five counties—yet all but a few of the counties were unionist. The convention was in session for two days as the members passed a secession ordinance and nailed together the framework of a provisional state "government" with George Johnson as governor and unionist-leaning Bowling Green as Kentucky's Confederate "capital." The *Courier*'s McKee was named secretary of state, and Haldeman was appointed state printer. Although the proceedings had no legal basis and clearly reflected only minority opinion, the Confederacy admitted Kentucky as its thirteenth "state" on December 10. A similarly bogus government got Missouri in as number twelve.[82]

The *Courier* was overjoyed when the Confederates welcomed Kentucky into the fold. "HUZZA! HUZZA!! Kentucky in the Confederacy!" its headline read on December 11. The *Courier* got the "joyous news" by telegraph from Richmond that Kentucky was "an equal member of the Confederate States." The announcement was sure to "cause a thrill of delight in every portion of our good old Commonwealth," it reported. Kentuckians "will feel a strong sense of security now that the powerful arm of the Confederate Government is extended over them and pledged to their protection and to the full and complete redemption of the State from the Abolition invaders who are now polluting a portion of her fair soil." The paper beat the war drum: "Let every man who is physically able, whatever his condition, at once shoulder his musket and give the aid of his strong right arm towards the immediate and unconditional redemption of glorious old Kentucky from the tyrant's clutches! Let your blows fall thick, fast and heavy! Let your soil be enriched by the blood of the Yankees who have insolently sought to conquer and subjugate you!"[83]

A Yankee victory would mean "the absolute and unconditional emancipation of the slaves," the *Courier* warned, sounding the tocsin of white supremacy anew. But first the paper focused on economics, claiming that freeing Kentucky's slaves "would be to destroy at one blow more than one-fifth of the taxable property of the State" and slash total revenues by 20 percent. Slaveholders would be reduced to beggary, Kentucky agriculture would be ruined, and "the whole Commonwealth [made] poorer." The race-baiting followed; already, Lincoln and his generals recognized blacks as human beings, not property, the paper hissed. Should the president and his blue-clad soldiers "obtain and maintain the ascendancy in Kentucky," they would free the state's 225,000 slaves "and confer upon them, as in Massachusetts, Ohio, and other free States, all the political privileges and immunities of free men!" Slaves would be led from their quarters and made "the equals in all respects of the white men, whose wisdom has given laws to the Commonwealth; and whose valor has made the name of Kentuckians forever famous!"[84]

The *Courier* again pandered to poor whites who had no slaves. It conjured the specter of "two hundred and twenty-five thousand negroes . . . taken from the service of their masters and made the equals of the non-slaveholder at the ballot box, on the witness stand, on the jury bench, in the Common schools, and in the halls of legislation, and his rivals in all the mechanical, agricultural, and professional pursuits of life!" In the end, state political power would thus "pass from the hands of the free white men into those of the black ones!" Kentucky would end up the same as Massachusetts and Ohio, except that the state "will have a free negro population five times as large in proportion to the whole number of her inhabitants as either of those States!" The screed ended with a call to arms: "Unless the free white men of Kentucky are ready to be reduced to equality, and compelled to fraternization with their emancipated negroes, they will answer from the mouths of their rifles." Any white son of Kentucky who donned Yankee blue or shrunk "meanly . . . from the bloody arbitrament" was "so abject in spirit, or debauched in feeling, and already so degraded in his own estimation, that the badge of a master, the insignia of slavery, would be to him a source of such pride as such a creature can feel and such consolation as a thing like him can enjoy."[85]

Meanwhile, the Union press gleefully ridiculed the Russellville convention for purporting to reflect the true sentiment of Kentucky. The *Louisville Democrat* jabbed at men who claimed to represent counties "whose people would spurn such representatives." The paper was "amused to see that these fellows are acting, not under any human Constitution, but under the law of God." The *Democrat* found it "strange if they don't improve on the laws of God. So much wisdom ought to amend the old code some." The paper declared that the secessionists had "tried their quack nostrums upon Kentucky, and failed. This last is a desperate effort in a desperate cause, and comes rather too late to be bold; it is only impudent." The disunionists, it charged, "run away and take up arms against Kentucky, and are then weak enough to complain that their rights are not respected—grunting that they are not protected by laws they defy." The *Democrat* dared, "Come and take your rights if you can get them."[86]

The *Observer & Reporter* also questioned the credentials of the conventioneers. The only ones who could claim any legitimacy were six deep western Kentucky house members elected in August—all but one from the Jackson

Purchase—plus a sitting Purchase senator and Congressman Burnett, who presided. "These men, few in number and with no extraordinary claims to public confidence to entitle their revolutionary designs to the slightest consideration, are undertaking to speak for the people of Kentucky, and to assume the powers which rightfully belong to their chosen representatives," the paper criticized. "It might well be asked, if the whole affair did not bear upon its face the imprint of the ludicrous, who constituted these forty or fifty refugees from their counties representatives to act for the people upon questions involving all that is sacred to them as individuals or as citizens? Who conferred upon them the power to determine not the future position, but the very existence of the Commonwealth?"[87]

The *Journal* threw its share of punches. After the October meeting adjourned, the paper confessed to being in the dark as to whether the movement to establish a Confederate government in Kentucky had fallen "to pieces in the meantime" or "fizzled regularly at Russellville or irregularly elsewhere." But the paper was certain "that the movement has ere now fizzled in one way or the other. Laughed to scorn by all good citizens as a freak of lawless effrontery and of braggart impotence, and stigmatized even by prominent rebels as tending 'to bring secession and revolution into contempt,' it must prove as shortlived as despicable. If it doesn't, the rebel mind is steeped in depravity and fatuity even further than we conceive. The movement displays all the folly of the meeting of 'The Three Tailors in Tooley Street' without any of the innocence."[88]

The *Journal*'s prognostication was correct. The provisional government, such as it was, collapsed in early 1862 when the Confederates gave up Kentucky. In February, Grant's capture of Fort Henry, on the Tennessee River just below the Kentucky state line, and Fort Donelson, on the Cumberland River at Dover, Tennessee, forced the Confederates out of the Bluegrass State. But in September, Southern armies under generals Braxton Bragg and Edmund Kirby Smith invaded Kentucky. When the rebels menaced Frankfort, the legislature and Governor James F. Robinson (Magoffin had resigned under pressure in August) decamped by train to Louisville. The rebels arrived on September 3; Frankfort was the only capital of a loyal state the Confederates captured during the war.[89]

Local secessionists, including *Yeoman* editor S. I. M. Major, welcomed the rebels. He stayed at the paper, but Kirby Smith authorized his brother, John B. Major, to raise a regiment of infantry. Perhaps anticipating a Yankee return, Major legally transferred ownership of the *Yeoman* and the rest of his business enterprises to his mother.[90]

The secessionists were not content just to see a Confederate flag flying over an empty capitol. They aimed to resurrect the provisional government. Johnson was dead; while fighting as a civilian volunteer, he was mortally wounded at the Battle of Shiloh. The Confederates settled on Richard Hawes of Paris as the new governor and scheduled his "inauguration" for October 4. The *Yeoman* provided publicity, reporting the arrival of Bragg, Kirby Smith, and other rebel brass on October 3. The paper claimed the citizenry could count on festivities "more imposing than have ever heretofore attended the installation of a chief magistrate of Kentucky." The *Yeoman* predicted that "the military display will far exceed anything of the kind ever witnessed at the State Capital; the throng of citizen spectators will be unusually large for a time of war." Bragg duly installed Hawes, but the rebel government at Frankfort was even shorter-lived than its initial incarnation at Russellville. Just as the ceremony was ending, messengers rushed in with news that General Joshua Sill's Union division was closing in on the capital, and the Confederates hastily withdrew. On October 8 at Perryville, Bragg's army collided with General Don Carlos Buell's Union forces in the bloodiest battle fought on Kentucky soil. Tactically, the fight was a draw, but Bragg retreated to Tennessee. Never again were the Confederates able to threaten Kentucky in such strength, although cavalry raiders and guerrillas plagued the state until the end of the war. Despite its open embrace of the rebel invaders, the *Yeoman* lasted until 1863, when it too was silenced, "not only on account of the browbeating its editor got at the hands of the military, but also on examining its subscription lists, it was found that the paper was pursuing a policy against the prevailing sentiment of the community."[91]

Meanwhile, in 1862 federal officials shut down two Louisville papers as disloyal. But these suppressed sheets were different from the others; they were religious publications—the *Baptist Recorder* and the *True Presbyterian*. The former survives as the *Western Recorder,* said to be the second oldest Baptist paper in the country. The latter reappeared in 1863, but federal authorities closed it for good in 1864. The Reverend Charles Y. Duncan edited the *Recorder,* and the Reverend Dr. Stuart Robinson was editor of the *True Presbyterian.* Robinson's Southern-sympathizing paper and Breckinridge's *Danville Quarterly Review*—which also ended in 1864—were fierce rivals. Duncan was lodged in the military prison in Louisville, but evidently not for long. Robinson, pastor at Louisville's Second Presbyterian Church, had fled to Canada.[92]

8

The Rebirth of the Old Rebel Press and the Thorny Issue of Censorship in Wartime

Kentucky became intensely pro-Southern after the war, a fact reflected in the resurgence of the old Confederate press. Although some of the papers did not survive the war, many did. Walter Haldeman returned to Louisville and resumed publishing the *Courier,* which soon had a greater circulation than both the *Journal* and the *Democrat.* In 1868 he bought out his rivals. The new paper, the Democratic *Louisville Courier-Journal,* was edited by Henry Watterson, a former Confederate soldier and journalist. The *Frankfort Yeoman* was back in business, too, though ironically, the *Kentucky Statesman's* new owners turned it Republican. Other secessionist publications such as the *Covington Journal, Cynthiana News, Hickman Courier,* and *Paducah Herald* became conservative Democratic organs. While the rebel editors and publishers represented the minority opinion during the war, they found themselves in step with most Kentuckians afterward. Yet from the war's end to today, the question has persisted: was the Lincoln administration justified in suppressing hostile newspapers?

The resurrection of the former secessionist press in postwar Kentucky mirrored the Bluegrass State's newfound nostalgia for the defeated Confederacy, whose armies surrendered in April and May 1865. "The conservative racial, social, political, and gender values inherent in Confederate symbols and the Lost Cause greatly appealed to many white Kentuckians, who despite their devotion to the Union had never entered the war in order to free slaves," historian Ann E. Marshall explained. "In a postwar world where racial boundaries were in flux, the Lost Cause and the conservative politics that went with it seemed not only a comforting reminder of a past free of late nineteenth-century insecurities but also a way to reinforce contemporary efforts to maintain white supremacy." Reflective of white sentiment, the Democratic and white supremacist General Assembly refused to ratify the Thirteenth Amendment to the Constitution, which ended the last vestiges of slavery; the Fourteenth, which made African Americans citizens; and the Fifteenth, which extended the vote to black males.[1]

Kentucky was filled with "belated Confederates," wrote Aaron Astor in *Rebels on the Border*. "Conservative Unionists who had fought against the Confederacy during the Civil War morally identified with their former Confederate foes in the war's aftermath," he observed. "They became, in essence, belated Confederates, and they shared with the genuine rebels a celebration of the Confederate cause, sacrifice and narrative of the Civil War." As Astor pointed out, the postwar period in the border states was marked by a "near total absence of white Unionist commemoration. . . . In essence former Unionists completely yielded public space to pro-Confederate propagandists."[2]

Likewise, in *The Rivers Ran Backwards*, Christopher Phillips wrote that "acceptance of Lost Cause precepts facilitated the evolution of southernness for wartime Confederates" in Kentucky and other border states. "As southerners they saw themselves as upholders of the founders' vision, as well as keepers of the social and cultural ideals on which the nation had formed and prospered." Phillips explained that "slavery was the lynchpin"; it had preserved white supremacy. At the same time, "proximity to northern social and political imperatives, including racial and ethnic pluralism, in contrast with the traditionalism of former slave states, heightened their sense of southernness."[3]

The *Courier*, the *Yeoman*, and the other ex-rebel papers that were back in print banged the drum for the Democratic Party and white supremacy. Most white Kentuckians, even Yankee veterans, eagerly stepped to the beat. At the same time, the late Thomas Bell Monroe Jr. would have been aghast at the changes at the *Statesman*. S. R. Smith, its new owner, had turned it into one of state's few Republican organs.[4]

William O. Goodloe, the *Statesman*'s editor, rebuked the rise of the Democrats, whose leaders included many ex-Confederate soldiers, officials of the state's short-lived rump rebel government, and outspoken Southern sympathizers: "What [Confederate General] Bragg failed to do in 1862, with his army and banners, the people of Kentucky, five years later, have done; they have given the State over into the hands of those who are and have been the enemies of the Union." The *Frankfort Commonwealth* complained, "The

'Lost Cause' is found again in Kentucky." Perhaps that rediscovery prompted Albert Gallatin Hodges to give his printing company to his son and move to Louisville in 1872. At any rate, a dismayed Republican wrote, "Kentucky is today as effectually in the hands of rebels as if they had every town and city garrisoned by their troops. . . . What is to become of the poor blacks and loyal white men God only knows."[5]

After fleeing Louisville in 1861, Haldeman vowed to return and restart the *Courier* when the Confederate flag flew over the Falls City. The Stars and Stripes stayed atop local flagpoles until the war's end, but after the guns fell silent in 1865, he came home in triumph. Helped by friends, Haldeman reestablished the *Courier* and enjoyed quick success. This might have surprised him, as Louisville had been a unionist stronghold. But after the war the city largely embraced the Lost Cause, and soon the *Courier* boasted a larger circulation than its old enemies the *Journal* and the *Democrat*. Haldeman bought out the competition in 1868, and the *Louisville Courier-Journal* was born, the first issue rolling off the presses on November 8. "The consolidation of two such presses enables us to produce a journal superior in every respect to its predecessors," readers were advised. Curiously, the announcement did not mention the *Democrat*, although for many years the *Courier-Journal*'s masthead proclaimed it to be a merger of the three papers. Haldeman would run the business, and Henry Watterson, Prentice's young editor, would assume the "editorial management." Sixty-seven-year-old Prentice would stay as one of the new paper's "complete and efficient corps of writers, reporters and correspondents." Three decades earlier, Haldeman had started in the newspaper business as a lowly clerk under Prentice at the *Journal*. Now Prentice would close out his career as one of Haldeman's junior-level editors.

Watterson had succeeded Prentice at the *Journal*. He, too, represented a different Louisville. He was an ex-rebel soldier, though evidently a reluctant one. The son of a Tennessee congressman, he had been born in Washington, DC, in 1840. When the war started, he went home to the Volunteer State, intending to fight for neither side. Apparently, peer pressure led him to enlist, and he spent the conflict on the staffs of generals Leonidas Polk, Joseph E. Johnston, John Bell Hood, and Nathan Bedford Forrest. But his pen proved more valuable to the South than his sword. Watterson ended up as editor of the *Chattanooga Rebel*, said to be the Confederate army's most widely read paper. Emulating his father, Watterson tossed his hat in the ring for the Confederate Congress from Tennessee's Fourth District. Naturally, he announced his candidacy in newspapers, including the October 17, 1861, edition of the *Courier*-in-exile. Editor Haldeman met editor Watterson in Chattanooga during the war. Thirty years after the shooting stopped, Watterson spoke at the opening of the national encampment of the Grand Army of the Republic (GAR) in Louisville. (The GAR was a Union veterans' organization similar to the American Legion, started by US veterans after World War I.) Marshall quoted the ex-rebel's greeting to those assembled: "You came and we resisted you . . . you come and we greet you; for times change and men change with them." The irony of a former Johnny Reb welcoming them was not missed by the old Union soldiers. Marshall pointed out another irony: "Along with many of his fellow white Kentuckians, Watterson seemed to overlook the fact that his home city stood with the Union during the Civil War and had served as a major supply center for the Union army." Marshall also noted that a tall, almost brand new Confederate monument stood just a few blocks from where the ex-Yankees met.[6]

Just as Prentice had always been the *Journal,* the *Courier-Journal* bore Watterson's indelible stamp. Supposedly, Prentice and Watterson became enemies, although both denied there was bad blood between them. Prentice was unwell physically and financially, if not emotionally. He apparently profited little from the sale of the *Journal.* His wife, Harriette, died in 1868 at age fifty. Perhaps symbolic of his fading health, happiness, fame, and fortune, Prentice let his gray beard and hair grow long and unkempt. His ex-rebel son Clarence added to his pecuniary woes. Clarence was less than successful in business and farming pursuits and frequently turned to his father for money. In turn, Prentice looked to Haldeman for help in bailing out Clarence. It is not difficult to imagine Prentice's mortification at having to go, cap in hand, to his old and bitter rival, a rebel he had vilified as a traitor worthy of the hangman's rope. Nonetheless, letters that Prentice wrote to Haldeman proved that his love for his sole surviving offspring trumped all. The entreaties survive in the Haldeman Family Papers at the Filson Historical Society in Louisville. Most of the missives are undated.[7]

Prentice was struggling to make ends meet himself; he lodged at the paper to save money, "working, eating, [and] sleeping" in a small room and seldom going out because of his poor health. In one letter he told Haldeman that he owed city and railroad taxes on $30,000 worth of property. If he did not pay up, his holdings would have to be sold. Prentice was scrupulously courteous to his boss. "I very much hate to put you to the slightest inconvenience but I should be exceedingly glad to get, to-day, what you find to be due me." In a postscript he jotted, "I shall try hard, on both our accounts, to make this the best year of my life."[8]

Clarence had started a distillery but was still struggling, prompting his father to ask Haldeman for a raise. "I was thirty-one dollars last week. I beg you to try to make it forty to-day even if it requires some effort." Prentice assured Haldeman, "You may always rely upon any efforts from me that can be of service to you." In other messages, Prentice sought money to help Clarence pay his farmhands. In every letter, Prentice apologized to Haldeman for inconveniencing him. In one, he ended his plea by pledging to "exhaust what remains of my life in work." Prentice was convinced "that no other editor toils as I do," explaining that he typically passed "24 hours a day in my room and should pass more if the days were longer."[9]

Prentice was nearing death by the waning weeks of 1869. On November 8 he wrote to Haldeman that he was not well but was "determined to resume hard work." Again, he mentioned that Clarence sorely needed money. On Christmas Day he asked Haldeman for $40. He had been too ill to work since the eighteenth but was confident that "most of the editorials have been mine." He closed by wishing the publisher "a Happy Christmas." Influenza claimed Prentice's life on January 22, 1870. He was sixty-seven. Clarence was killed in 1873 in a buggy accident in Louisville. He was thirty-four.[10]

Prentice's *Courier-Journal* obituary took up almost four columns. "It becomes our duty, and we have never had a more melancholy duty, to announce the death of George D. Prentice," it began. The death notice was a paean to Prentice from start to finish and glossed over his longtime feud with Haldeman's *Courier*. Prentice had scorched Confederates and secessionist Kentuckians, including the *Courier* chief, as the rankest of villains and traitors. According to his obituary, Prentice "did not conceal his warm sympathies for the Southern people, who had so steadfastly befriended him for thirty years." It described his unionism in heroic terms. "But nothing could turn him from his devotion to the Union, as it then was, and for which he repeatedly declared he would lay down his life." The next two sentences apparently referred to Haldeman and Prentice: "These friends parted in coolness, the one to battle in a lost cause, the other to sustain the winning side. But when the war ended Mr. Prentice was one of the first to greet his old friend with accustomed cordiality."[11]

With Watterson in charge of the morning *Courier-Journal*, the millionaire Haldeman started the afternoon *Louisville Times* in 1884. The idea was to complement the *Courier-Journal* and challenge the upstart *Evening Post*. Afterward, he forsook Louisville and headed south again—this time voluntarily—and helped found Naples, Florida, as a vacation spot. During a visit back home, a Louisville streetcar struck the eighty-one-year-old Haldeman on May 10, 1902, and he succumbed three days later.[12]

Whereas Haldeman had opted for sunnier climes, his old friend Samuel Major stayed in Frankfort. The political climate had warmed up considerably for office seekers like the old rebel editor. In 1867 he was elected mayor of

Frankfort and the capital city's representative in the state house. He served four years in city hall but apparently did not run for reelection to the state house in 1869. Nonetheless, the voters returned him to the house in 1885. He also resumed his old job as public printer and held that post for several years. Both Major and the *Yeoman* expired in 1886. "In the social circle Col. S. I. M. Major was one of the most agreeable and entertaining men we ever knew," read his obituary in the *Frankfort Roundabout*. "It was there that his friends knew and loved him best. Under the warming influence of their enjoyment his conversation, wit and wisdom would flow from his lips in a brilliant stream." As a "Democrat of the strictest school," Major "always gave and received the sturdiest blows that could fall, but in private life his personal friendships were not bounded by his political horizon. He scorned the little meanness of narrow-minded men, and was charitable in his judgements to all." Major died impoverished and despondent, said the paper. "In late years, misfortunes fell thick and fast about his pathway. He saw his fortune drift away, until at last his house, home, and library were all gone, and then, a broken-hearted man, he laid himself down in sorrow to breathe his last."[13]

Elsewhere in the state, the *Covington Journal*, which had ceased operations in 1862, came back conservative and Democratic; it lasted until 1876. The *Paducah Herald*'s John C. Noble returned to the city in 1865 and published the paper as a Democratic daily, triweekly, and weekly. He sold the *Herald*'s news and printing departments to two other local papers in 1871. Ink still coursing through his veins, Noble restarted the *Herald* sometime around 1874, but the paper survived only a few months. He died on January 21, 1901, at age eighty-six, succumbing to "general debility, after a brief illness," according to his obituary in the *Paducah Sun*. It described Noble as Kentucky's oldest newspaperman. "Dissolution was calm and peaceful, but the demise of this well known and popular man came as a great shock to his hundreds off friends throughout the city, who thought his illness was only temporary, and not in any way dangerous," the *Sun* explained. Noble and his wife had celebrated their sixty-second anniversary on December 3 and his birthday the next day. Besides his spouse, eight children survived him. Also in the Purchase, the *Hickman Courier* reappeared in 1866 with George Warren as editor. The *Henderson Reporter* hung on until 1883.[14]

Unlike the *Paducah Herald* and the *Hickman Courier*, there was no rebirth for the *Columbus Crescent–Confederate News* or the *Mayfield Southern Yeoman*, which had perished during the war. Len Faxon, formerly of the *Crescent*, returned to the Purchase after the war, settling in Paducah and editing the *Herald* for his old friend Noble. "After making himself the master bantam of that town," he supposedly "dropped his faber [pencil]" to pursue "other and more promising schemes." He died on November 27, 1895, apparently in Paducah.[15]

More than halfway across the state, the prodigal A. J. Morey came home to Cynthiana and revived the *News.* The paper had resumed publishing in October 1865 as the *Cynthiana Times.* After Morey became the editor, he renamed it the *News;* the first issue came out on December 7. In it, he pledged to use the paper to help "heal up the differences which have divided this nation." He became a disciple of Watterson's "New Departure" editorializing, which had the *Courier-Journal* chief entreating Kentuckians to put the war and slavery behind them, support a state and federal role in the economy, accept at least limited African American rights, and modernize and industrialize like the Yankees were doing up north. Watterson had another ally in the *Lexington Observer & Reporter,* even though it, the *Courier-Journal,* the *Cynthiana News,* and other Democratic papers supported white supremacy and opposed the federal Reconstruction program for the defeated South. Like the *Statesman,* the *Observer & Reporter* had switched sides, but in the opposite direction. Under the editorship of W. C. P. Breckinridge and later George Washington Ranck, the paper turned Democratic. Breckinridge was a Confederate veteran and a son of Robert J. Breckinridge.[16]

Despite his sop toward reconciliation, Morey could be as irascible as ever and was not prone to forgive Yankees such as Major General Stephen G. Burbridge of Georgetown, whom Southern sympathizers in the Bluegrass State still despised as the "Butcher of Kentucky." Burbridge had become commander in Kentucky in 1864, when the state was overrun with Confederate raiders and guerrillas. He cracked down hard on the marauders and on citizens who helped them. Burbridge imprisoned a number of civilians as traitors and had guerrillas and spies executed. On November 15, 1864, he ordered Walter Ferguson hanged in Lexington for spying. Three years later, when Burbridge was apparently trying to vindicate himself, the *News* responded with "a very abusive and bitter article." The piece, published on November 21, 1867, taunted Burbridge; its anonymous author—Morey—demanded to know if Ferguson's ghost haunted him. "Can he forget the appeals the ladies of Lexington made to him in behalf of this youth, and how he spurned them from his presence, and doomed him to an infamous death?" Could Burbridge "have forgotten so early how he sent young Jameson and Reece, of Harrison co., to eternity for no other cause than that they were rebel soldiers?" On the article went, mocking: "Has the death of Thornt. Lafferty passed out of his mind? And many others we could mention." If so, the writer warned, "let him be assured the people have not filled their places yet; and that their homes are desolate and dreary to-day on account of their absence, and that their memory is fresh and green in the hearts of the people of Ky."[17]

Oscar H. Burbridge of Bourbon County took up for his brother, confronting Morey as he stepped off a streetcar in Covington. He demanded to know who had written the article. Morey offered to name the author if Burbridge would come to Cynthiana. Then Morey agreed to tell Burbridge in Covington the next day. They met on the morrow, both armed with pistols. Burbridge whacked Morey with his cane, causing the editor "to reel toward the street." Both men went for their pistols, but Burbridge was quicker. He shot Morey in the right arm, the bullet burrowing "into his side, inflicting a dangerous wound" and forcing Morey to drop his firearm. He recovered and later described the gunfight as "a contest as to which should get the first shot." Burbridge was charged with shooting Morey with intent to kill, but a Covington jury found him not guilty. Morey continued to publish the *News* until 1886; ten years later, he ran unsuccessfully for Congress as a Democrat. Morey died on November 25, 1907, at age eighty. Eccentric to the end of his newspaper career, the editor had in his office at the *News* "an imposing stone taken from a graveyard," the *Maysville Public Ledger* noted in his death notice. "On the bottom of the stone were the words: 'Sacred to the memory of —.' Etc." Before the Civil War, the *Louisville Courier* had praised Morey as "a blooming specimen of the rural editorial fraternity."[18]

Haldeman, Morey, Breckinridge, and Major were typical of many ex-Confederates who excelled in the press in postwar Kentucky. Other rebel veterans and Southern sympathizers were business and political leaders. Postwar governors included Simon Bolivar Buckner, a former Confederate general, and James B. McCreary, a rebel lieutenant colonel. Scorned as traitors during the war, the former secessionist civilians and soldiers became heroes afterward. Republicans, many of them the most ardent unionists in 1861–1865, would be marginalized for many years. African Americans would suffer as second-class citizens for a century. Kentucky would become the northern border of the white supremacist, Democratic, Jim Crow "Solid South."[19]

The First Amendment to the US Constitution, often called "the sheet anchor of the republic," guarantees a free press. But Article III, section 3 empowers the federal government to punish traitors. The trick, of course, is balancing the former with the latter. Such equilibrium was never more difficult to maintain than during the Civil War, especially in loyal border states like Kentucky, where sentiment was divided.[20]

Kentucky's Confederate press argued that the state should separate from both the Constitution and the nation. In three elections in 1861, Kentucky spurned secession. In September 1861, after Confederate and then Union forces invaded neutral Kentucky, the Union-majority legislature—most of whose members had been elected or reelected the month before—ordered only the Confederates to withdraw, thus putting Kentucky squarely on the Union side in the war. So despite the objections of a noisy secessionist minority, Kentucky remained under the US Constitution, which defines treason as making war on the United States "or in adhering to their enemies, giving them aid and comfort." The rebel editors and publishers embraced an armed rebellion against the United States, and they encouraged Kentucky to join it.[21]

In the last analysis, arguments over the issue of press censorship in wartime boil down to where to draw the line between a free people's right to know and a democratic government's right to defend itself. At no point in American history was the Union more imperiled than during the Civil War. Did hostile newspapers—notably Kentucky's rebel press—significantly add to that peril? Was the Lincoln administration, through General Anderson, justified in silencing the *Louisville Courier* and other secessionist sheets?

"It may also be argued that the Lincoln administration exercised *less* newspaper control than it might have imposed during so widespread a civil war," Harold Holzer wrote in *Lincoln and the Power of the Press*. "The government never attempted to impose formal limits on dissent, or to suggest precisely where criticism ended and treason began." Elsewhere in the book he asked, "Did press dissent really pose an existential threat to national security?" His answer: "Probably not, certainly not in the free, loyal Northern states."[22]

Of course, there was no danger of New York or Ohio or Illinois joining the Confederacy or furnishing the South with large numbers of soldiers. Kentucky was decidedly different; it was a border slave state. Although the state ultimately stayed under the Stars and Stripes, it was hard to predict which way Kentucky might go in the secession crisis. A president less patient than Lincoln might have invaded Kentucky when it adopted neutrality and refused to furnish troops to help save the Union of which it was a part. Lincoln thought Kentucky was unionist at heart, but he could not be sure. The state's large and vociferous secessionist press made disunion sentiment seem stronger than it actually was. While Kentucky ultimately rejected secession, many of its citizens—including some of the rebel editors—donned Confederate gray. Many others remained unrepentantly rebel to the war's end.

Kentucky's rebel editors and publishers preached unvarnished treason, yet they, like secessionists everywhere, saw themselves as patriots fighting for "liberty" in the mold of the nation's revolutionary founders. They were, as historian James M. McPherson points out, counterrevolutionaries fighting for the right of whites to keep African Americans in bondage. The Confederate press called for armed rebellion against the federal government, applying to Lincoln epithets like "dictator," "usurper," and "tyrant." The same and similar words have been used to describe the likes of Adolf Hitler, Joseph Stalin, Muammar Gadhafi, and Saddam Hussein. Those men routinely shot, hanged, tortured, and meted out long prison sentences to offending journalists. Lincoln did not. His suppression of critical newspapers in Kentucky and elsewhere in the Union may have been undemocratic in the strictest sense. But his larger goal was the preservation of the Union and American democracy—however imperfect. As the conflict progressed, he broadened the Union's war aims to include the elimination of slavery, the most undemocratic of institutions.

Holzer is an eminent scholar. He is perhaps the nation's foremost authority on Lincoln and the press. But he, like all of us who write history from a twenty-first-century perspective, has the advantage of hindsight. We know how the war turned out. Lincoln was fighting to save the Union with almost nothing to guide his footsteps. The Constitution is silent about what the federal government is supposed to do in the event of secession and civil war. One part of the national charter safeguards a free press, and another grants the government the power to protect itself against traitors. Did Lincoln overreact in silencing hostile papers in the free states? Perhaps he did. But federal authorities acted correctly and prudently in suppressing the *Courier* and the rest of Kentucky's rebel press. There was no chance of any Northern free state exiting the Union to join an independent confederacy of Southern slave states. But the possibility of Kentucky forsaking the Stars and Stripes for the Stars and Bars was real.

Even though their actions fell under the constitutional definition of treason, Kentucky's rebel editors and publishers suffered only the mildest of consequences. They could no longer print their papers—but otherwise, they were free men. A few, like Reuben Durrett, spent relatively short stretches behind bars and were allowed to go home after pledging allegiance to the Union. Had Haldeman and Morey been caught and imprisoned, it seems almost certain that they, too, would have been turned loose upon swearing the loyalty oath. After the war ended, many of the secessionist editors and publishers resurrected their papers and resumed their careers.

The fate of the secessionist editors would have been decidedly less happy in most other countries. In the mid-nineteenth century the crowned heads of Europe (except for Great Britain, which had a constitutional monarchy) and Emperor Napoleon III of France heavily censored the press in war and peace. Offending journalists forfeited their freedom and sometimes their lives, or they were forced to flee. The common punishment for treason was death or long-term, even lifetime, imprisonment.

According to a posting on the First Amendment Center's website, "Lincoln's governing principle—that a nation must be able to protect itself in wartime against expression that causes insubordination or actually obstructs the raising of armies—was 'absolutely opposed,' said [noted free-speech scholar Zechariah] Chafee [Jr.], to the continuation of such practices once 'the emergency had passed.'" The happy postwar fate of most of Kentucky's Confederate editors and publishers is ample proof of that. "However problematic the actions of the president and his subordinates, at least Lincoln had the good sense to cease censorship once the underlying danger had abated." The posting continued: "While President Lincoln's wartime First Amendment record is certainly controversial, it is nonetheless remarkable how much restraint he exercised in the face of truly nation-threatening challenges. Admittedly, there were sporadic instances when the president, or more often his subordinates, censored anti-administration criticism. But far more often, Lincoln's critics were allowed to publicly express calumnious sentiments and hurl epithets such as 'despot,' 'tyrant,' 'butcher,' 'fiend,' 'monster,' 'liar,' 'pirate,' 'swindler' and 'ignoramus.' 'Surely, Lincoln did not enjoy such criticism,' Professor Geoffrey Stone has written, 'but he kept it in perspective and did not [always] overreact.'"[23]

Acknowledgments

"I get by with a little help from my friends," says the famous Beatles song. So it goes with writing a book. This one has my byline on it. But writing it required more than a little help from more than a few friends—and family. I am indebted to Melinda Hocker Craig, my wife, best friend, and retired senior English teacher at Mayfield High School, for diligently proofreading the manuscript and to our son, Berry Craig IV of Louisville, for again cheerfully and patiently guiding his aged and technologically challenged father through the shoal waters of writing another book with a computer. Writers worth their salt also appreciate good copyediting. I was blessed with an outstanding copyeditor in Linda Lotz of Hannacroix, New York. My other able support troops included university library staff. I thank Laura Hall, Tawni Miller, Aliya Williams, and Jacob Toloczko, all of the University of Kentucky Library, Lexington; Dieter Ullrich, Morehead State University Library, Morehead, Kentucky; LaDonna Hammontree and Wesley Bolin, both of Murray State University Library, Murray, Kentucky; and Elizabeth B. Dunn, Duke University Library, Durham, North Carolina. I am equally grateful for city and county public library staff, including Nathan Lynn, McCracken County Public Library, Paducah, Kentucky; Natalie Watts, Mercer County Public Library, Harrodsburg, Kentucky; Ernie Dixon, Paul Sawyier Public Library, Frankfort, Kentucky; Erin West, J. P. Johnson, Mariam Addarrat, Eli Riveire Warner, and Brian Hudson, all of the Lexington Public Library; Nate McGee, Kenton County Public Library, Covington, Kentucky; and Kim Fortner, John L. Street Public Library, Princeton, Kentucky. Too, I am grateful for valuable aid rendered by Jennifer Cole, Filson Historical Society, Louisville; Marti Martin, Woodford County Historical Society, Versailles, Kentucky; Jackie Penny, American Antiquarian Society, Worcester, Massachusetts; Russ Hatter, Frankfort Civil War Museum; Professor Melony Shemberger, Murray State University; Professor David Sachsman, University of Tennessee–Chattanooga; Cindy Lynch, manager at Columbus-Belmont State Park, Columbus, Kentucky; researcher Carolyn Dyer of Georgetown; and Hickman County historian John Ross of Clinton.

Notes

Introduction

1. E. Merton Coulter, *The Civil War and Readjustment in Kentucky* (1926; reprint, Gloucester, MA: Peter Smith, 1966), vii.

2. Lowell H. Harrison and James C. Klotter, *A New History of Kentucky* (Lexington: University Press of Kentucky, 1997), 167.

3. Ford Risley, *Civil War Journalism*, (Santa Barbara, CA: Praeger, 2012), xiii; Lewis Collins and Richard Collins, *History of Kentucky: By the Late Lewis Collins, Judge of the Mason County Court, Revised, Enlarged Four-Fold and Brought Down to the Year 1874, by His Son, Richard H. Collins, A.M., LL.B. Embracing Pre-Historic Annals for 331 Years, Outline, and by Counties, Statistics, Antiquities, and Natural Curiosities, Geographical and Geological Descriptions, Sketches of the Court of Appeals, the Churches, Freemasonry, Odd Fellowship, and Internal Improvements, Incidents of Pioneer Life, and Nearly Five Hundred Biographical Sketches of Distinguished Pioneers, Soldiers, Statesmen, Jurists, Lawyers, Surgeons, Divines, Merchants, Historians, Editors, Artists, etc., etc.,* 2 vols. (1874; reprint, Berea, KY: Kentucke Imprints, 1976), 2:263.

4. "American Newspapers, 1800–1860: A Guide to Understanding and Using Antebellum American Newspapers," University Library, University of Illinois at Urbana-Champaign, http://guides.library.illinois.edu/c.php?g=347656&p=2348310 (accessed January 30, 2016).

5. Lorman A. Ratner and Dwight L. Teeter Jr., *Fanatics & Fire-Eaters: Newspapers and the Coming of the Civil War* (Urbana: University of Illinois Press, 2004), 7–9; Risley, *Civil War Journalism,* xiv; J. Cutler Andrews, *The North Reports the Civil War* (Pittsburgh: University of Pittsburgh Press, 1955), 6–7.

6. J. Cutler Andrews, *The South Reports the Civil War* (Pittsburgh: University of Pittsburgh Press, 1985), 24; Robert Emmett McDowell, *City of Conflict: Louisville in the Civil War, 1861–1865* (Louisville, KY: Louisville Civil War Roundtable, 1962), 5, 147; Zachariah Frederick Smith, *The History of Kentucky from Its Earliest Discovery and Settlement, to the Present Day, Embracing Its Prehistoric and Aboriginal Periods; Its Pioneer Life and Experiences; Its Political, Social, and Industrial Progress; Its Educational and Religious Development; Its Military Events and Achievements, and Biographic Mention of Its Historic Characters* (Louisville, KY: Courier-Journal Job Printing Co., 1886), 765–66; Amy Murrell Taylor, *The Divided Family in Civil War*

America (Chapel Hill: University of North Carolina Press, 2005), 30–31; *Louisville Journal,* October 10, 1862; George D. Prentice, "The Death-Day of William Courtland Prentice," in *The Poems of George D. Prentice,* ed. John James Piatt (Cincinnati: Robert Clarke, 1877), 182–85.

7. *Louisville Journal,* September 5, 1861; Sir William Howard Russell, *My Diary North and South* (Boston: T. O. H. P. Burnham, 1863), 335.

8. *Louisville Courier,* August 19, 1861; James M. McPherson, *Battle Cry of Freedom: The Civil War Era* (New York: Ballantine Books, 1988), 273.

9. Andrews, *South Reports,* 24.

10. US Bureau of the Census, "Population of the 100 Largest Urban Places: 1860," table 9, June 15, 1998, https://www.census.gov/population/www/documentation/twps0027/tab09.txt (accessed June 25, 2015); Donald E. Reynolds, *Editors Make War: Southern Newspapers in the Secession Crisis* (Carbondale: Southern Illinois University Press, 2006), 5; Collins and Collins, *History of Kentucky,* 1:105; D. F. Murphy, reporter, *Presidential Election 1864: Proceedings of the National Union Convention Held in Baltimore, Md., June 7th and 8th, 1864* (New York: Barker and Godwin, 1864), 5; *Western Recorder* advertising information http://westernrecorder.org/advertising-home.page (accessed June 25, 2015).

11. "American Newspapers, 1800–1860"; John E. Kleber, ed., *The Kentucky Encyclopedia* (Lexington: University Press of Kentucky, 1992), 398, 736.

12. Andrews, *North Reports,* 8; *Louisville Journal,* September 5, 1861.

13. *The News Manual: A Professional Resource for Journalists and the Media,* chap. 8, http://www.thenewsmanual.net/Manuals%20Volume%201/volume1_08.htm (accessed June 12, 2015).

14. Andrews, *South Reports,* 25; Risley, *Civil War Journalism,* xv; "American Newspapers, 1800–1860."

15. "American Newspapers, 1800–1860."

16. Harrison and Klotter, *New History of Kentucky,* 318.

17. Reynolds, *Editors Make War,* 67; David B. Sachsman, ed., *A Press Divided: Newspaper Coverage of the Civil War* (New Brunswick, NJ: Transaction Publishers, 2014) xi; Ratner and Teeter, *Fanatics & Fire-Eaters,* 33.

18. Harold Holzer, *Lincoln and the Power of the Press: The War for Public Opinion* (New York: Simon and Schuster, 2014), xvi.

19. Ibid., xx.

20. Collins and Collins, *History of Kentucky,* 2:241, 280; Ratner and Teeter, *Fanatics & Fire-Eaters,* 21; "Secretary of State Thomas B. Monroe," Kentucky Secretary of State website, http://apps.sos.ky.gov/secdesk/sosinfo/default.aspx?id=36 (accessed June 25, 2015); William Henry Perrin, *The Pioneer Press of Kentucky, from the First Paper West of the Alleghenies, August 11, 1787, to the Establishment of the Daily Press in 1830* (Louisville, KY: John P. Morton for the Filson Club, 1888), 51; *The Biographical Encyclopaedia of Kentucky of the Dead and Living Men of the Nineteenth Century* (Cincinnati: J. Armstrong, 1878), 552; George W. Ranck, *History of Lexington, Kentucky, Its Early Annals and Recent Progress Including Biographical Sketches and Personal Reminisces of the Pioneer Settlers, Notices of Prominent Citizens, etc., etc.* (Cincinnati: Robert Clarke, 1872), 236; Murphy, *Presidential Election 1864,* 25, 93.

21. Reynolds, *Editors Make War*, 9–10; Ratner and Teeter, *Fanatics & Fire-Eaters*, 19; Holzer, *Lincoln and Power of the Press*, xxii.

22. Sachsman, *Press Divided*, xii; Ratner and Teeter, *Fanatics & Fire-Eaters*, 19.

23. Ratner and Teeter, *Fanatics & Fire-Eaters*, x, 19.

24. Ibid., 19.

1. The Rebel Press, and Some Yankee Papers, Too

1. Collins and Collins, *History of Kentucky*, 2:260–61; Coulter, *Civil War and Readjustment*, 13.

2. Allen C. Guelzo, *Abraham Lincoln as a Man of Ideas* (Carbondale: Southern Illinois University Press, 1909), 91; James C. Klotter and Freda C. Klotter, *A Concise History of Kentucky* (Lexington: University Press of Kentucky, 2008), 101–2.

3. Collins and Collins, *History of Kentucky*, 2:401–2; Paul F. Boller Jr., *Presidential Campaigns from George Washington to George W. Bush* (Oxford: Oxford University Press, 2004), 64; *Biographical Sketch of Hon. Linn Boyd of Kentucky, the Present Speaker of the House of Representatives of the United States by a Virginian* (Washington, DC: Congressional Globe Office, 1855), 15.

4. Harrison and Klotter, *New History of Kentucky*, 102, 130; US Bureau of the Census, "Population of the 100 Largest Urban Places: 1860," table 9.

5. Thomas D. Clark, *Agrarian Kentucky* (Lexington: University Press of Kentucky, 1977), 44–45; Klotter and Klotter, *Concise History of Kentucky*, 127.

6. Harrison and Klotter, *New History of Kentucky*, 167–68.

7. J. G. Randall and David Donald, *Civil War and Reconstruction*, 2nd ed. (Lexington, MA: D. C. Heath, 1969), 228; Aaron Astor, *Rebels on the Border: Civil War, Emancipation, and the Reconstruction of Kentucky and Missouri* (Baton Rouge: Louisiana State University Press, 2012), 29.

8. Gary R. Matthews, *More American than Southern: Kentucky, Slavery, and the War for an American Ideology, 1828–1861* (Knoxville: University of Tennessee Press, 2014), 24.

9. Coulter, *Civil War and Readjustment*, 55; Harrison and Klotter, *New History of Kentucky*, 195.

10. Harrison and Klotter, *New History of Kentucky*, 318; Thomas D. Clark, *A History of Kentucky* (Lexington, KY: John Bradford Press, 1960), 241; Coulter, *Civil War and Readjustment*, 452.

11. *New York Times*, May 14, 1902; Clark, *History of Kentucky*, 241; J. Stoddard Johnston, *Memorial History of Louisville from Its First Settlement to the Year 1896* (Chicago: American Biographical Publishing, 1896), 2:493–95; John E. Kleber, ed., *The Encyclopedia of Louisville* (Lexington: University Press of Kentucky, 2001), 365; Perrin, *Pioneer Press*, 84–87.

12. *Louisville Journal*, July 20, 1857; *Louisville Courier*, July 21, 23, 1857; Alvin Seekamp and Roger Burlingame, eds., *Who's Who in Louisville* (Louisville, KY: Anziger Press, 1918), 25.

13. Kleber, *Encyclopedia of Louisville*, 365. Proposed by Senator Stephen A. Douglas, the Kansas-Nebraska Act created the territories of Kansas and Nebraska and allowed settlers to decide the slavery issue by "popular sovereignty." In other words,

the citizens could vote slavery in or out. The measure passed but created a firestorm of controversy in the North because Kansas and Nebraska were above 36 degrees, 30 minutes latitude, the boundary between slave and free territory established by the Missouri Compromise of 1820, which Clay had helped broker.

14. Clark, *History of Kentucky*, 243; "Secretary of State Thomas B. Monroe"; Ed Porter Thompson, *History of the Orphan Brigade* (Louisville, KY: Lewis N. Thompson, 1898), 461–62, 464. Wounded at the Battles of Shiloh and Stone's River, Tennessee, in 1862, Thompson rose from private to captain in the Sixth Kentucky Infantry Regiment. See also William C. Davis, *A History of the Orphan Brigade: The Kentuckians Who Couldn't Go Home* (New York: Doubleday, 1980).

15. L. P. Johnson, *The History of Franklin County, Ky.* (Frankfort, KY: Roberts Printing, 1912), 141–42; Perrin, *Pioneer Press,* 50–51. According to *Who's Who in Louisville,* the shoot-out was supposed to take place not in Virginia but in Indiana. It was stopped "by the mediation of friends in Louisville, where the would-be combatants and their seconds arrived enroute to the field of honor" (25).

16. J. H. Battle, W. H. Perrin, and G. C. Kniffen, *Kentucky: A History of the State,* 1st ed. (Louisville, KY: F. A. Battey, 1885), 7.

17. *Daily Nashville Patriot,* October 25, 1858; *Detroit Free Press,* June 26, 1887; William Henry Perrin, *History of Alexander, Union and Pulaski Counties, Illinois* (Chicago: O. L. Baskin, 1883), 129–30.

18. *Fayetteville (TN) Observer,* May 14, 1857; *Cairo Times and Delta,* n.d., quoted in *Bloomington (IL) Pantagraph,* September 4, 1857.

19. *Cairo Times and Delta,* n.d., quoted in *Bloomington (IL) Pantagraph,* November 23, 1857.

20. *Louisville Courier,* February 14, 1859; Perrin, *History of Alexander, Union and Pulaski Counties,* 130.

21. Battle, Perrin, and Kniffen, *Kentucky,* 67, 249–50; Berry Craig, *Kentucky Confederates: Secession, Civil War, and the Jackson Purchase* (Lexington: University Press of Kentucky, 2014), 171.

22. *Louisville Daily Union Press,* February 1, 1865.

23. *Louisville Journal,* July 20, 1863, September 27, 1864.

24. Kleber, *Kentucky Encyclopedia,* 736; Clark, *History of Kentucky,* 238.

25. Thomas D. Clark, *The Rampaging Frontier: Manners and Humors of Pioneer Days in the South and Middle West* (Indianapolis: Bobbs-Merrill, 1939), 123–25; Perrin, *Pioneer Press,* 76–79. "Big Ben" Brain and Daniel Mendoza were famous eighteenth-century British boxers.

26. Perrin, *Pioneer Press,* 76–77; Johnston, *Memorial History of Louisville,* 2:63; Clark, *History of Kentucky,* 238–39.

27. Perrin, *Pioneer Press,* 73; Clark, *History of Kentucky,* 239–40.

28. Perrin, *Pioneer Press,* 73–74.

29. McDowell, *City of Conflict,* 11.

30. *Louisville Journal,* July 8, 1855; *Louisville Courier,* August 9, 1855; Harrison and Klotter, *New History of Kentucky,* 123.

31. *Louisville Democrat,* July 1, 1863; Coulter, *Civil War and Readjustment,* 255.

32. Johnston, *Memorial History of Louisville,* 2:68; Perrin, *Pioneer Press,* 87–88; *Louisville Journal,* August 3, 1861.

33. *Frankfort Commonwealth,* July 27, 1863, June 27, 1864.

34. Kleber, *Kentucky Encyclopedia,* 436; Collins and Collins, *History of Kentucky,* 2:279–80; Clark, *History of Kentucky,* 243–44. The Old Court–New Court battle grew out of hard times resulting from the Panic of 1819. Debtors got the legislature to pass a law permitting them to postpone the payment of loans and mortgages and creating a cheap-money Bank of the Commonwealth. Creditors claimed the relief measures were unconstitutional, and the Court of Appeals, the state's highest court, agreed. A Relief Party arose and backed Joseph Desha, who won the governorship in 1824. Afterward, the legislature abolished the old court and replaced it with a new one comprising pro-relief justices. The old court refused to disband, throwing the state into turmoil. Ultimately, supporters of the old court won a majority in the legislature, restored the old court and its decisions, and abolished the new court. See Harrison and Klotter, *New History of Kentucky,* 109–11; Clark, *History of Kentucky,* 140–46.

35. Perrin, *Pioneer Press,* 53–54; Ranck, *History of Lexington,* 234–36.

36. McDowell, *City of Conflict,* 11–12; Betty Carolyn Congleton, "George D. Prentice: 19th Century Southern Editor," *Register of the Kentucky Historical Society* 65 (April 1967): 94.

37. McDowell, *City of Conflict,* 10.

2. The Press and the Presidential Election of 1860

1. Collins and Collins, *History of Kentucky,* 1:84.

2. McPherson, *Battle Cry of Freedom,* 215–16; *Covington Journal,* June 2, 1860; Collins and Collins, *History of Kentucky,* 1:84.

3. *Frankfort Yeoman,* June 26, July 19, 1860.

4. *Woodford Pennant,* June 29, 1860, quoted in *Frankfort Yeoman,* July 3, 1860; *Woodford Pennant,* July 20, 1860.

5. *Frankfort Yeoman,* July 3, 1860; *History of Daviess County, Kentucky, Together with Sketches of Its Cities, Villages, and Townships, Educational, Religious, Civil, Military, and Political History, Portraits of Prominent Persons, Biographies of Representative Citizens, and an Outline History of Kentucky* (Chicago: Inter-state Publishing, 1883), 198.

6. *Frankfort Yeoman,* July 5, 1860.

7. Ibid.

8. *Kentucky Statesman,* June 26, 1860.

9. *Louisville Courier,* July 4, 1860.

10. *Louisville Democrat,* July 4, 1860.

11. *Princeton Bulletin,* n.d., quoted in *Louisville Courier,* July 3, 1860. Marshall was in Congress from 1855 to 1859. The former Whig turned Know-Nothing turned Opposition man supported Breckinridge and, like his candidate, became a Confederate general in 1861. See Kleber, *Kentucky Encyclopedia,* 610–11.

12. *Louisville Journal,* July 4, 6, 1860.

13. Ibid.

14. *Cadiz Organ,* n.d., quoted in *Louisville Courier,* July 6, 1860; William Henry Perrin, *History of Trigg County, Kentucky* (reprint, Westminster, MD: Heritage Press, 2008), 55–56.

15. *Georgetown Gazette,* n.d., quoted in *Louisville Courier,* July 6, 1860; *Covington Journal,* May 26, July 7, 1860; *Lebanon Democrat,* n.d., quoted in *Louisville Courier,* July 6, 1860.

16. *Louisville Courier,* July 6, 1860.

17. *Covington Journal,* July 14, 1860.

18. *Kenton County Democrat,* n.d., quoted in *Louisville Courier,* July 9, 1860; Charles B. Eilerman, *Historic Covington: Proposed Subjects for Registration and Historic Marking* (reprint, Covington, KY: Charles B. Eilerman, 1975), 46.

19. *Owensboro Democrat,* n.d., quoted in *Louisville Courier,* July 9, 1860.

20. *Louisville Courier,* July 9, 1860. Born in Madison County in 1810, Cassius Marcellus Clay, a cousin of Henry Clay, attended Yale University. There, an 1832 speech by famous Boston abolitionist William Lloyd Garrison converted him to the anti-slavery cause. Back home in Kentucky, Clay joined the Whig Party and got elected to the state house of representatives in 1835. But his outspoken criticism of slavery cut short his political career and nearly cost him his life. In 1841 he fought a duel with Robert Wickliffe Jr. of Bardstown, but neither combatant was hurt. At a political meeting in 1843, a man thought to be a hired assassin shot Clay, and Clay stabbed him with a bowie knife—a weapon that became part of the Clay legend in Kentucky. Charged with mayhem, Clay was acquitted. His legal team included his cousin Henry. In 1845 he founded the *True American,* an anti-slavery newspaper in Lexington. A mob led by James B. Clay, Henry's son, attacked Clay's newspaper office while he was home in bed, ill with typhoid fever. The printing equipment was shipped to Cincinnati, and Clay briefly published the paper there. After fighting in the Mexican-American War, Clay returned to Kentucky and continued to speak out on slavery both at home and in the North. He befriended abolitionist James G. Fee and gave him land on which to found a school for white and African American students. That school became Berea College. Clay was one of the few Kentuckians to join the Republican Party. See Kleber, *Kentucky Encyclopedia,* 199–200.

21. *Paris State Flag,* n.d., quoted in *Louisville Courier,* July 16, 1860; *Louisville Courier,* July 11, 1860; William Henry Perrin, *History of Bourbon, Scott, Harrison and Nicholas Counties, Kentucky, with an Outline Sketch of the Bluegrass Region by Robert Peter, M.D., Ed.* (Chicago: O. L. Baskin, 1882), 111.

22. *Louisville Courier,* July 14, 1860.

23. *Harrodsburg Press,* n.d., quoted in *Louisville Courier,* July 16, 1860; "The Press of Harrodsburg," *Register of the Kentucky Historical Society* 20 (January 1922): 47.

24. *Henderson Reporter,* n.d., quoted in *Louisville Courier,* July 16, 1860; Edmund L. Starling, *History of Henderson County, Kentucky: Comprising History of County and City, Precincts, Education, Churches, Secret Societies, Leading Enterprises, Sketches and Recollections, and Biographies of the Living and Dead* (Henderson, KY: n.p., 1887), 822.

25. *Mayfield Southern Yeoman,* n.d., quoted in *Louisville Courier,* July 17, 1861;

Battle, Perrin, and Kniffen, *Kentucky,* 53. The Jackson Purchase, comprising the eight Kentucky counties west of the Tennessee River, became part of the Bluegrass State via an 1818 treaty with the Chickasaw Indians. Andrew Jackson and former Kentucky governor Isaac Shelby represented the federal government in negotiations to buy the land, which also included west Tennessee. For reasons that are not clear, the deal became known as Jackson's Purchase or the Jackson Purchase.

26. *Louisville Courier,* July 19, 1860.

27. *Paris Citizen,* n.d., quoted in *Lexington Observer & Reporter,* July 25, 1860.

28. *Winchester Union,* n.d., quoted in *Lexington Observer & Reporter,* July 25, 1860.

29. *Nicholasville Democrat,* n.d., and *Mount Sterling Whig,* n.d., quoted in *Lexington Observer & Reporter,* July 21, 1860.

30. *Russellville Herald,* n.d., quoted in *Lexington Observer & Reporter* July 21, 1860.

31. *Louisville Courier,* July 21, 23, 1860.

32. Ibid., July 23, 1860. Adams had been secretary of state; so had the three preceding presidents: Thomas Jefferson, James Madison, and James Monroe.

33. Ibid.

34. *Kentucky Statesman,* July 31, 1860.

35. *Louisville Courier,* July 24, 1860.

36. Ibid., July 26, 1860. In February 1859, during his first term in Congress, Lovejoy famously replied to charges from a Southern congressman that he was a "Negro stealer":

> Yes, I do assist fugitive slaves to escape! Proclaim it upon the house-tops; write it upon every leaf that trembles in the forest; make it blaze from the sun at high noon, and shine forth in the radiance of every star that bedecks the firmament of God. Let it echo through all the arches of heaven, and reverberate and bellow through all the deep gorges of hell, where slave catchers will be very likely to hear it. Owen Lovejoy lives at Princeton, Illinois, and he aids every fugitive that comes to his door and asks it. Thou invisible demon of slavery! dost thou think to cross my humble threshold, and forbid me to give bread to the hungry and shelter to the houseless? I bid you defiance in the name of God!

Isaac Newton Arnold, *The History of Abraham Lincoln and the Overthrow of Slavery* (Chicago: Clarke, 1866), 225.

37. *Louisville Courier,* August 2, 1860; Battle, Perrin, and Kniffen, *Kentucky,* 91. In ancient Greek mythology, Nestor was the king of Pylos. In the *Iliad,* he famously gives advice to the young warriors.

38. Collins and Collins, *History of Kentucky,* 1:84. Other candidates won 1,154 votes.

39. *Louisville Courier,* August 8, 1860.

40. *Kentucky Statesman,* August 17, 1860.

41. *Louisville Journal,* August 9, 1860.

42. Ibid.

43. *Louisville Courier,* August 22, 1860.

44. Ibid., August 31, 1860.

45. *Southern Democratic Banner,* n.d., quoted in *Louisville Courier,* September 6, 1860.

46. *Louisville Courier,* September 12, 1860.

47. Ibid., September 20, 1860.

48. Ibid., October 1, 1860.

49. McPherson, *Battle Cry of Freedom,* 230–231; Gerhard Peters and John T. Woolley, "Republican Party Platform of 1860," May 17, 1860, American Presidency Project, http://www.presidency.ucsb.edu/ws/?pid=29620. Point four in the platform read: "That the maintenance inviolate of the rights of the states, and especially the right of each state to order and control its own domestic institutions according to its own domestic institutions according to its own judgment exclusively." Point eight stated,"We deny the authority of Congress, of a territorial legislature, or of any individuals, to give legal existence to slavery in any territory of the United States."

50. *Louisville Courier,* October 12, 1860.

51. Ibid.

52. Ibid.

53. *Kentucky Statesman,* October 2, 1860.

54. *Frankfort Yeoman,* October 18, 1860.

55. *Kentucky Statesman,* November 2, 1860.

56. *Louisville Democrat,* November 4, 1860.

57. *Frankfort Yeoman,* November 1, 1860.

58. *Louisville Journal,* November 5, 1860.

59. Ibid.

60. *Louisville Courier,* November 5, 1860. Garrison's *Liberator* was one of the country's leading anti-slavery organs.

61. Jasper B. Shannon and Ruth McQuown, *Presidential Politics in Kentucky 1824–1948 Studies in Political Behavior Number 1* (Lexington: Bureau of Government Research, College of Arts and Sciences, University of Kentucky, 1960), 32–36.

3. South Carolina, Secession, and Lincoln's Inauguration

1. *Kentucky Statesman,* November 9, 1860.

2. Ibid.

3. Ibid.

4. *Louisville Courier,* November 10, 1860.

5. *Covington Journal,* November 10, 1860.

6. *Frankfort Yeoman,* November 10, 1860. Governor Magoffin sued to force Dennison to give up Lago, and the case wound up in the Supreme Court. The eight justices ruled unanimously in *Kentucky v. Dennison* that the Court lacked the power to compel Dennison to surrender Lago.

7. Ibid.

8. Collins and Collins, *History of Kentucky,* 1:84.

9. *Kentucky Statesman,* November 13, 1860.

10. *Louisville Courier,* November 13, 1860.

11. *Cadiz Organ,* November 17, 1860, quoted in *Louisville Courier,* November 21, 1860.

12. *Henderson Reporter,* n.d., quoted in *Louisville Courier,* November 17, 1860. The Old Testament (Judges 16) tells the story of Samson, a judge of the ancient Israelites. After Delilah cut off his hair—the source of his superhuman strength—the Philistines captured Samson, blinded him, and took him to the temple of Dagon, one of their gods. Once his hair grew back, Samson destroyed the temple by toppling its main pillars, but he died when the temple collapsed. On March 15, 44 BCE, Julius Caesar was stabbed to death in the Roman forum by a conspiracy of Roman senators led by Marcus Junius Brutus and Gaius Cassius Longinus. Joshua Giddings was an Ohio abolitionist and former Whig congressman who helped found the Republican Party.

13. *Cynthiana News,* n.d., quoted in *Louisville Courier,* November 17, 1860.

14. *Bowling Green Standard,* n.d., quoted in *Louisville Courier,* November 19, 1860.

15. *Paducah Herald,* n.d., quoted in *Louisville Courier,* November 20, 1860.

16. *Georgetown Journal,* n.d., quoted in *Louisville Courier,* November 27, 1860.

17. *Louisville Courier,* November 29, December 1, 1860; *Lexington Statesman,* December 4, 1860; *Frankfort Yeoman,* December 8, 1860.

18. *Kentucky Statesman,* December 4, 1860.

19. Coulter, *Civil War and Readjustment,* 25–26; Collins and Collins, *History of Kentucky,* 1:85.

20. *Bowling Green Standard,* n.d., quoted in *Kentucky Statesman,* January 4, 1861.

21. *The Address of the People of South Carolina, Assembled in Convention, to the People of the Slaveholding States of the United States* (Charleston, SC: Evans and Cogswell, 1860), 16; Charles B. Dew, *Apostles of Disunion: Southern Secession Commissioners and the Causes of the Civil War* (Charlottesville: University Press of Virginia, 2001), 93, 96–98.

22. *Frankfort Yeoman,* January 3, 1861.

23. Ibid.; Coulter, *Civil War and Readjustment,* 25–26.

24. *Kentucky Statesman,* December 21, 1860.

25. *Frankfort Yeoman,* December 29, 1860.

26. *Kentucky Statesman,* January 1, 1861.

27. *Maysville Express,* n.d., quoted in *Kentucky Statesman,* January 1, 1861.

28. Coulter, *Civil War and Readjustment,* 29.

29. *Louisville Journal,* August 16, 1859.

30. Coulter, *Civil War and Readjustment,* 27–28.

31. *Louisville Courier,* January 10, 1861.

32. *Covington Journal,* January 12, 1861.

33. *Kentucky Statesman,* January 11, 1861.

34. *Hickman Courier,* n.d., quoted in *Louisville Courier,* January 11, 24, 1861; Craig, *Kentucky Confederates,* 22, 41–42; "About the Hickman Courier (Hickman, Ky.) 1859–Current," *Chronicling America,* http://chroniclingamerica.loc.gov/lccn/sn85052141/ (accessed August 12, 2015). The *Courier, Hickman Gazette,* and *Fulton Leader* merged to become the *Current.*

35. *Columbus Crescent,* n.d., *Owensboro Democrat,* n.d., quoted in *Louisville Courier,* January 17, 1861.

36. *Woodford Pennant,* n.d., quoted in *Louisville Courier,* January 17, 1861.

37. *Henderson Reporter,* n.d., quoted in *Louisville Courier,* January 17, 1861.

38. Ibid.

39. Starling, *History of Henderson County,* 199–201, 822; H. Levin, ed., *The Lawyers and Lawmakers of Kentucky* (Chicago: Lewis, 1897), 388; Ezra J. Warner and W. Buck Yearns, *Biographical Registry of the Confederate Congress* (Baton Rouge: Louisiana State University Press, 1975), 65–66. According to Starling, the *Reporter* was founded in 1853 and "was a tower of strength in Henderson" for thirty years before Judge J. F. Simmons bought the paper and took it to Sardis, Mississippi.

40. *Henderson Reporter,* n.d., quoted in Starling, *History of Henderson County,* 201.

41. Coulter, *Civil War and Readjustment,* 29–34; *Frankfort Yeoman,* February 4, 1861.

42. Constitution of the Confederate States, March 11, 1861, http://avalon.law. yale.edu/19th_century/csa_csa.asp (accessed October 13, 2016).

43. *Louisville Democrat,* February 14, 1861.

44. *Hickman Courier,* n.d., quoted in *Louisville Courier,* February 6, 1861.

45. *Winchester Review,* n.d., quoted in *Louisville Courier,* February 18, 1861.

46. *Southern Kentucky Register,* n.d., quoted in *Kentucky Statesman,* February 22, 1861.

47. McPherson, *Battle Cry of Freedom,* 261–62; *Frankfort Yeoman,* February 28, 1861.

48. *Paducah Herald,* February 16, 1861, quoted in *Louisville Courier,* February 22, 1861; Craig, *Kentucky Confederates,* 51. According to Dew, Davis did not mention slavery in his inaugural address of February 18, 1861. But on April 29, 1861, he told the Confederate Congress in Richmond, Virginia, that "fanatical organizations . . . were assiduously engaged in exciting amongst the slaves a spirit of discontent and revolt; means were furnished for their escape from their owners; and agents secretly employed to entice them to abscond." Davis claimed that "a spirit of ultra fanaticism" gripped the Republicans. The party was determined to keep slavery out of the federal territories and hem in the South with "states in which slavery should be prohibited . . . thus rendering property in slaves so insecure as to be comparatively worthless." Davis described slavery as an institution through which "a superior race" had converted "brutal savages into docile, intelligent, and civilized agricultural laborers"— close to 4 million in number. He concluded: "With interests of such overwhelming magnitude imperiled, the people of the Southern States were driven by the conduct of the North to the adoption of some course of action to avert the danger which they were openly menaced." Dew, *Apostles of Disunion,* 13–15.

49. *Kentucky Statesman,* February 19, 1861.

50. *Russellville Herald,* n.d., quoted in *Louisville Courier,* February 22, 1861.

51. Joint Congressional Committee on Inaugural Ceremonies, "Address by Abraham Lincoln, 1861," http://www.inaugural.senate.gov/swearing-in/address/address-by-abraham-lincoln-1861 (accessed July 5, 2015); McPherson, *Battle Cry of Freedom,* 262–63; Eric Foner, *The Fiery Trial: Abraham Lincoln and American Slavery* (New York: W. W. Norton, 2010), 158.

52. *Louisville Courier,* March 5, 1861. In seventeenth-century England, Protestants used the term *Jesuitism* to mean to "equivocating." Jesuits are an order of Catholic priests.

53. Ibid., March 9, 1861.

54. *Frankfort Yeoman,* March 7, 1861; McPherson, *Battle Cry of Freedom,* 263.

55. *Kentucky Statesman,* March 8, 1861.

56. *Lexington Observer & Reporter,* March 6, 1861.

57. *Cadiz Organ,* n.d., quoted in *Louisville Courier,* March 7, 1861.

58. *Princeton Bulletin,* n.d., quoted in *Louisville Courier,* March 7, 1861.

59. *Hickman Courier,* n.d. quoted in *Louisville Courier,* March 7, 1861.

60. *Elizabethtown Democrat,* n.d., quoted in *Louisville Courier,* March 8, 1861.

61. *Paris Flag,* n.d., quoted in *Louisville Courier,* March 8, 1861.

62. *Louisville Journal,* March 5, 1861.

63. *Louisville Democrat,* March 6, 1861.

4. Fort Sumter to Neutrality

1. *Columbus Crescent,* n.d., quoted in *Louisville Courier,* March 14, 1861; Craig, *Kentucky Confederates,* 51–52. The whole Kentucky house and half of the senate had been elected in 1859; voters had elected the rest of the senate in 1857.

2. Coulter, *Civil War and Readjustment,* 37.

3. Ibid., 27.

4. Kleber, *Kentucky Encyclopedia,* 120; Robert J. Breckinridge, "Our Country—Its Peril—Its Deliverance," *Danville Quarterly Review* (March 1861): 74–75, 87, 94, 105–6, 112, 114–15. Old School Presbyterians were theologically conservative and, unlike their New School counterparts, opposed the emotionalism that marked the Second Great Awakening, a revival movement that swept the country in the early nineteenth century. Although Breckinridge's unionism never flagged, two of his sons fought for the Confederacy (and two for the Union), and his nephew, John C. Breckinridge, was a Confederate general and secretary of war.

5. *Louisville Courier,* March 15, 1861.

6. Ibid.

7. *Kentucky Statesman,* March 12, 1861.

8. *Louisville Courier,* March 21, 1861.

9. Ibid.

10. *Frankfort Yeoman,* March 23, 1861.

11. *Frankfort Commonwealth,* March 23, 1861.

12. Coulter, *Civil War and Readjustment,* 37.

13. *Louisville Journal,* April 5, 1861.

14. *Kentucky Statesman,* April 12, 1861; McPherson, *Battle Cry of Freedom,* 267–68.

15. Collins and Collins, *History of Kentucky,* 1:87; McPherson, *Battle Cry of Freedom,* 273–74.

16. *Louisville Courier,* April 13, 1861; "Abraham Lincoln Inaugural Address," http://www.inaugural.senate.gov/swearing-in/address/address-by-abraham-lincoln-1861 (accessed July 11, 2015).

17. *Frankfort Yeoman,* April 16, 1861.

18. Ibid. Myrmidons were Greek warriors led by Achilles at the siege of Troy.

19. *Kentucky Statesman,* April 16, 1861.

20. *Covington Journal,* April 20, 1861.

21. Ibid.

22. *Paris Flag,* n.d., and *Georgetown Journal,* n.d., quoted in *Covington Journal,* April 20, 1861; *Cynthiana News,* n.d., quoted in *Covington Journal,* April 27, 1861.

23. *Louisville Journal,* April 15, 1861. "Hotspur" was the nickname of English soldier Sir Henry Percy (1364–1403). He is one of the most famous characters in William Shakespeare's *Henry IV, Part 1.*

24. *Frankfort Yeoman,* April 16, 1861.

25. *Maysville Eagle,* n.d., quoted in *Covington Journal,* April 20, 1861.

26. *Louisville Democrat,* April 16, 1861.

27. Collins and Collins, *History of Kentucky,* 1:87–88; McDowell, *City of Conflict,* 26–28.

28. *Louisville Courier,* April 18, 1861; Coulter, *Civil War and Readjustment,* 82–83.

29. Ibid.

30. *Louisville Courier,* April 19, 1861.

31. Ibid.

32. *Paducah Herald,* n.d., quoted in *Louisville Courier,* April 29, 1861; McPherson, *Battle Cry of Freedom,* 285; Craig, *Kentucky Confederates,* 57.

33. Coulter, *Civil War and Readjustment,* 54; Collins and Collins, *History of Kentucky,* 1:88.

34. *Kentucky Statesman,* April 26, 1861.

35. Ibid.

36. *Russellville Herald,* April 24, 1861, quoted in *Louisville Courier,* April 26, 1861; *Kentucky Statesman,* April 26, 1861.

37. *Covington Journal,* April 27, 1861.

38. *Louisville Courier,* May 4, 1861.

39. Ibid., May 3, 4, 1861.

40. Collins and Collins, *History of Kentucky,* 1:89; Shannon and McQuown, *Presidential Politics,* 35–36.

41. *Louisville Courier,* May 6, 1861.

42. *Paducah Herald,* n.d., quoted in *Richmond (VA) Daily Dispatch,* May 14, 1861.

43. *Louisville Courier,* May 6, 1861.

44. Ibid., May 8, 1861.

45. *Frankfort Commonwealth,* May 8, 1861.

46. *Frankfort Yeoman,* May 6, 1861.

47. Ibid., May 10, 1861.

48. *Columbus Crescent,* n.d., quoted in *Louisville Courier,* March 14, 1861; Craig, *Kentucky Confederates,* 51–52; *Frankfort Commonwealth,* May 15, 1861.

49. Coulter, *Civil War and Readjustment,* 54–56, 87–89.

50. *Louisville Courier,* May 27, 1861.

51. Ibid.

52. *Kentucky Statesman,* May 17, 1861.

53. Ibid., May 21, 1861.

54. *Frankfort Yeoman,* May 22, 1861.

5. Neutrality Summer

1. Coulter, *Civil War and Readjustment,* 81–82; Collins and Collins, *History of Kentucky,* 1:91–92; *Louisville Courier,* May 30, 1861.

2. *Louisville Courier,* May 30, 1861.

3. Robert J. Breckinridge, "State of the Country," *Danville Quarterly Review* (June 1861): 294–95.

4. Craig, *Kentucky Confederates,* 93–94.

5. *Louisville Courier,* June 8, 1861.

6. *Covington Journal,* June 8, 1861.

7. Craig, *Kentucky Confederates,* 96.

8. *Cairo Gazette,* n.d., quoted in *Davenport (IA) Daily Gazette,* May 29, 1861.

9. Ibid.

10. Ibid.

11. Russell, *My Diary North and South,* 335–36.

12. Ibid.

13. Ibid.

14. *Louisville Courier,* June 19, 1861.

15. Craig, *Kentucky Confederates,* 90, 71–92.

16. *Covington Journal,* June 15, 1861.

17. *Louisville Courier,* June 20, 1861.

18. Ibid.

19. Craig, *Kentucky Confederates,* 99–100; Collins and Collins, *History of Kentucky,* 1:92; Shannon and McQuown, *Presidential Politics,* 35–36.

20. *Paducah Herald,* n.d., quoted in *Louisville Democrat,* July 3, 1861; Craig, *Kentucky Confederates,* 99–100.

21. *Louisville Courier,* June 21, 1861.

22. Ibid.

23. *Frankfort Yeoman,* June 22, 1861.

24. McPherson, *Battle Cry of Freedom,* 241.

25. *Frankfort Yeoman,* June 22, 1861.

26. *Covington Journal,* June 22, 1861; Collins and Collins, *History of Kentucky,* 1:92.

27. *Kentucky Statesman,* June 21, 1861; Collins and Collins, *History of Kentucky,* 1:92.

28. *Kentucky Statesman,* June 21, 1861.

29. Ibid.; Coulter, *Civil War and Readjustment,* 91.

30. *Louisville Courier,* July 2, 1861.

31. Ibid., July 3, 1861.

32. Ibid.

33. Ibid., July 4, 1861.

34. McPherson, *Battle Cry of Freedom,* 244.

35. *Louisville Courier,* July 5, 1861; "George Washington's Mount Vernon: Slavery," http://www.mountvernon.org/george-washington/slavery/ (accessed August 20, 2015). In his famous speech against the pro-slavery provisions of the Compromise of 1850, Seward said, "There is a Higher Law than the Constitution," meaning the law of God.

36. *Covington Journal,* July 13, 1861.

37. *Frankfort Yeoman,* July 16, 1861. Lincoln's Emancipation Proclamation, which took effect on January 1, 1863, ultimately led to the enlistment of about 179,000 African American soldiers—10 percent of the whole Union army during the war. Another 19,000 blacks were in the navy. All told, 23,700 black Kentuckians donned Union blue—about 13 percent of all African Americans in the army. See "Black Soldiers in the Civil War," National Archives Online, https://www.archives.gov/education/lessons/blacks-civil-war (accessed October 25, 2016); Harrison and Klotter, *New History of Kentucky,* 180.

38. *Frankfort Yeoman,* July 16, 1861; "The 1860 Presidential Vote in Virginia," West Virginia Archives and History Online, extracted from *The Tribune Almanac and Political Register for 1861* (New York: Tribune Association, 1861), http://www.wvculture.org/history/statehood/1860presidentialvote.html (accessed October 25, 2016).

39. *Frankfort Yeoman,* June 11, July 16, 1861.

40. *Covington Journal,* July 20, 1861; *Carrollton Signs of the Times,* n.d., quoted in *Covington Journal,* July 20, 1861.

41. *Louisville Courier,* July 23, 1861.

42. Ibid., July 26, 1861.

43. Ibid., July 27, 1861.

44. Ibid., August 1, 1861.

45. Ibid., August 2, 1861.

46. Ibid., August 5, 1861.

47. Ibid.

48. Collins and Collins, *History of Kentucky,* 1:92; Craig, *Kentucky Confederates,* 114.

49. *Louisville Courier,* August 6, 1861.

50. Ibid.

51. *Frankfort Yeoman,* August 8, 1861.

52. *Kentucky Statesman,* August 6, 1861.

53. Ibid.

54. Ibid., August 9, 1861.

55. *Paducah Herald,* n.d., quoted in *Louisville Democrat,* July 3, 1861; *New York Times,* August 10, 1861.

56. *Louisville Journal,* August 8, 9, 1861.

6. The Twilight of the Rebel Press

1. Collins and Collins, *History of Kentucky,* 1:92; Coulter, *Civil War and Readjustment,* 103–104.

2. *Louisville Courier,* August 19, 1861.

3. Ibid.

4. *Frankfort Yeoman,* August 17, 1861.

5. *Kentucky Statesman,* August 9, 1861.

6. *Covington Journal,* August 17, 1861.

7. Ibid., August 31, 1861.

8. *Louisville Courier,* September 2, 1861.

9. *Louisville Journal,* August 19, 1861.

10. Ibid.

11. *Frankfort Yeoman,* August 17, 1861.

12. *Louisville Courier,* August 15, 1861.

13. Ibid., September 2, 1861.

14. Ibid. September 3, 1861; Coulter, *Civil War and Readjustment,* 112.

15. Coulter, *Civil War and Readjustment,* 113.

16. *Louisville Journal,* August 19, 1861.

17. Ibid.

18. *Louisville Courier,* August 19, 1861.

19. *Louisville Journal,* September 5, 1861.

20. *Frankfort Yeoman,* September 9, 1861.

21. *Louisville Democrat,* September 10, 1861.

22. Harrison and Klotter, *New History of Kentucky,* 190.

23. Craig, *Kentucky Confederates,* 132–33.

24. Coulter, *Civil War and Readjustment,* 109.

25. *Louisville Journal,* September 7, 1861.

26. Ibid., September 9, 1861.

27. *Louisville Courier,* September 9, 1861.

28. Ibid., September 10, 1861.

29. *Frankfort Yeoman,* September 9, 1861.

30. *Louisville Democrat,* September 10, 1861; *Louisville Courier,* September 11, 1861.

31. *Frankfort Commonwealth,* September 11, 1861.

32. *Frankfort Yeoman,* September 10, 1861; Coulter, *Civil War and Readjustment,* 109–10.

33. *Louisville Democrat,* September 21, 1861.

34. *Kentucky Statesman,* September 10, 1861.

35. Coulter, *Civil War and Readjustment,* 114; Harrison and Klotter, *New History of Kentucky,* 192. Thomas L. Crittenden's brother, George B. Crittenden, was a Confederate general.

36. *Louisville Democrat,* September 20, 1861; *Louisville Journal,* September 19, 1861. Both of Prentice's sons, Courtland and Clarence, were Confederate officers. Courtland was mortally wounded in battle, and Clarence was captured. Their mother, Harriett, was a Southern sympathizer.

37. *Frankfort Commonwealth,* September 21, 1861.

7. The Death of the Rebel Press

1. *The War of the Rebellion: A Compilation of the Official Records of the Union and Confederate Armies* (Washington, DC: War Department, 1880–1902), ser. 2, vol. 2, 806; hereafter cited as *O.R.*

2. *Louisville Courier,* September 18, 1861.

3. Ibid.; Harrison and Klotter, *New History of Kentucky,* 195.

4. *Louisville Courier,* September 18, 1861.

5. Ibid.

6. Ibid.

7. *Louisville Journal,* September 19, 1861.

8. McDowell, *City of Conflict,* 48.

9. Ibid., 49.

10. *Frankfort Commonwealth,* September 20, 1861.

11. *Louisville Democrat,* September 20, 1861.

12. Ibid.

13. *Louisville Journal,* September 20, 1861.

14. *Louisville Democrat,* September 21, 1861.

15. *Louisville Journal,* September 21, 26, 1861.

16. *O.R.,* ser. 2, vol. 2, 807–8.

17. Ibid., 808–9.

18. Ibid., 809.

19. Ibid., 811.

20. Ibid., 810–12.

21. *Nashville Union and American,* October 2, 1861.

22. Ibid.

23. Ibid.

24. Ibid.

25. Ibid.

26. Ibid.

27. Collins and Collins, *History of Kentucky,* 1:94; *O.R.,* ser. 1, vol. 4, 296.

28. *Louisville Journal,* October 9, 1861.

29. Ibid.

30. Ibid.

31. Ibid.

32. Ibid.

33. Ibid.

34. Ibid.

35. Ibid.

36. Ibid. The Greek Kalends were times that did not and would not exist.

37. Coulter, *Civil War and Readjustment,* 255; *Louisville Courier,* October. 14, 1861.

38. *Louisville Courier,* October 14, 1861.

39. Ibid., October 16, 1861.

40. Ibid.

41. W. N. Haldeman to Gen. F. K. Zollicoffer, October 19, 1861, Haldeman Family Papers, Filson Historical Society, Louisville.

42. *Louisville Courier,* October 17, 1861.

43. Ibid., October 18, 1861.

44. Ibid., October 25, 1861.

45. Ibid.

46. Ibid.

47. Ibid.

48. Ibid., November 16, 1861.

49. Ibid.

50. Ibid.

51. Ibid.

52. Ibid., November 20, 1861.

53. *O.R.*, ser. 2, vol. 2, 805–6.

54. William A. Penn, *Kentucky Rebel Town: The Civil War Battles of Cynthiana & Harrison County* (Lexington: University Press of Kentucky, 2016), 65, 69; Collins and Collins, *History of Kentucky*, 1:95.

55. Penn, *Kentucky Rebel Town*, 65; Collins and Collins, *History of Kentucky*, 1:95; *Daily Ohio State Journal*, October 4, 1861.

56. *Daily Ohio State Journal*, October 4, 1861; Collins and Collins, *History of Kentucky*, 1:105.

57. *Daily Ohio State Journal*, October 4, 1861; *Lexington Leader*, November 28, 1907.

58. *Daily Ohio State Journal*, October 4, 1861.

59. *O.R.*, ser. 2, vol. 1, 544; James Ford Rhodes, *History of the United States from the Compromise of 1850*, vol. 5, *1864–1866* (New York: Macmillan, 1904), 507–8.

60. *O.R.*, ser. 2, vol. 1, 545–46; Penn, *Kentucky Rebel Town*, 65–66.

61. Ibid.

62. Ibid.

63. *Louisville Journal*, October 8, 1861.

64. *Louisville Courier*, October 14, 1861; *O.R.*, ser. 2, vol. 1, 545.

65. Penn, *Kentucky Rebel Town*, 70.

66. *Kentucky Statesman*, September 24, 1861. The *Statesman* reappeared in September and October 1862, when the Confederates occupied Lexington. See William Henry Perrin, ed., *History of Fayette County, Kentucky, with an Outline Sketch of the Bluegrass Region by Robert Peter, M.D.* (Chicago: O. L. Baskin, 1882), 372.

67. Thompson, *History of the Orphan Brigade*, 460–66.

68. Ibid., 463–64.

69. Ibid., 462, 464–65.

70. Henry George, *History of the 3d, 7th, 8th and 12th Kentucky C.S.A.* (Louisville, KY: Dearing Press, 1911), 182; *Paducah Sun*, December 21, 1901; Craig, *Kentucky Confederates*, 153.

71. Craig, *Kentucky Confederates*, 153.

72. Ibid.

73. Ibid., 160; *Louisville Courier*, October 29, 1861.

74. Craig, *Kentucky Confederates*, 171.

75. Ibid., 176–77; Battle, Perrin, and Kniffen, *Kentucky*, 91, 249.

76. Coulter, *Civil War and Readjustment*, 255.

77. *Paris Flag*, September 25, 1861, quoted in *Frankfort Yeoman*, October 27, 1861.

78. Ibid.

79. *Lexington Observer & Reporter,* October 19, 1861.

80. Coulter, *Civil War and Readjustment,* 137–38; *Resolution of the [Confederate] Congress [in Kentucky]* (reprint, Lyndon, KY: Mull-Wathen Historic Press, 1970), 9.

81. *Louisville Courier,* October 31, 1861.

82. Ibid., October 31, November 1, 4, 11, 21, 23, 1861; Coulter, *Civil War and Readjustment,* 137–38; 111; *Resolution of the [Confederate] Congress,* 5, 9.

83. *Louisville Courier,* December 11, 1861.

84. Ibid.

85. Ibid.

86. *Louisville Democrat,* November 21, 1861; Coulter, *Civil War and Readjustment,* 138.

87. *Lexington Observer & Reporter,* November 10, 1861; Craig, *Kentucky Confederates,* 157–59.

88. *Louisville Journal,* November 23, 1861. Three tailors who worked on Tooley Street in London presented a petition of grievances to the House of Commons while George Canning was prime minister. It grandly began, "We, the people of England." The phrase was applied to any small group that had the temerity to claim that it represented all the people.

89. James M. Pritchard, *Embattled Capital: Frankfort Kentucky in the Civil War* (Frankfort, KY: Frankfort Heritage Press, 2014), 75.

90. Ibid., 74.

91. Ibid., 75–78. See also Kenneth W. Noe, *Perryville: This Grand Havoc of Battle* (Lexington: University Press of Kentucky, 2001); Coulter, *Civil War and Readjustment,* 255.

92. Collins and Collins, *History of Kentucky,* 1:105; McDowell, *City of Conflict,* 74; Coulter, *Civil War and Readjustment,* 121, 152; Preston D. Graham Jr., *A Kingdom Not of This World: Stuart Robinson's Struggle to Distinguish the Sacred from the Secular during the Civil War* (Macon, GA: Mercer University Press, 2002), 57–58; Kleber, *Kentucky Encyclopedia,* 777; Lewis George Vander Velde, *The Presbyterian Churches and the Federal Union, 1861–1869* (Cambridge, MA: Harvard University Press, 1932), 141.

8. The Rebirth of the Old Rebel Press and the Thorny Issue of Censorship in Wartime

1. Ann E. Marshall, *Creating a Confederate Kentucky: The Lost Cause and Civil War Memory in a Border State* (Chapel Hill: University of North Carolina Press, 2010), 5.

2. Astor, *Rebels on the Border,* 195, 198–99.

3. Christopher Phillips, *The Rivers Ran Backwards: The Civil War and the Remaking of the American Middle Border* (New York: Oxford University Press, 2016), 312.

4. Coulter, *Civil War and Readjustment,* 452.

5. Harrison and Klotter, *New History of Kentucky,* 241–42; Kleber, *Kentucky Encyclopedia,* 436.

6. Kleber, *Encyclopedia of Louisville,* 365–66; Kleber, *Kentucky Encyclopedia,*

936; *Louisville Courier,* October 17, 1861; Marshall, *Creating a Confederate Kentucky,* 1.

7. Kleber, *Encyclopedia of Louisville,* 723. A Prentice son and daughter had died in childhood. See Prentice, *Poems of George D. Prentice,* xvii.

8. George D. Prentice to Walter N. Haldeman, n.d., Haldeman Family Papers, Filson Historical Society, Louisville; Prentice, *Poems of George D. Prentice,* xli.

9. Prentice to Haldeman, August 27, [1869?], other letters, n.d., Haldeman Family Papers.

10. Prentice to Haldeman, November 8, [1869], December 25, [1869?], ibid.; Smith, *History of Kentucky,* 766; Prentice, *Poems of George D. Prentice,* xlii.

11. *Louisville Courier-Journal,* January 23, 1870.

12. Kleber, *Encyclopedia of Louisville,* 366. The *Post* died in 1893; the *Times* survived until 1987.

13. *Frankfort Roundabout,* June 26, 1886; "About the Weekly Kentucky Yeoman Frankfort, Ky.) 1854–1886," *Chronicling America,* http://chroniclingamerica.loc.gov/lccn/sn82015454/ (accessed August 24, 2015); Collins and Collins, *History of Kentucky,* 2:241; Perrin, *Pioneer Press,* 51.

14. "About the Covington Journal (Covington, Ky.) 1848–1876," *Chronicling America,* http://chroniclingamerica.loc.gov/lccn/sn84037822/ (accessed August 24, 2015); Battle, Perrin, and Kniffen, *Kentucky,* 91, 311; *Paducah Sun,* December 21, 1901; *Memorial Record of Western Kentucky, II* (Chicago: Lewis Publishing, 1904), 693; Starling, *History of Henderson County,* 822.

15. Perrin, *History of Alexander Union and Pulaski Counties,* 130; Martin L. Newell, *Reports of Cases Determined in the Appellate Courts of Illinois,* vol. 87 (Chicago: Callaghan, 1900), 263.

16. Harrison and Klotter, *New History of Kentucky,* 243; Coulter, *Civil War and Readjustment,* 452; Penn, *Kentucky Rebel Town,* 244–45.

17. Kleber, *Kentucky Encyclopedia,* 142; Collins and Collins, *History of Kentucky,* 1:182.

18. Collins and Collins, *History of Kentucky,* 1:182; *Cincinnati Enquirer,* January 27, 1868; *Louisville Courier,* January 31, 1868; *Louisville Journal,* February 1, 1868; *Lexington Leader,* November 28, 1907; *Maysville Evening Bulletin,* April 22, 1896; *Maysville Public Ledger,* November 30, 1907; *Louisville Courier,* November 15, 1855; Penn, *Kentucky Rebel Town,* 245–48.

19. Harrison and Klotter, *New History of Kentucky,* 241–42.

20. America's Founding Documents, National Archives and Records Administration, https://www.archives.gov/founding-docs (accessed October 31, 2016).

21. Ibid.

22. Holzer, *Lincoln and Power of the Press,* 337, 356.

23. "Civil War Tested Lincoln's Tolerance for Free Speech, Press," First Amendment Center, Nashville, TN, February 11, 2009, http://www.firstamendmentcenter.org/civil-war-tested-lincolns-tolerance-for-free-speech-press (accessed October 31, 2016).

Bibliography

Collections

Haldeman Family Papers. Filson Historical Society, Louisville.

Published and Online Sources

"About the Covington Journal (Covington, Ky.) 1848–1876." *Chronicling America.* http://chroniclingamerica.loc.gov/lccn/sn84037822/.

"About the Hickman Courier (Hickman, Ky.) 1859–Current." *Chronicling America.* http://chroniclingamerica.loc.gov/lccn/sn85052141/.

"About the Weekly Kentucky Yeoman (Frankfort, Ky.) 1854–1886." *Chronicling America.* http://chroniclingamerica.loc.gov/lccn/sn82015454/.

"Abraham Lincoln Inaugural Address." http://www.inaugural.senate.gov/swearing-in/address/address-by-abraham-lincoln-1861.

The Address of the People of South Carolina, Assembled in Convention, to the People of the Slaveholding States of the United States. Charleston, SC: Evans and Cogswell, 1860.

"American Newspapers, 1800–1860: A Guide to Understanding and Using Antebellum American Newspapers." University Library, University of Illinois at Urbana-Champaign. http://guides.library.illinois.edu/c.php?g=347656&p=2348310.

America's Founding Documents. National Archives and Records Administration. https://www.archives.gov/founding-docs.

Andrews, J. Cutler. *The North Reports the Civil War.* Pittsburgh: University of Pittsburgh Press, 1955.

———. *The South Reports the Civil War.* Pittsburgh: University of Pittsburgh Press, 1985.

Arnold, Isaac Newton. *The History of Abraham Lincoln and the Overthrow of Slavery.* Chicago: Clarke, 1866.

Astor, Aaron. *Rebels on the Border: Civil War, Emancipation, and the Reconstruction of Kentucky and Missouri.* Baton Rouge: Louisiana State University Press, 2012.

Battle, J. H., W. H. Perrin, and G. C. Kniffen. *Kentucky: A History of the State.* 1st ed. Louisville, KY: F. A. Battey, 1885.

The Biographical Encyclopaedia of Kentucky of the Dead and Living Men of the Nineteenth Century. Cincinnati: J. Armstrong, 1878.

Biographical Sketch of Hon. Linn Boyd of Kentucky, the Present Speaker of the House of Representatives of the United States by a Virginian. Washington, DC: Congressional Globe Office, 1855.

"Black Soldiers in the Civil War." National Archives Online. https://www.archives .gov/education/lessons/blacks-civil-war.

Boller, Paul F., Jr. *Presidential Campaigns from George Washington to George W. Bush.* Oxford: Oxford University Press, 2004.

Breckinridge, Robert J. "Our Country—Its Peril—Its Deliverance." *Danville Quarterly Review* (March 1861).

———. "State of the Country." *Danville Quarterly Review* (June 1861).

"Civil War Tested Lincoln's Tolerance for Free Speech, Press." First Amendment Center, Nashville, TN, February 11, 2009. http://www.firstamendmentcenter .org/civil-war-tested-lincolns-tolerance-for-free-speech-press.

Clark, Thomas D. *Agrarian Kentucky.* Lexington: University Press of Kentucky, 1977.

———. *A History of Kentucky.* Lexington, KY: John Bradford Press, 1960.

———. *The Rampaging Frontier: Manners and Humors of Pioneer Days in the South and Middle West.* Indianapolis: Bobbs-Merrill, 1939.

Collins, Lewis, and Richard Collins. *History of Kentucky: By the Late Lewis Collins, Judge of the Mason County Court, Revised, Enlarged Four-Fold and Brought Down to the Year 1874, by His Son, Richard H. Collins, A.M., LL.B. Embracing Pre-Historic Annals for 331 Years, Outline, and by Counties, Statistics, Antiquities, and Natural Curiosities, Geographical and Geological Descriptions, Sketches of the Court of Appeals, the Churches, Freemasonry, Odd Fellowship, and Internal Improvements, Incidents of Pioneer Life, and Nearly Five Hundred Biographical Sketches of Distinguished Pioneers, Soldiers, Statesmen, Jurists, Lawyers, Surgeons, Divines, Merchants, Historians, Editors, Artists, etc., etc.* 2 vols. 1874. Reprint, Berea, KY: Kentucke Imprints, 1976.

Congleton, Betty Carolyn. "George D. Prentice: 19th Century Southern Editor." *Register of the Kentucky Historical Society* 65 (April 1967).

Constitution of the Confederate States. March 11, 1861. http://avalon.law.yale. edu/19th_century/csa_csa.asp.

Coulter, E. Merton. *The Civil War and Readjustment in Kentucky.* 1926. Reprint, Gloucester, MA: Peter Smith, 1966.

Craig, Berry. *Kentucky Confederates: Secession, Civil War, and the Jackson Purchase.* Lexington: University Press of Kentucky, 2014.

Davis, William C. *A History of the Orphan Brigade: The Kentuckians Who Couldn't Go Home.* New York: Doubleday, 1980.

Dew, Charles B. *Apostles of Disunion: Southern Secession Commissioners and the Causes of the Civil War.* Charlottesville: University of Virginia Press, 2001.

"The 1860 Presidential Vote in Virginia." West Virginia Archives and History Online. Extracted from *The Tribune Almanac and Political Register for 1861.* New York: Tribune Association, 1861. http://www.wvculture.org/history/ statehood/1860presidentialvote.html.

Eilerman, Charles B. *Historic Covington: Proposed Subjects for Registration and Historic Marking.* Reprint, Covington, KY: Charles B. Eilerman, 1975.

Foner, Eric. *The Fiery Trial: Abraham Lincoln and American Slavery.* New York: W. W. Norton, 2010.

George, Henry. *History of the 3d, 7th, 8th and 12th Kentucky C.S.A.* Louisville, KY: Dearing Press, 1911.

"George Washington's Mount Vernon: Slavery." http://www.mountvernon.org/georgewashington/slavery.

Graham, Preston D., Jr. *A Kingdom Not of This World: Stuart Robinson's Struggle to Distinguish the Sacred from the Secular during the Civil War.* Macon, GA: Mercer University Press, 2002.

Guelzo, Allen C. *Abraham Lincoln as a Man of Ideas.* Carbondale: Southern Illinois University Press, 1909.

Harrison, Lowell H., and James C. Klotter. *A New History of Kentucky.* Lexington: University Press of Kentucky, 1997.

History of Daviess County, Kentucky, Together with Sketches of Its Cities, Villages, and Townships, Educational, Religious, Civil, Military, and Political History, Portraits of Prominent Persons, Biographies of Representative Citizens, and an Outline History of Kentucky. Chicago: Inter-state Publishing, 1883.

Holzer, Harold. *Lincoln and the Power of the Press: The War for Public Opinion.* New York: Simon and Schuster, 2014.

Johnson, E. Polk. *A History of Kentucky and Kentuckians: The Leaders and Representative Men in Commerce, Industry and Modern Activities.* Chicago: Lewis Publishing, 1912.

Johnson, L. P. *The History of Franklin County, Ky.* Frankfort, KY: Roberts Printing, 1912.

Johnston, J. Stoddard. *Memorial History of Louisville from Its First Settlement to the Year 1896.* Chicago: American Biographical Publishing, 1896.

Joint Congressional Committee on Inaugural Ceremonies. "Address by Abraham Lincoln, 1861." http://www.inaugural.senate.gov/swearing-in/address/address-by-abraham-lincoln-1861.

Kleber, John E., ed. *The Encyclopedia of Louisville.* Lexington: University Press of Kentucky, 2001.

———. *The Kentucky Encyclopedia.* Lexington: University Press of Kentucky, 1992.

Klotter, James C., and Freda C. Klotter. *A Concise History of Kentucky.* Lexington: University Press of Kentucky, 2008.

Levin, H., ed. *The Lawyers and Lawmakers of Kentucky.* Chicago: Lewis Publishing, 1897.

Marshall, Ann E. *Creating a Confederate Kentucky: The Lost Cause and Civil War Memory in a Border State.* Chapel Hill: University of North Carolina Press, 2010.

Matthews, Gary R. *More American than Southern: Kentucky, Slavery, and the War for an American Ideology, 1828–1861.* Knoxville: University of Tennessee Press, 2014.

McDowell, Robert Emmett. *City of Conflict: Louisville in the Civil War, 1861–1865.* Louisville, KY: Louisville Civil War Roundtable, 1962.

McPherson, James M. *Battle Cry of Freedom: The Civil War Era.* New York: Ballantine Books, 1988.

Memorial Record of Western Kentucky, II. Chicago: Lewis Publishing, 1904.

Murphy, D. F., reporter. *Presidential Election 1864: Proceedings of the National Union Convention Held in Baltimore, Md., June 7th and 8th, 1864.* New York: Barker and Godwin, 1864.

Newell, Martin L. *Reports of Cases Determined in the Appellate Courts of Illinois.* Vol. 87. Chicago: Callaghan, 1900.

The News Manual: A Professional Resource for Journalists and the Media. http://www .thenewsmanual.net.

Noe, Kenneth W. *Perryville: This Grand Havoc of Battle.* Lexington: University Press of Kentucky, 2001.

Penn, William A. *Kentucky Rebel Town: The Civil War Battles of Cynthiana & Harrison County.* Lexington: University Press of Kentucky, 2016.

Perrin, William Henry. *History of Alexander, Union and Pulaski Counties, Illinois.* Chicago: O. L. Baskin, 1883.

———. *History of Bourbon, Scott, Harrison and Nicholas Counties, Kentucky, with an Outline Sketch of the Bluegrass Region, by Robert Peter, M.D., Ed.* Chicago: O. L. Baskin, 1882.

———. *History of Fayette County, Kentucky, with an Outline Sketch of the Bluegrass Region by Robert Peter, M.D., Ed.* Chicago: O. L. Baskin, 1882.

———. *History of Trigg County, Kentucky.* Reprint, Westminster, MD: Heritage Press, 2008.

———. *The Pioneer Press of Kentucky, from the First Paper West of the Alleghenies, August 11, 1787, to the Establishment of the Daily Press in 1830.* Louisville, KY: John P. Morton for the Filson Club, 1888.

Peters, Gerhard, and John T. Woolley. "Republican Party Platform of 1860," May 17, 1860. American Presidency Project. http://www.presidency.ucsb.edu/ws/?pid=29620.

Phillips, Christopher. *The Rivers Ran Backwards: The Civil War and the Remaking of the American Middle Border.* New York: Oxford University Press, 2016.

Prentice, George D. *The Poems of George D. Prentice.* Edited by John James Piatt. Cincinnati: Robert Clarke, 1877.

"The Press of Harrodsburg." *Register of the Kentucky Historical Society* 20 (January 1922): 47.

Pritchard, James M. *Embattled Capital: Frankfort Kentucky in the Civil War.* Frankfort, KY: Frankfort Heritage Press, 2014.

Ranck, George W. *History of Lexington, Kentucky, Its Early Annals and Recent Progress Including Biographical Sketches and Personal Reminisces of the Pioneer Settlers, Notices of Prominent Citizens, etc., etc.* Cincinnati: Robert Clarke, 1872.

Randall, J. G., and David Donald. *The Civil War and Reconstruction.* 2nd ed. Lexington, MA: D. C. Heath, 1969.

Ratner, Lorman A., and Dwight L. Teeter Jr. *Fanatics & Fire-Eaters: Newspapers and the Coming of the Civil War.* Urbana: University of Illinois Press, 2004.

Resolution of the [Confederate] Congress [in Kentucky]. Reprint, Lyndon, KY: Mull-Wathen Historic Press, 1970.

Reynolds, Donald E. *Editors Make War: Southern Newspapers in the Secession Crisis.* Carbondale: Southern Illinois University Press, 2006.

Rhodes, James Ford. *History of the United States from the Compromise of 1850.* Vol. 5, *1864–1866.* New York: Macmillan, 1904.

Risley, Ford. *Civil War Journalism.* Santa Barbara, CA: Praeger, 2012.

Russell, Sir William Howard. *My Diary North and South.* Boston: T. O. H. P. Burnham, 1863.

Sachsman, David B., ed. *A Press Divided: Newspaper Coverage of the Civil War.* New Brunswick, NJ: Transaction Publishers, 2014.

"Secretary of State Thomas B. Monroe." Kentucky Secretary of State website. http://apps.sos.ky.gov/secdesk/sosinfo/default.aspx?id=36.

Seekamp, Alvin, and Roger Burlingame, eds. *Who's Who in Louisville.* Louisville, KY: Anziger Press, 1918.

Shannon, Jasper B., and Ruth McQuown. *Presidential Politics in Kentucky 1824–1948.* Lexington: Bureau of Government Research, College of Arts and Sciences, University of Kentucky, 1960.

Smith, Zachariah Frederick. *The History of Kentucky from Its Earliest Discovery and Settlement, to the Present Day, Embracing Its Prehistoric and Aboriginal Periods; Its Pioneer Life and Experiences; Its Political, Social, and Industrial Progress; Its Educational and Religious Development; Its Military Events and Achievements, and Biographic Mention of Its Historic Characters.* Louisville, KY: Courier-Journal Job Printing Co., 1886.

Starling, Edmund L. *History of Henderson County, Kentucky: Comprising History of County and City, Precincts, Education, Churches, Secret Societies, Leading Enterprises, Sketches and Recollections, and Biographies of the Living and Dead.* Henderson, KY: n.p., 1887.

Taylor, Amy Murrell. *The Divided Family in Civil War America.* Chapel Hill: University of North Carolina Press, 2005.

Thompson, Ed Porter. *History of the Orphan Brigade.* Louisville, KY: Lewis N. Thompson, 1898.

US Bureau of the Census. "Population of the 100 Largest Urban Places: 1860." https://www.census.gov/population/www/documentation/twps0027/tab09.txt.

Vander Velde, Lewis George. *The Presbyterian Churches and the Federal Union, 1861–1869* Cambridge, MA: Harvard University Press, 1932.

The War of the Rebellion: A Compilation of the Official Records of the Union and Confederate Armies. Washington, DC: War Department, 1880–1902.

Warner, Ezra J., and W. Buck Yearns. *Biographical Registry of the Confederate Congress.* Baton Rouge: Louisiana State University Press, 1975.

Western Recorder advertising information. http://westernrecorder.org/advertising-home.page.

Index

CPSIA information can be obtained
at www.ICGtesting.com
Printed in the USA
LVHW111054140821
695300LV00001B/7

9 780813 174594